SIP Beyond VoIP

Henry Sinnreich
Alan B. Johnston
Robert Sparks

VON Publishing LLC
115 Broadhollow Road
Suite 225
Melville, New York 11747 USA

SIP Beyond VoIP

Published by VON Publishing LLC
115 Broadhollow Road
Suite 225
Melville, New York 11747 USA
Web: http://www.vonmag.com

ISBN Number: 0-9748130-0-1

July 2005

First Edition

Cover by Derek Davalos

Dedication

The authors are grateful to Fabienne, Lisa and Jean for their continuous support and patience that has enabled us to write this book and also for tolerating our SIP-ish conversations at all times.

Table of Contents

Table of Contents

List of Figures

List of Tables

Acknowledgements

The authors would like to thank all our colleagues from numerous companies working in the Internet Engineering Task Force (IETF) on SIP-related standards for freely sharing their insight in public Internet documents and in private conversations. We hope this book is an accurate view of SIP based communications and applications as envisaged by their developers in the Internet community.

We would also like to thank our colleagues from dynamicsoft, MCI and Xten for the hands on experience gained by working with them in the development of SIP products and services.

The sponsorship of Vint Cerf from MCI and Jeff Pulver from pulver.com has encouraged us to write this book.

Gunnar Hellström has kindly contributed with valuable information on text over IP (ToIP) and the use of SIP for the disabled people in Chapter 10. Vint Cerf has helped with critical comments on Presence, as described in Chapter 5.

Foreword

by Vint Cerf

In a stunning repetition of the transition between the 19th and 20th Centuries as the telephone reached its quarter century mark, the Internet is crossing into the 21st Century at about the same age as its century old counterpart, and is also transforming the world of communication in the process. Standards lie at the heart of the Internet and Session Initiation Protocol (SIP) is one of the newer and most fundamental. It is enabling the Internet to negotiate an endless range of modalities (voice, video, data, collaborative tools, peer-to-peer applications...).

While early experiments with the Internet and its predecessor, the ARPANET, explored use of the net to carry packetized voice and video in the 1970s and 1980s, the capacity of the system to carry these modalities was limited. But the concepts have taken on new significance with the increasing capacity of the network to carry traffic, the increasing penetration of the Internet around the world and the growing ability to supply high capacity at the edges of the net for residential and business users. Perhaps equally important is the ability of the edge devices to be programmed for increasingly rich functionality. Unlike the traditional voice network, the devices on the Internet are typically programmable and therefore adaptable to new applications sometimes in real time through the downloading of new Java code or other high level language to run on high level interpreters such as a Java.

Although SIP has been most prominent as a tool for the establishment of voice communications among pairs or groups of correspondents, the protocol itself is vastly more versatile and extensible. Indeed, SIP is exactly what its name says it is: a Session Initiation Protocol. Parties use SIP to find each other on the Internet (rendezvous) and then engage in any sort of "session," exchanging parametric and other information by means of the SIP protocol. The primary objective is to assure that both (or all) parties are in agreement as to how the resulting communication or application is to be conducted. Other pairwise or group protocols may be invoked as a consequence of this session initiation exchange. SIP is extensible so that new features can be added with modest effort. And because it is text-based (with a message format similar to HTTP), it is generally easy to debug problems by examining the actual packets exchanged during the SIP setup.

The authors of this volume have been personally and deeply involved in the introduction of SIP into the Internet lexicon. One could not write a foreword without acknowledging Henning Schulzrinne as the principal author and inventor of SIP. He recognized early on that SIP was about more than voice over IP but it could be adapted readily to that task in particular.

I had the good fortune to be introduced to Schulzrinne in the relatively early stages of the development of SIP and insisted on having him come to brief key engineering staff at MCI. Some of the authors of this book were part of the team that was exposed to SIP and embraced it early on as a tool to support VoIP. It is my honest opinion that we have barely scratched the surface of the various applications to which SIP may be adapted. If we have seen 1% of the applications of SIP so far, then there are still 99% waiting to be invented, developed or deployed. The generality of SIP will make it a major workhorse for the Internet of this century.

This book will take you on a journey of discovery. Like guides through an as yet uncharted jungle, the authors will take on an unsettled continent waiting to be populated with new applications. VoIP is only the beginning.

Vint Cerf
McLean, Virginia
June 2005

Introduction

SIP-related standards have matured and SIP has become the dominant Voice over IP (VoIP) protocol in wired and wireless communications. The authors have already written several books about SIP, so why do we have this new book?

This book is about how the initial promise of SIP has finally started to take shape:

- Internet communications based on SIP is about far more than just VoIP and is redefining how people and processes communicate,
- Internet communications are having a tremendous impact on the whole telecommunication industry, including wireless and enterprise communications.

The time stamp for this book

SIP standards and technology enjoys the benefit of a large and creative flow of contributions from all over the world. This book reflects the state of SIP as published in many IETF documents and commercial literature up to the 62 IETF meeting, March 6-11, 2005 in Minneapolis, MN, USA. It may take several years for the some of standards reported here to emerge as commercial products.

SIP and its Competitors

The statement that SIP is now the dominant VoIP protocol is better understood by looking at the state of other major protocols that may be competing with SIP.

H.323 H.323 was defined by the ITU-T as the protocol for multimedia over IP LANs and was initially adopted by telecom vendors for VoIP. The legacy from the circuit switched family of ISDN protocols has proven however to be quite complex to implement in an Internet environment, where solving specific problems, such as NAT traversal is much harder for H.323. Besides the implementation challenges, the fact that H.323 is not suited for presence, instant messaging and integration with applications has made it already a legacy protocol.

Master-slave protocols: SGCP, MCGP, MEGACO/H.248

The old concept of an intelligent central control (master) and dumb terminals (slaves) does not make sense on the Internet or indeed anywhere else, given the ever-increasing computing power and intelligence of all possible types of networked devices. Besides, the users of such systems are not exposed to any IP experience or IP application. The master-slave protocols are however still deployed in emulations of telephone switches over IP networks, but the lack of new services, beyond voice, has proven in our opinion to be in the long run a costly planning mistake in the traditional telephone industry when trying to adapt to IP.

Jabber and other IM

There are several successful instant messaging (IM) protocols in the market that are not based on SIP. Jabber is just one representative example. What all non-SIP IM protocols have in common is they are designed only for text communications. This forces their users to turn to other systems when using voice and video, such as SIP. Since SIP extensions in SIMPLE[1] are already a most comprehensive standards family for events, presence and IM, non-SIP IM may persist for a while, but most public and enterprise services are deploying SIMPLE or migrating to it.

Skype

The presence, IM and VoIP service deployed by Skype Technologies, S.A. is a most remarkable competitor to SIP-based products. Skype is arguably the biggest VoIP provider worldwide. Skype is a brilliant proof of concept for peer-to-peer (P2P) Internet communications in the real world. The proprietary nature of Skype prevents it from being part of the communication revolution enabled by open standards and assertions of security cannot be proven in a closed environment. Access to the rich media and presence capabilities of SIP can only be achieved through gateways. We believe for these reasons that P2P SIP as described in Chapter 14 is the better alternative to Skype.

---

[1] SIMPLE is an acronym that stands for "*S*IP for *I*nstant *M*essaging and *P*resence *L*everaging *E*xtensions." This is the name of an IETF standards working group. See the home page at http://ietf.org/html.charters/simple-charter.html

In conclusion, there are good reasons for choosing SIP as the single protocol when buying or designing communication systems, be they ground-up new designs or the migration from various existing legacy systems to IP.

SIP in the Marketplace

Considerations such as those above have made SIP the dominant voice and multimedia protocol in the industry:

- Practically all requests for proposals (RFP) from service providers and enterprise networks have SIP support as a mandatory item.
- Most communications vendors claim to support SIP, though the degree of SIP product depth and maturity may still differ widely.
- The mobile phone industry has specified the IP Multimedia Subsystems (IMS) based on SIP.
- Most of the large enterprise vendors, such as (in alphabetical order) ALCATEL, Avaya, Cisco, IBM, Microsoft, Siemens and many others have SIP-based enterprise communication systems as their flagship products. As mentioned however, the degree of maturity and standards compliance may vary.
- Large carriers, such as MCI, BT and AT&T were among the first to roll out SIP-based services. The number of SIP-based VoIP providers worldwide has grown to a point where we have a hard time keeping track of them.

What has changed in SIP

Besides the base standard for SIP in RFC 3261, there are close to 70 other RFCs related to SIP as of this writing and hundreds of Internet Draft documents in various stages of progress. As a result, SIP is not only a very detailed family of specifications, but such a large one, that considerable work is required to understand SIP thoroughly.

Chapters 1 and 2 deal with SIP Fundamentals and the Summary of VoIP using SIP.

SIP supports not only basic VoIP, but also the various requirements to match the complex voice features of the PBX and Centrex, the various and manifold wireless services, mobility across multiple user devices, networks and locations, conferencing and multimedia. SIP enables new modalities in communications, such as presence and events. Presence and events make up the emerging field of context aware communications. Applications for SIP are described in Chapter 4 and Context Aware Communications are described in Chapter 5.

As we show in the book, SIP events and presence enable new communication behaviors and the integration of applications, both personal and business processes, with communications. Indeed, presence may be the dial tone of the 21st century and people may now communicate with various processes and applications, besides communicating with other people.

Conferencing and collaboration on the Internet gave the initial impact for developing SIP and the well-developed status for conference and collaboration today using SIP is described in Chapter 6.

Most SIP-enabled VoIP and IM networks are still isolated islands at present. Chapter 7 describes connecting the SIP islands using DNS and ENUM.

Many SIP documents such as for presence and policy are based on XML. XCAP is the protocol for manipulating XML documents and is described in Chapter 8.

Most people associate wireless networks with mobility. We describe in Chapter 9 the various types of mobility and how SIP application level mobility will complement mobility solutions at the network and link layers in both wireless and wired links to the Internet.

Accessibility to communications by the disabled persons using multimedia and SIP transcoding services is described in Chapter 10.

The Internet is completely reshaping customer care by all businesses in stark contrast to the legacy voice-centric call centers that provided a rather discouraging customer experience. This is discussed in Chapter 11.

Last but not least, SIP is not like your email when it comes to privacy and protection from telemarketing, spam and malicious attacks. These topics are treated in Chapter 13. The related but distinct topic on how to deal correctly with NAT and firewall traversal is described in Chapter 13.

The Changing of the Communications Industry

The Internet has already drastically changed many of our work and leisure habits and has profoundly impacted many industries. Probably few industries however are as heavily impacted as the global Trillion Dollar industry of telecommunications. The media and analysts are using the rather fuzzy term of *convergence* of telecoms and the Internet.

Contrary to convergence, the authors believe all communications traffic, both wired and wireless, is irrevocably moving away from telecom networks onto the Internet and its attached private IP networks and millions of Internet connected computing devices. The Internet and its applications are thus replacing the telecommunications services and telecommunications industry. *Replacement* and not *convergence* is therefore happening in the industry.

Depending on the reader's preferences, the replacement of the traditional telecom industry by the Internet can be documented in many economical studies, or can be better understood by reading this book. Besides the specific applications described in various other chapters, a sample summary of fundamental disruptions can be found in Chapter 14 on P2P SIP.

Wrong Turns When Using SIP

Not all products and services using SIP will however be successful. We will expand here on the possible wrong turns when implementing SIP to underline the fact that partial use of SIP and its principles is definitely not a recipe for success.

Bypassing of Standards: There are many products and services based on "our special SIP" or "our SIP strategy." Such statements hide the avoidance of the hard work required for fully implementing 100% standards compliant interoperability in all products and services.

Ignoring the End-to-End Principle: Besides lack of full compliance with standards (one cannot be 99% compliant, but only 0% or fully 100% standards compliant, given all the complexity), we have also observed many designs that are trying to use Internet technology, but at the same time are trying to avoid the basic architectural principles of the Internet such as the end-to-end principle. The end-to-end principle assures transparency for new applications, thus fostering innovation, as well as security.

All kinds of boxes and intermediaries introduced "in the network" to presumably solve a problem or give a near term competitive advantage fall in this category. Various closed networks that are "walled gardens" *versus* the Internet are also avoiding the very principles that make the Internet successful, in spite of using IP technology. By the time some providers finish up building their walled garden, the customers will be safely outside of them.[2]

Legacy Designs over IP: Trying to port legacy telecom concepts, such as central control and voice-only complex Class 5 switch, PBX and Centrex features over IP will not prove in our opinion to be competitive with native IP communications that are both much lower in cost and richer in new services. Too much reliance on telephone numbers instead of using URLs,

[2] "Reflections from 2005 International SIP Conference in Paris," by A. Georgescu. *IP Center News*, February 2005. http://www.sipcenter.com/sip.nsf/html/2005+International+SIP

for example, has not only many technical drawbacks but is also an open invitation for litigation with the legacy telephone industry, government regulation and taxation.

Unnecessary Complexity: Overly complex systems occur not only from trying to emulate circuit-switched voice-over-IP, but also from short-sighted business plans to 'make it first to market' and pay later for the consequences, such as out-of-bound complexity, costly operations and very expensive regression testing for new services.

One of the most common sources of complexity is to compensate inadequate bandwidth on Internet access links or other parts of the network with complex quality of service (QoS) software systems and with overly complex voice quality monitoring systems to check on these very network QoS systems. However, QoS does not create bandwidth and in most cases provisioning adequate bandwidth and avoiding both congestion and under-provisioned networks is far more preferable.

One of the reasons for writing this book is to help our readers to detect the wrong turns when buying, implementing or operating SIP-based communication systems.

References in this Book

Most references in this book are either Internet standards published as RFCs or Internet Drafts that may or may not make it on the IETF standards track.

Internet standards published as RFCs can be found searching by RFC number or key words at: http://www.rfc-editor.org/rfcsearch.html

Internet drafts that are work in progress can be found searching by the title, subject or authors at: http://search.ietf.org/

Some Internet drafts referenced in this book may no longer be available on the IETF web site. For all IETF drafts as well as for RFCs, we recommend using a search engine such as Google to find the document in various archives on the Internet.

Chapter 1

SIP Fundamentals

Internet Standards and SIP

Session Initiation Protocol, SIP,[1] was developed by the standards body of Internet protocols, the Internet Engineering Task Force or the IETF. SIP occupies the application layer and fits into the Internet architecture as shown in Figure 1.1, which shows the basic five-layer model used for the Internet.

The lowest layers are the physical and link layers. For SIP, common physical/link layers are Ethernet or 802.11a, b, or g wireless LANs, or V.90 dialup using the PPP protocol. This layer provides basic network connectivity between network elements. Physical layer routing is performed using identifiers such as MAC (Media Access Control) addresses. The next layer is the Internet layer which provides routing between local area networks as a datagram service. SIP can be used with either IPv4 or the new IPv6. IP addresses are used for routing at this layer. The third layer is the transport layer, which provides application multiplexing using port numbers. Transport layer protocols can also provide reliability and other services. Common transports used with SIP include unreliable UDP (User Datagram Protocol),[2] reliable TCP (Transmission Control Protocol),[3] and SCTP (Stream Control Transport Protocol).[4]

The hourglass architecture of the Internet protocols has changed since the early design of the Internet and the changes are referred to as the coming of age of the Internet.[5] The main reasons for such concerns are as follows:

- The Internet may be 'putting on weight' with the deployment of such protocols as Multi-Protocol Label Switching (MPLS) and various QoS enhancements in the backbone and edge networks.
- The absorption of complex telecom technologies, such as SONET and ATM, may even lead to a 'midlife crisis'.[6]

---

[1] RFC 3261: Rosenberg, J., Schulzrinne, H., Camarillo, G., Johnston, A., Peterson, J., Sparks, R., Handley, M. and E. Schooler, "SIP: Session Initiation Protocol." IETF, June 2002.

[2] RFC 0768: "User Datagram Protocol," by J. Postel. IETF, August 1980.

[3] "RFC 793: Transmission Control Protocol," by J. Postel. IETF, September 1981. Updated by RFC 3168.

[4] RFC 2960: "Stream Control Transmission Protocol," by R. Stewart, et al. IETF, October 2000. Updated by RFC 3309.

[5] *The Internet's Coming of Age.* Book published by the National Academy Press, Washington, DC, 2001. See http://bob.nap.edu/html/coming_of_age/

[6] "Modern Internet architecture and technology," by H. Schulzrinne. Columbia University, Fall 2003. See http://www.cs.columbia.edu/~coms6181/slides/1/internet.ppt

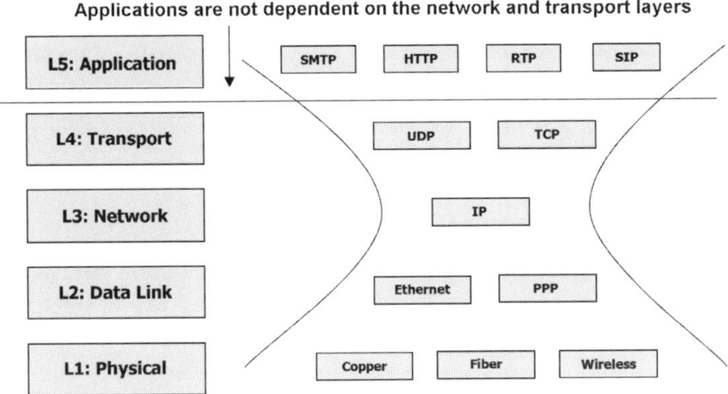

Figure 1.1 – The hourglass architecture of the Internet protocols

Key Functions of SIP

SIP is a very rich and extensible protocol. We will review in this chapter only the principal functions that could be used as a baseline for SIP implementations.

The SIP Rendezvous Function

SIP has many additional capabilities beyond just signaling, useful for applications other than just VoIP. SIP is a true "rendezvous" protocol for establishing sessions over the Internet. This means it allows one SIP-enabled endpoint (known as a User Agent or UA) to:

- Locate another User Agent.
- Locate a SIP server to facilitate the finding of another User Agent.
- Establish a media session using an offer/answer exchange.
- Modify an existing session using an offer/answer exchange.
- Express the UAs capabilities and features.
- Request 3rd party (remote) call control operations.
- Find out the status, capabilities, and availability of another UA.
- Request future updates on the status and availability of another UA.
- Exchange mid call signaling information.
- Exchange short instant messages with another UA.

From this list, it is clear that SIP is much more than just a signaling protocol, and is useful other than in a single application such as VoIP.

Table 1.1 – SIP Request Methods

Request purpose	Method	Reference
Establish a session with offer/answer	INVITE	RFC 3261[1]
Acknowledge a response to an INVITE	ACK	RFC 3261
Query the capabilities of a server or UA	OPTIONS	RFC 3261
Cancel a pending request	CANCEL	RFC 3261
Terminate an existing SIP session	BYE	RFC 3261
Temporarily bind a device URI to an AOR	REGISTER	RFC 3261
Establish a session to receive future information updates	SUBSCRIBE	RFC 3265[7]
Deliver information after a SUBSCRIBE	NOTIFY	RFC 3265
Upload status information to a server	PUBLISH	RFC 3903[8]
Request another UA to act upon a URI	REFER	RFC 3515[9]
Transport an Instant Message (IM)	MESSAGE	RFC 3428[10]
Update session state information	UPDATE	RFC 3311[11]
Acknowledge a provisional response	PRACK	RFC 3262[12]
Transport mid call signaling information	INFO	RFC 2976[13]

SIP Requests

SIP requests can be standalone or they can be used to establish a long-lasting relationship between two UAs known as a dialog. Requests sent within an established dialog receive special treatment. A SIP dialog may result in a media session being established. Basic request types (known as methods) are listed in Table 1.1.

---

[7] RFC 3265: Roach, A., "Session Initiation Protocol (SIP)-Specific Event Notification." RFC 3265, June 2002.

[8] RFC 3903: Niemi, A., "Session Initiation Protocol (SIP) Extension for Event State Publication." RFC 3903, October 2004.

[9] RFC 3515: Sparks, R., "The Session Initiation Protocol (SIP) Refer Method." RFC 3515, April 2003.

[10] RFC 3428: Campbell, B., Rosenberg, J., Schulzrinne, H., Huitema, C. and D. Gurle, "Session Initiation Protocol (SIP) Extension for Instant Messaging." RFC 3428, December 2002.

[11] RFC 3311: Rosenberg, J., "The Session Initiation Protocol (SIP) UPDATE Method." RFC 3311, October 2002.

[12] RFC 3262: Rosenberg, J. and H. Schulzrinne, "Reliability of Provisional Responses in Session Initiation Protocol (SIP)." RFC 3262, June 2002.

[13] RFC 2976: "The SIP INFO Method," by S. Donovan. IETF, October 2000.

Table 1.2 – SIP Response Codes

Class	Code	Examples
Informational or Provisional	1xx	100 Trying 180 Ringing 183 Session Progress
Success	2xx	200 OK 202 Accepted
Redirection	3xx	300 Moved 302 Multiple Choices 305 Use Proxy
Client Error	4xx	401 Unauthorized 403 Forbidden 415 Unsupported Media Type 486 Busy Here 428 Use Identity Header
Server Error	5xx	501 Not Implemented 503 Service Unavailable
Global Error	6xx	600 Busy Everywhere 603 Decline

SIP Responses

SIP responses are three-digit numerical codes. The first digit indicates the class of the response. In addition to the code, a reason phrase is included which can be displayed or rendered to the user. Each response code has a default reason phrase, but often the reason phrase is customized to provide more details about the result of the request.

The classes and examples are shown in Table 1.2.

A SIP transaction consists of a request and a final response. A final response is a non-1xx response. (A UA may only generate one final response per SIP request. An unlimited number of provisional responses can be generated.)

Example SIP Call Flow

An example SIP call flow is shown in Figure 1.2.

In this flow, two UAs establish a media session between them using two SIP proxy servers. This interdomain arrangement with each domain having a proxy server is known as the "SIP Trapezoid" because of the shape.

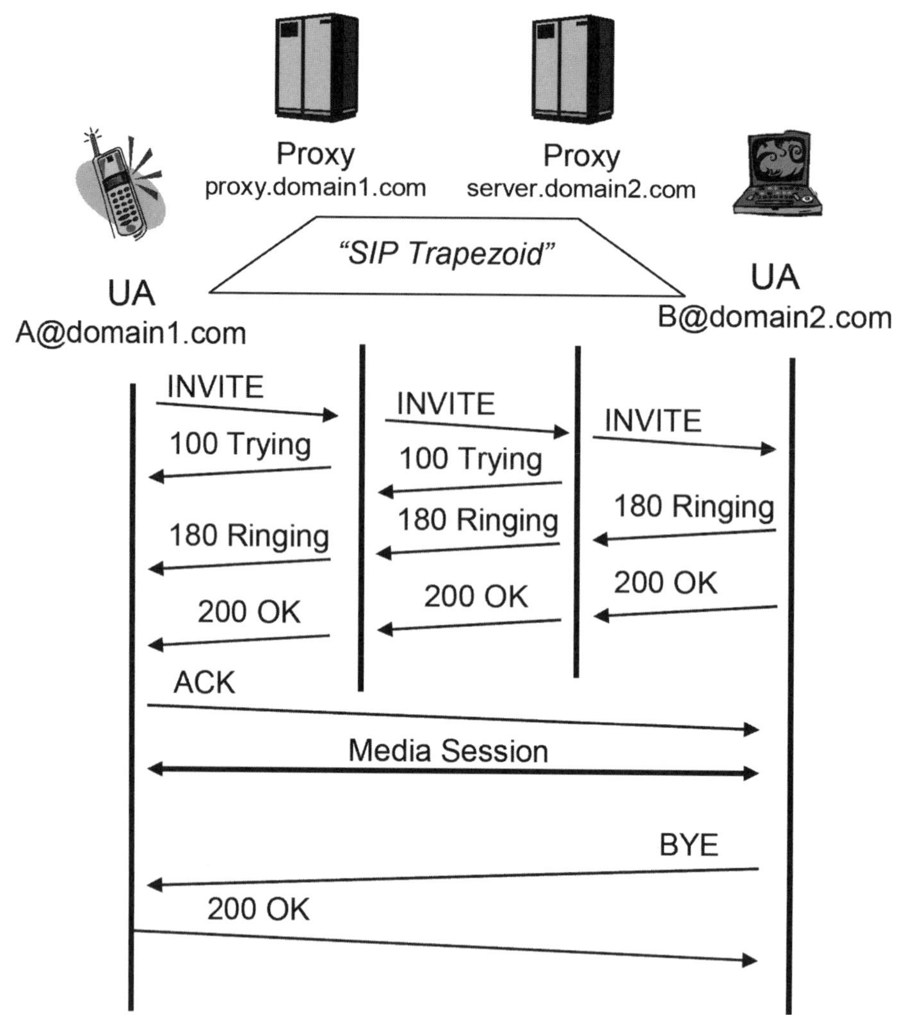

Figure 1.2 – Basic SIP call flow with the "SIP trapezoid"

In this flow, A requests the establishment of a session with B by sending an INVITE request. By default, the request is sent to the proxy server for domain1.com. The 100 Trying provisional responses are generated by the proxy servers to indicate that they have received and processed the SIP INVITE request. The called UA sends a 180 Ringing response to indicate alerting is taking place. When the session invitation is accepted, a 200 OK response is sent.

Note that all responses to the INVITE are routed through the same set of proxy servers that forwarded the INVITE (An exception is the 100 Trying response which is defined to be a single hop response and is never proxied).

The INVITE and 200 OK messages contain device URIs for each UA; as a result, the ACK and all future SIP messages sent by either party during the rest of this dialog may be sent directly to the other user agent, bypassing the proxies that performed the initial discover and database lookups.

The dialog and the media session ends when one UA sends a BYE. To acknowledge the BYE, a 200 OK response is generated. No ACK is sent, as ACKs are sent only to acknowledge final (non-1xx) responses to INVITE requests.

Example Message Detail

A SIP message has a similar structure to an email message. The type of request is indicated in the first line, followed by the Request-URI, the destination of the request. The type of request line is followed by several SIP header fields, some of which appear in an email message such as To, From, Subject, etc. Most of the header fields are unordered with a few exceptions such as Via. After the list of header fields, a SIP message may contain a message body. SIP transports bodies the same way that email does—using Multipart Internet Mail Extensions (MIME). If a body is present, a Content-Type and Content-Length must be present, and a Content-Disposition (indicating the usage of the body) and Content-Encoding header fields may also be present. An example SIP message is shown beginning below:

```
INVITE sip:912036072778@mci.globalipcom.com SIP/2.0
From: sip:ajohnston@mci.globalipcom.com;tag=1c28785
To: sip:912036072778@mci.globalipcom.com
Call-Id: call-1102633900-11@207.206.144.74
Cseq: 2 INVITE
Contact: <sip:ajohnston@207.206.144.74>
Content-Type: application/sdp
Content-Length: 310
Accept-Language: en
Allow: INVITE, ACK, CANCEL, BYE, REFER, OPTIONS, NOTIFY, REGISTER,
SUBSCRIBE
Supported: timer, replaces
User-Agent: Pingtel/2.1.11 (VxWorks)
Date: Thu, 09 Dec 2004 23:11:40 GMT
```

```
Proxy-Authorization: DIGEST USERNAME="ajohnston", REALM="mci.com",
NONCE="6a97cae3acd771fe44326184cc0de7ea.1102633901",
URI="sip:912036072778@mci.globalipcom.com",
RESPONSE="dac5861e6734b006e8548acdbf98173a"
Via: SIP/2.0/UDP 207.206.144.74

v=0
o=Pingtel 5 5 IN IP4 207.206.144.74s=phone-call
c=IN IP4 207.206.144.74
t=0 0
m=audio 8766 RTP/AVP 96 97 0 8 18 98
a=rtpmap:96 eg711u/8000/1
a=rtpmap:97 eg711a/8000/1
a=rtpmap:0 pcmu/8000/1
a=rtpmap:8 pcma/8000/1
a=rtpmap:18 g729/8000/1
a=fmtp:18 annexb=no
a=rtpmap:98 telephone-event/8000/1
```

For example, to establish a media session, SIP uses Session Description Protocol (SDP)[14] message bodies which contain descriptions of the media session. One party in the session makes an SDP offer, and the other party replies with an SDP answer, which must be a subset of the media types and codecs in the offer. Normally, the INVITE request contains the offer, and a 200 OK answer carries the answer. However, SIP offers a lot of flexibility in that:

- The sender of the INVITE can omit the offer; the 200 OK answer must then carry the offer, and the ACK then carries the answer. (Note that this approach is a little problematic because an ACK must be sent in response to the 200 OK, no error messages can be generated based on the offer. Instead, all the caller can do is decline the media and then send a BYE to terminate the dialog and session.)
- To support "early media," an answer may be delivered in a reliably-sent provisional response (that is, a 18x response containing a RSeq header field which results in a PRACK[15] response—if the PRACK is not received, the 18x response is retransmitted.)
- Offers and answers can also be carried in UPDATE requests.

---

[14] RFC 2327: "SDP: Session Description Protocol," by M. Handley, V. Jacobson. IETF, April 1998.

[15] RFC 3262: Rosenberg, J. and H. Schulzrinne, "Reliability of Provisional Responses in Session Initiation Protocol (SIP)." RFC 3262, June 2002.

Despite these options, the basic offer/answer exchange is preserved. The rules governing SIP's use of SDP in this offer answer exchange are detailed elsewhere.[16]

The SUBSCRIBE method is the only other SIP method that establishes a dialog. As described in detail in Chapter 5, NOTIFY methods sent in response to a SUBSCRIBE are sent within the dialog. A SUBSCRIBE dialog is not terminated with a BYE; instead it is terminated with a SUBSCRIBE with Expires:0 or a NOTIFY with a Subscription-State: terminated.

SIP and URIs

Another very important part of SIP is its use of URIs. A Uniform Resource Indicator or URI is a general type of address used on the Internet. It contains information about the resource or server and provides information about how to contact the server. The protocol used to access the resource is known as the URI scheme. Common URI schemes are shown in Table 1.1, and include common protocols such as HTTP (Hyper Text Transport Protocol). SIP has defined its own URI scheme. Most signaling protocols understand their own addressing schemes, and some have added URI support as an afterthought. However, SIP was initially designed to work with URIs, and not just SIP URIs. SIP systems commonly use URI schemes of other protocols such as tel URIs[17] with telephone numbers, h323 URIs[18] with H.323 aliases. This use of URIs for interworking is extremely powerful.

SIP URIs are also extremely general and powerful addressing schemes. For example, consider the URI

sip:fred@stoneage.org;rock-size=rubble

The URI has a user part (fred) and a host part (stoneage.org) and a URI parameter (rock-size). The domain part is resolved using the Internet's Domain Name System (DNS) which is an extremely powerful and general scheme. For example, DNS lookups based on this domain name can be used to determine the following:

- The transport protocols supported in the stoneage.org domain (using NAPTR records)

---

[16] RFC 3264: Rosenberg, J. and H. Schulzrinne, "An Offer/Answer Model with Session Description Protocol (SDP)," RFC 3264, June 2002.

[17] RFC 3999: "The TEL URI for Telephone Numbers," by H. Schulzrinne, IETF, June 2004.

[18] RFC 3508: "H.323 Uniform Resource Locator (URL) Scheme Registration," by O. Levin, IETF, April 2003.

- The Internet IP address of a SIP server or UA used to locate the user (using SRV or A records), or
- The Internet transport port used to reach the SIP server or UA.

Once these DNS resolutions are performed on the host part, the SIP request can be forwarded using the resolved transport, IP address, and port number.

For the representation of telephone numbers and dialed digit strings, the user part of a SIP URI may contain digits. For example:

sip:+19725551212@example.com;user=phone

The presence of the "+" indicates that this telephone number is in the global E.164 telephone number format, starting with the country code (1 in this case for the North American Numbering Plan), then the remaining digits. The "user" URI parameter is a hint that this URI contains a telephone number. The host part of the URI is the domain to which the request should be routed so that the telephone number in the user part may be analyzed and routed. Alternatively a 'tel' URI could be used in a SIP message as discussed in the following section.

Types of SIP URIs

SIP also has built into it a number of different types of URIs. There are three main types of SIP URIs: user, device, and service. Note that it is not possible to tell the type of SIP URI by inspection. The only way to tell is to resolve the URI and use it.

Address of Record URI

A user URI represents a human user, the user utilizing the User Agent. The user has an identity, and that identity URI is known as an Address of Record or AOR. The AOR URI has a long-lived nature, might be published in a directory, included on a web page, or printed on a business card. Since a user can utilize multiple devices, one-to-many mapping is possible and even common.

Contact or Device URI

A device URI represents a single SIP UA instance. For example a user might have a mobile phone, a PDA, a laptop, and a desktop phone or PC. Each of these devices would have a unique device URI that might be temporarily associated with the user. This binding of a device URI to an Address of Record is another function provided by SIP which is used for routing incoming requests.

Service URI

The final kind of URI is a service URI. For example, SIP defines a Conference URI as a URI that can be used to join a SIP conference. A SIP request sent to this URI results in a media session that is part of the conference. SIP conferencing is described in detail in Chapter 6.

Other URI Schemes

SIP can handle a number of other URI schemes. They are listed in Table 1.3. The ability of SIP to work with non-SIP addresses is a great help in handling interworking and dealing with mixed environments.

To understand how SIP resolves or dereferences URIs, one must understand the basic types of SIP servers.

Types of SIP Servers

The request may reach one of a number of types of SIP devices. It might reach a proxy server, a redirect server, or a user agent. These types of servers are briefly described in the next section. Note that other service specific types of SIP entities will be introduced in other chapters including State Agents, Presence Servers, Watchers, Presentity, Focus, etc.

Basic User Agent

A User Agent (UA) is a SIP endpoint which receives the SIP request and generates a response. The simplest UA can be a SIP phone or a gateway which interacts with the PSTN. A SIP phone will likely only support voice and no other media types. Services will typically be limited to emulation of PSTN/PBX features such as call hold, transfer, pickup, etc. A numeric keypad allows telephone numbers and extensions to be entered for dialing.

Advanced User Agent

A more advanced SIP UA will support multiple media types, including voice, video, and text messaging. Advanced services such as presence and conferencing can be supported. Remote call control from a web page or a resource list allows URI dialing in addition to telephone numbers.

Table 1.3 – URI schemes

URI Scheme	Use	Reference
sip:, sips:	SIP and Secure SIP Addresses	RFC 3261
tel:	Telephone numbers and dial strings	RFC 3999[17]
pres:	Presence resource	RFC 3861[19]
im:	Instant Message resource	RFC 3861[19]
http:	Hyper Text Tranport Protocol for web pages	RFC 2616[20]
xmpp:	Jabber IM and presence URIs	[[21]]
h323:H323:	H.323 URL	RFC 3508[18]

SIP Proxy Server

A proxy server is, a server which receives SIP requests, performs various database lookups then forwards or proxies the request on its next hop. There is virtually no explicit limit[22] to the number of proxy servers which can be chained together to deliver a request to its ultimate destination, though large numbers of SIP proxies in the path are not desirable. This design allows a request to traverse a number of servers, each providing a specific function or consulting a special database in providing SIP routing services. This design is easily exploited to build decomposed SIP application servers, inter-service provider handoffs, etc. SIP proxy servers only need to stay in the SIP messaging path during the initial exchange; after that, they can safely drop out and allow the two UAs to communicate directly. Alternatively, a proxy server can request to stay in the signaling path for all future SIP signaling messages. In this way, SIP provides "IP router"

---

[19] RFC 3861: "Address Resolution for Instant Messaging and Presence," by J. Peterson. IETF, August 2004.

[20] RFC 2616: "Hypertext Transfer Protocol—HTTP/1.1," by R. Fielding, J. Gettys, J. Mogul, H. Frystyk, L. Masinter, P. Leach, T. Berners-Lee. IETF, June 1999.

[21] P. Saint-Andre, "A Uniform Resource Identifier (URI) Scheme for the Extensible Messaging and Presence Protocol (XMPP)." IETF Internet-Draft, Work in progress, December 2004.

[22] Daisy chaining large numbers of proxy servers can introduce significant request processing delay and often adds little value. Also, note that the default value for Max-Forwards is 70, effectively limiting the number of proxy hops to 70.

type of functionality, but at the application layer to a SIP application. This can be used to route SIP messages through network discontinuities such as firewalls and Network Address Translators (NATs).

SIP Redirect Server

A redirect server is a server which receives a SIP request, performs various database lookups, then returns the results back to the requesting UA. As such, it provides a kind of "database query" functionality to SIP messaging. If the database lookups provide multiple locations, the set of possible locations can be provided back to the requesting UA.

Registrar

A SIP registrar server is a SIP endpoint that receives and processes REGISTER requests. Registration is the temporary binding or linking of a device URI (provided in the Contact header field in a REGISTER message) to a user URI (defined as an Address of Record in the section below, provided in the To: header field). The lifetime of a registration is indicated in an *expires* parameter which is returned to the UA in the 200 OK response. Multiple device URIs may be registered against the same user URI, giving proxy and redirect servers a choice of destinations for incoming requests.

Note that these server types are all logical; a given server can act as a User Agent, Redirect, or Proxy Server to a given request based on the nature of the request.

Any URI parameters can be used to convey specific information about the resource being contacted, or perhaps the service being requested.

SIP Capability Discovery

Using SIP, a request can contain extensive information about the capabilities of the UAC. Most UAs support basic VoIP with a common set of codecs. However, SIP provides a mechanism in which much more powerful UAs can discover the capabilities of other UAs. For example, it can include the following:

- The types of SIP requests (methods) the UAC will accept (Accept header field).
- Any SIP extensions and capabilities (Supported header field).
- The characteristics of the UAC such as whether it is mobile or fixed, a conference server, etc. (feature tags in the Contact header field).
- Any SIP event packages supported (Allow-Events header field).[7]

- Any SIP extensions and capabilities required to complete the request (Required header field).
- The type of message bodies accepted (Accept-Content header field).
- Remote Call Control.

A SIP request can convey context information about another existing dialog. For example, the Replaces header field[23] can be used in an INVITE to replace an existing dialog. An example is in an attended transfer or a call pickup. If the Replaces header field matches an existing dialog and has been authorized, the INVITE is accepted and the referenced dialog is terminated with a BYE.

In a similar way, an INVITE containing a Join header field[24] requests that the media session referenced by the dialog in the Join header field be joined. As a result, a point-to-point call can be turned into a conference, and a conference can add an additional participant.

Message Body Payloads

SIP can carry a variety of other message body types. For example, some SIP event packages carry XML encoded message bodies that carry a variety of content. Examples of common content types are shown in Table 1.4.

A SIP message can contain multiple message bodies using a technique called Multipart MIME. Using this approach, an INVITE can contain an SDP offer and another message body. For example, it is possible to include both S/MIME encrypted SDP and SDP without encryption.

A SIP request can contain information for related applications. The simplest example is the Call-Info header field which can contain a URI which should be rendered to a user. This could be used for "screen pops" in a call center type application containing, for example, a web page.

In another approach, an application can send a REFER with a Refer-To URI of a web page that would be rendered to the user.

---

[23] RFC 3891: Mahy, R., Biggs, B. and R. Dean, "The Session Initiation Protocol (SIP) 'Replaces' Header," RFC 3891, September 2004.

[24] RFC 3911: Mahy, R. and D. Petrie, "The Session Initiation Protocol (SIP) 'Join' Header," RFC 3911, October 2004.

Table 1.4 – Common SIP message body types

Content	Content Type	Used in Methods
Simple text encoded	text/plain	MESSAGE
Marked up text	text/html	MESSAGE
Delivery of UA registration info	application/reginfo+xml[25]	NOTIFY
Delivery of Message Waiting Indications (MWI)	application/simple-message-summary[26]	NOTIFY
Used to transport an ISUP message for SIP-T	application/ISUP[27]	INVITE, BYE, INFO
Presence data information	application/pidf+xml[28]	PUBLISH, NOTIFY
Dialog state information	application/dialog+xml[29]	NOTIFY
Conference state information	application/conf+xml[30]	NOTIFY
VoIP session summary report	application/voip-rpt[31]	PUBLISH, NOTIFY

[25] RFC 3680: Rosenberg, J., "A Session Initiation Protocol (SIP) Event Package for Registrations," RFC 3680, March 2004.

[26] RFC 3842: Mahy, R., "A Message Summary and Message Waiting Indication Event Package for the Session Initiation Protocol (SIP)," RFC 3842, August 2004.

[27] RFC 3204: Zimmerer, E., Peterson, J., Vemuri, A., Ong, L., Audet, F., Watson, M. and M. Zonoun, "MIME media types for ISUP and QSIG Objects," RFC 3204, December 2001.

[28] RFC 3863: "Presence Information Data Format (PIDF)," by H. Sugano, S. Fujimoto, G. Klyne, A. Bateman, W. Carr, J. Peterson, IETF, August 2004.

[29] Rosenberg, J., "An INVITE Inititiated Dialog Event Package for the Session Initiation Protocol (SIP)," draft-ietf-sipping-dialog-package-05 (work in progress), November 2004.

[30] Rosenberg, J., Schuzrinne, H., and O. Levin., "A Session Initiation Protocol (SIP) Event Package for Conference State," draft-ietf-sipping-conference-package-08 (work in progress), December 2004.

[31] A. Johnston, H. Sinnreich, A. Clark, and A. Pendleton, "SIP Service Quality Reporting Event." IETF Internet-Draft, October 2004, Work in progress.

Table 1.4 *(continued)*

Content	Content Type	Used in Methods
Location Information extension to PIDF	application/cpim-pidf+xml[32]	PUBLISH, NOTIFY
Common presence data format	Message/CPIM[33]	PUBLISH, NOTIFY
Part of SIP message used to convey status	Message/sipfrag[34]	NOTIFY
Resource List	application/resource-lists+xml[35]	SUBSCRIBE, MESSAGE, INVITE, REFER

Another type of message body is a URI list. A URI list can be used to list a set of destinations for a single request. For example, an INVITE containing a URI list to a conference server can cause an *ad hoc* conference to be created and the conference server to "dial out" to connect the list members to the conference.[36] A SUBSCRIBE containing a URI list can cause a server to initiate multiple subscriptions.[37]

SIP Header Fields

Information carried in various SIP header fields can carry a variety of information used by SIP applications. Note that Table 1.5 does not contain a complete list of SIP header fields; rather, it is a list of interesting SIP header fields that give some idea of the power of SIP.

---

[32] J. Peterson, "A Presence-based GEOPRIV Location Object Format." IETF Internet-Draft, Work in progress, September 2004.

[33] RFC 3862: "Common Presence and Instant Messaging (CPIM): Message Format." G. Klyne, D. Atkins. IETF, August 2004.

[34] RFC 3842: Sparks, R., "Internet Media Type message/sipfrag." RFC 3420, November 2002.

[35] Camarillo, G. and A. Roach, "Requirements and Framework for Session Initiation Protocol (SIP) Uniform Resource Identifier (URI)-List Services." draft-ietf-sipping-uri-services-02 (work in progress), December 2004.

[36] Camarillo, G. and A. Johnston, "Conference Establishment Using Request-Contained Lists in the Session Initiation Protocol (SIP)." draft-ietf-sipping-uri-list-conferencing-02 (work in progress), December 2004.

[37] Garcia-Martin, M. and G. Camarillo, "Multiple-Recipient MESSAGE Requests in the Session Initiation Protocol (SIP)." draft-ietf-sipping-uri-list-message-02 (work in progress), December 2004.

Table 1.5 – SIP header fields

Header Field	Use	Reference
Alert-Info	Customized ringing.	RFC 3261
Call-Info	Screen Pops.	RFC 3261
Replaces	Call control, transfer, pickup.	RFC 3891
Join	Conferencing.	RFC 3911
Privacy	Request privacy.	RFC 3233
Reason	Indicate reason for failure response.	RFC 3326
Accept-Contact	Used by a caller to indicate Contact URI preferences.	RFC 3841
Referred-By	Provide the identity of a third party who initiated the request.	RFC 3892
Error-Info	Provides a URI with more information about an error condition.	RFC 3261
Supported	Provides list of feature tags supported by a UA.	RFC 3261
P-OSP-Auth-Token	Carries an Open Settlements Protocol token for clearing-house networks.	[[38]]
Event	Indicates the SIP event package the subscription or notification is in reference to.	RFC 3265
Resource-Priority	Used to indicate the priority of a request.	[[39]]
History-Info	Information on how and why a call arrives at a specific application or user. Used to provide information about the history of a request and how and why re-targeting has occurred.	[[40]]

[38] Johnston, A., Rawlins , D., Sinnreich, H., Thomas, S., and Brennan, R., "Session Initiation Protocol Private Extension for an OSP Authorization Token." IETF Internet-Draft, Work in progress, June 2004.

[39] H. Schulzrinne and J. Polk, "Communications Resource Priority for the Session Initiation Protocol (SIP)." IETF Internet-Draft, Work in progress, October 2004.

[40] Barnes, M., "An Extension to the Session Initiation Protocol for Request History." IETF Internet-Draft, Work in progress, January 2005.

SIP Interactions

A typical SIP session involves two UAs and often one or more proxy servers. However, SIP also supports a number of other communication modes. This includes pure peer-to-peer, multicast, conferencing, and resource list communications.

Peer-to-Peer Properties

Despite the use of SIP intermediaries such as proxy servers, SIP can operate in a peer-to-peer mode as well. In fact, it has been observed that many SIP functions implemented by a proxy server can be implemented by a redirect server, which allows direct peer-to-peer dialog establishment.

Using techniques such as dynamic DNS, it is possible for a UA to utilize a SIP URI and still be nomadic and continue to receive incoming requests without having to REGISTER with a SIP server. The authors believe that these properties of SIP will likely be increasingly utilized in the future, as the peer-to-peer model has the following advantages:

- Highest level of security: minimized opportunities for man in the middle attacks.
- Lowest latency in connection.
- Highest availability: no fate sharing at the application layer besides the peer.
- Lowest cost and highest scalability.

A detailed look at Peer-to-Peer SIP is in Chapter 14.

Multicast

SIP messages can be sent over multicast streams as well as in unicast mode in an IP network. For example, a REGISTER could be sent over multicast to the well-known SIP multicast address sip.mcast.net. Any SIP registrar server listening on this address could respond. It is also possible to send other SIP requests via multicast. This type of conferencing is a source of experimentation, but conventional conferencing and collaboration systems actually use unicast, and a single centralized point for authorization and access control known as a focus. This is described in the following section.

Conferencing

SIP has defined a number of conferencing modes, the most commonly deployed is one in which there is a single centralized point known as a focus. Note that the media sessions may themselves utilize multicast media, or be a full mesh between conference participants. The centralized signaling point provides a stable, controllable, manageable system.

In this arrangement, as described in detail in Chapter 6, each participant in a conference establishes an individual dialog with the focus. The focus logically groups the set of dialogs and can share media, participant, and state information about the conference using SIP and some non-SIP mechanisms.

Resource Lists

SIP supports the use of Resource Lists, which are lists of URIs for group operations. For example, a resource list could be a list of contacts in a presence "buddy" list. A SIP UA can send a single SUBSCRIBE request, with a message body which will result in individual subscriptions being established with each of the URIs in the resource list. Or, resource lists can also be used in an INVITE request sent to establish an *ad hoc* conference. This would result in the creation of an *ad hoc* conference and the resources identified in the resource list would be "dialed out" to join the conference.

The Design Principles of SIP

This short introduction to SIP will now better enable the reader to understand the design principles of SIP. These principles are useful in most design decisions and are helpful in avoiding wrong choices and design mistakes. We provide on the following pages a short summary of the reference contained in some Internet Drafts.[41] There also exists a complementary document on guidelines for the authors of SIP extensions.[42]

[41] "Architecture and Design Principles of the Session Initiation Protocol (SIP)," by J. Rosenberg and H. Schulzrinne. Internet Drafts, IETF, February 2005.

[42] "Guidelines for Authors of Extensions to the Session Initiation Protocol (SIP)," by J. Rosenberg and H. Schulzrinne. Internet Drafts, IETF, July 2004.

Table 1.6 – SIP objectives, architecture and design principles

Objectives	Enable new features and Services	The main objective of SIP is to enable new services, such as presence as part of the events architecture. This can support the integration of communications and applications.
	Not a PSTN replacement	SIP is designed for the Internet and can provide new services that are not possible on the PSTN. SIP can provide also PSTN-like services, but in a different manner.
	Heterogeneous clients	SIP clients may differ widely in regard to computing power and interfaces to the user. SIP can accommodate new extensions and capability negotiation for new option tags, new body types, new methods and new codecs.
	Multiple clients	Users can have many devices, such as desktop phones, PC/laptops, PDAs and mobile phones. Devices can be connected to different networks, such as wired and wireless. Multiple calls and SIP forking enable the use of many SIP devices.
	Multimedia	SIP can support all media used for communications, such as various modalities for text, voice and video.
Architecture	Proxies are for routing	The function of SIP proxies is call routing as opposed to call control, state and management which is the role of the endpoints.
	Endpoint call state and features	The SIP endpoints maintain the call state and are under local control by the application. This is in harmony with the end-to-end control principle of the Internet.
	Dialog model, not call model	SIP presumes that the application is a separate layer above the SIP dialog that accomplishes the signaling functions. This is in contrast to the telephony call model, where the application and signaling are merged in a vertical manner.

Table 1.6 *(continued)*

Architecture *(continued)*	Endpoint fate sharing	The application and the call state are situated in the endpoints and do not depend on any "network services." The call can fail, only if the endpoints fail. This makes a SIP-based system highly available and conforms to a key architectural principle of the Internet.
	Components-based design	SIP defines primitives out of which complex functions can be built. For example, the notifications about the states for registration, dialog, conference, messaging, presence and subscriptions enable endpoints to support context aware communications.
	Components are logical, not physical	The logical components of SIP, such as user agents, registrars, proxies and redirect servers can be placed in various functional packages. SIP specifications define purely logical functions.
	Designed for the Internet	SIP makes use of core Internet services such as DNS for resource discovery and load balancing as well as security using TLS.
	Generality over efficiency	The flexibility for introducing new services takes precedent over computing and network bandwidth utilization, given the ever increasing computing power and Internet bandwidth.
	Separating Signaling and media	The route of signaling packets thorough various servers is determined by specific services, while the media will always be routed directly between the endpoints. Complex topologies are thus enabled without impairing quality.
Design	Proxy transparency	Proxies are transparent to the methods, headers and bodies in SIP messages. This ensures transparency to the applications in the endpoints.

Table 1.6 ***(continued)***

Design *(continued)*	INVITE is stateful	Each INVITE message conveys the full state of the session to enable the invoking of underlying network resources, as appropriate. For example, an INVITE for an audio and video session may require more bandwidth.
	SIP URI's	A SIP URI may identify a user, a device, a service or some combination of those. Only the owner of the domain can identify the resource specified at the left side of the @ in the URI. Various and complex services can thus be invoked.
	Extensibility and compatibility	SIP is supporting a framework for new extensions on the assumption that new usage scenarios and new services cannot be predicted.
	International-ization	SIP is designed for the international setting of the Internet and can support UTF-8 encoding of text and the negotiation of languages.
	Explicit intermediaries	Proxies operate only at the explicit requests of the endpoints. Via and Record-Route headers are used for this purpose by proxies to keep their role well defined and bounded.
	Guided proxy routing	A user agent or proxy can predetermine the downstream proxies in the signaling path to the destination. This is also called *loose routing*.
	Transport Protocol independence	SIP can use various transport protocols, such as UDP, TCP and SCTP.
	Protocol reuse	SIP reuses many HTTP header fields and semantics. SIP also reuses other Internet protocols, such as SDP and MIME. This eases the learning curve and development of SIP implementations.

Conclusion

This chapter has introduced basic SIP behavior and capabilities as well as the design principles for SIP. Many of the message types and message bodies will be discussed in detail in the following chapters.

Chapter 2

Summary of SIP-based VoIP

Introduction

VoIP is a common application for SIP. Although this book is primarily about SIP services beyond VoIP, these services are part of the basic feature set of SIP. In addition, since SIP can handle multiple media types, most of the services in this chapter can be applied to video and text sessions in addition to just voice. This chapter will cover a typical set of VoIP services such as call transfer, forwarding, voicemail, etc. Finally, some quality of service (QoS) issues will be covered.

VoIP Service Description

A typical VoIP service involves the elements described in Table 2.1 on the next page.

Users in a VoIP network utilize SIP Phones, Clients, Adapters, or Enterprise Gateways to place voice calls. These devices must be configured with a minimum set of information that includes:

- Identity of the user. This will typically be a telephone number or extension, and may also include a user's URI. This information is used to populate the From: header field in requests.
- Shared secret, provided by the VoIP provider which identifies the individual user. This shared secret is provided after an authentication challenge by a server.
- SIP Server URI or address information. If a URI is provided, a DNS SRV lookup can be used to return the proxy server address IP address and port number. Simple load balancing in a proxy farm can be achieved using multiple SRV records. Instead of a URI, the IP address, port number, and transport protocol can be provisioned.
- Configuration URL or address. The detailed configuration details of the SIP UA can be provided by a configuration server. A framework for configuration of UAs has been developed.[45]

User authentication is usually performed upon registration and for certain requests such as INVITE requests. While UA certificates can be used, typically this is done using a shared secret and SIP Digest. REGISTER requests are sent at regular intervals to the default outbound proxy server for the service provider. Registration intervals are configurable, and typically

---

[45] D. Petrie, "A Framework for Session Initiation Protocol User Agent Profile Delivery." Internet Draft, October 2004, Work in progress.

Table 2.1 – VoIP network elements

Element	Description
SIP Phone	A SIP UA that looks like a normal phone except for an Ethernet connection or wireless link that connects into the user's broadband Internet connection. Terminates and originates SIP calls. A SIP Phone may have a screen and additional services such as directory access. See Fig. 2.1.
SIP Phone Adapter	A small appliance that has an Ethernet jack for the user's broadband connection. The device also has an RJ-11 telephone port (FXO—Foreign Exchange Office) that a conventional POTS telephone or telephone line can be plugged into.
SIP Soft Client	A PC or PDA software application that provides SIP UA functionality. Often a nomadic device that connects to the Internet in a variety of ways.
SIP/PSTN Gateway	Provides gateway services for between the Internet and the PSTN. May have SS7 or PRI (Primary Rate Interface) trunks to PSTN
Enterprise Gateway	Used to SIP enable a conventional PBX (Private Branch Exchange) or Key system. May have analog trunks or PRIs (ISDN Primary Rate Interface).
SIP Servers	Provide core proxy, registration, and services to the VoIP user. A STUN Server may also be utilized by endpoints to traverse NATs.
Media Relays	Used to relay VoIP RTP media traffic. Required in some NAT/Firewall traversal scenarios.
SIP-Enabled Firewall or Application Layer Gateway (ALG)	Used between the SIP UA and the broadband network.
AAA Server	Authentication, Authorization, and Accounting Server. Stores user credentials, call detail records, logs, etc.
Voicemail Server	A SIP UA that includes media servers for playing prompts and recording messages.

Figure 2.1 – Examples of a SIP phone: snom 360 (left) and Zultys ZIP 4x4
(Photos courtesy of snom Technology AG and Zultys Technologies.)

range from 60 minutes to 10 minutes depending on the scenario. The presence of a NAT can be determined from the registration information and be used to introduce a network-based NAT traversal technique involving a media relay. Alternatively, the UAs can implement endpoint-based NAT discovery and traversal using STUN, TURN, and ICE as described in Chapter 13.

SIP and PSTN interworking allows a phone call originated on the Internet to be routed to a PSTN telephone, and a phone call on the PSTN to route to a VoIP device. The gateway must map both the SIP signaling messages and RTP media into the equivalent trunk. Gateways can be decomposed into a media component (Media Gateway) and a signaling component (Media Gateway Controller), sometimes with a control protocol used between the two elements.

A basic call flow for SIP to PSTN is shown in Figure 2.2. The first step consists of the user dialing a phone number. While some SIP phones and adapters have dial plans, most of these devices just rely on a simple time-out or else use a "send" or "#" key to terminate the dial string. The dialed digits are then put into either a SIP URL[46], or a tel URL.[47]

---

[46] RFC 3261: Rosenberg, J., Schulzrinne, H., Camarillo, G., Johnston, A., Peterson, J., Sparks, R., Handley, M. and E. Schooler, "SIP: Session Initiation Protocol." IETF, June 2002.

[47] RFC 3966: "The tel URI for Telephone Numbers," by H. Schulzrinne. IETF, December 2004.

Examples are as follows:

sip:13145551212@voip.example.com
tel:011441235534

This URL is used as the Request-URI for the INVITE, which is usually sent to the default outbound proxy server that has been provisioned into the SIP phone or adapter.

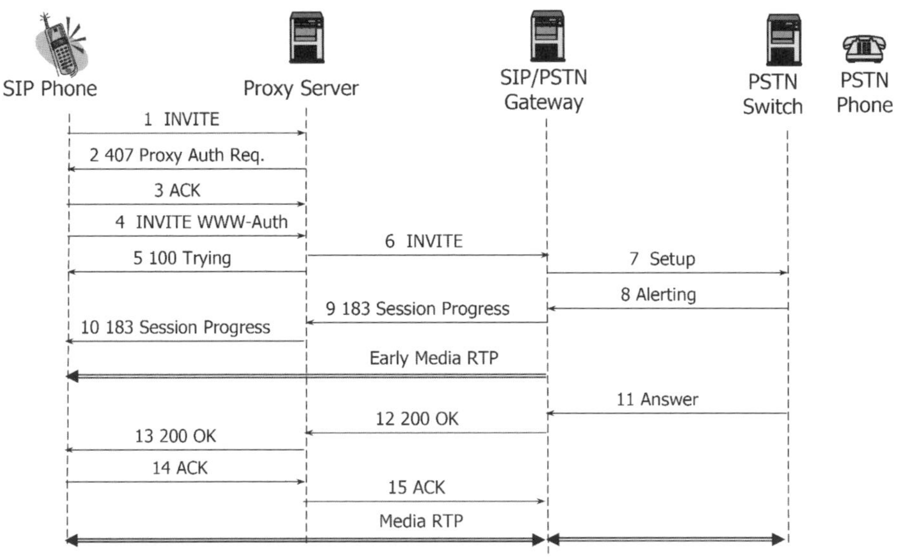

Figure 2.2 – SIP-to-PSTN call flow

The proxy server issues a 407 Proxy Authentication Required authentication Digest challenge to the UA, which then resends the INVITE with the shared secret. Only if the authentication is successful is the INVITE processed by the proxy. The proxy server can utilize an AAA (Authorization, Authentication, and Accounting) server using a protocol such as Radius[48] to retrieve stored credentials.

If the dial string corresponds to another VoIP user, the INVITE may be proxied to the destination SIP phone or adapter. Other databases such as

[48] RFC 3702: Loughney, J. and G. Camarillo, "Authentication, Authorization, and Accounting Requirements for the Session Initiation Protocol (SIP)." IETF, February 2004.

ENUM[49] may be queried to see if there is a SIP URI associated with the telephone number. If not, the INVITE will be routed to a SIP/PSTN gateway. Having performed the authentication of the user, the proxy server can include identity information in the request. For example, as discussed in the Network Asserted Identity section in Chapter 12, the P-Asserted-Identity header field[50] can be populated with the originating telephone number of the caller.

The VoIP service provider's proxy server and gateway will usually have a security association, so the gateway does not need to authenticate the UA again. For example, they may share private keys over an IPsec[51] tunnel. The gateway will map dialed digits in the Request-URI into the PSTN signaling protocol. For example, the detailed mapping of SIP to ISUP is covered in RFC 3398.[52] Mapping of SIP to ISDN is similar and also straightforward. Indications of ringback in the PSTN map to the 180 Ringing response. A phone number in a P-Asserted-Identity header field may be mapped into a Calling Party identification field for PSTN Caller ID services.

If there is a possibility of in-band progress indications in the PSTN then early media must be used. Early media is defined as RTP flows during a SIP session prior to the 200 OK answer response. Typically, if early media is present, a gateway will send a 183 Session Progress containing an SDP answer and at the same time stream RTP media back to the calling UA. Note that if the INVITE did not contain an SDP offer, early media cannot be sent by the gateway. Early media interacts poorly with a number of SIP services. As a result, a longer term approach using the Content-Disposition header field has been defined.[53]

---

[49] RFC 3761: "The E.164 to Uniform Resource Identifiers (URI) Dynamic Delegation Discovery System (DDDS) Application (ENUM)," by P. Falstrom and M. Mealing. IETF, April 2004.

[50] RFC 3325: Jennings, C., Peterson, J. and M. Watson, "Private Extensions to the Session Initiation Protocol (SIP) for Asserted Identity within Trusted Networks." IETF, November 2002.

[51] RFC 2401: "Security Architecture for the Internet Protocol," by S. Kent, R. Atkinson. IETF, November 1998.

[52] RFC 3398: Camarillo, G., Roach, A., Peterson, J. and L. Ong, "Integrated Services Digital Network (ISDN) User Part (ISUP) to Session Initiation Protocol (SIP) Mapping." IETF, December 2002.

[53] RFC 3959: Camarillo, G., "The Early Session Disposition Type for the Session Initiation Protocol (SIP)." IETF, December 2004.

An answering of the call in the PSTN results in a 200 OK and an ACK being exchanged which completes the call setup.

In order to route a PSTN telephone number to a VoIP device, the PSTN routing must cause the call to terminate on a PSTN-to-SIP gateway. To the PSTN network, the gateway will appear as the termination point—a local or Class 5 switch, for example. Forwarding or number portability can be used to move a telephone number from a PSTN device to a VoIP device.

A PSTN/SIP Gateway receiving an incoming call from the PSTN will generate an INVITE, populate information about the Called Party Number and the Calling Party Number, and forward to the proxy server.

A proxy server will consult the registration database to find the latest registration for the device assigned to that telephone number. The INVITE is then proxied to that SIP phone or adapter which then rings. A SIP phone or adapter typically does not send a 183 Session Progress with early media; instead it will send a 180 Ringing and allow the gateway to either provide this alerting indication or generate ringback tone, depending on the interworking.

Accounting for calls to the PSTN can be done at either the gateway or the proxy server. CDRs (Call Detail Records) can be generated and stored for later rating and billing operations. However, many VoIP services utilize flat rate billing for simplicity.

If local services such as local operator, local directory assistance, or emergency services are provided, trunking to these local services must be established to the gateway.

A signaling "keep alive" mechanism known as the Session Timer[54] can be used to force UAs to send periodic re-INVITEs. If a re-INVITE is not received, the proxy can assume that the session has failed and can destroy any state information stored.

Media – RTP and RTCP

VoIP media sessions are established using an offer/answer SDP exchange transported by SIP, as discussed in Chapter 1. The voice media is transported using RTP—Real Time Transport Protocol.[55] Usually, a small set of

---

[54] S. Donovan and J. Rosenberg, "Session Timers in the Session Initiation Protocol (SIP)." IETF Internet-Draft, July 2004, Work in progress.

[55] RFC 3550: "RTP: A Transport Protocol for Real-Time Applications," by H. Schulzrinne, S. Casner, R. Frederick, V. Jacobson. IETF, July 2003.

codecs are offered and a single codec is accepted in the exchange. VoIP networks commonly support both uncompressed and compressed codecs. Some examples are given in Table 2.2. The codecs with RTP/AVP Profile numbers are defined in RFC 3551.[56]

Table 2.2 – Common VoIP codecs

Codec Name	RTP/AVP Payload Type	Description
G.711 μ-Law	0	Uncompressed Pulse Coded Modulation (PCM) Codec with μ-Law companding. No transcoding necessary for calls to PSTN in North America and Japan.
G.711 A Law	8	Uncompressed PCM Codec with A-Law companding. No transcoding necessary for calls to PSTN in Europe.
G.729	18	Code Excited Linear Prediction Model (CELP) compressed codec.
G.723	4	Compressed codec with Voice Activity Detection (VAD).
AMR	Dynamic	Adaptive Multirate Codec.[57] Used as default codec by 3GPP mobile networks.
iLBC	Dynamic	Internet Low Bit Rate Codec.[58] A low bit rate codec available as freeware.

In addition to RTP, UAs also use RTP Control Protocol or RTCP[55] to communicate quality and other information. RTCP messages can also be used as a media "keep alive" as RTCP messages are exchanged at regular intervals, even when a silence suppressing codec is used, or if the media session is on hold.

---

[56] RFC 3551: "RTP Profile for Audio and Video Conferences with Minimal Control," by H. Schulzrinne and S. Casner. IETF, July 2003.

[57] RFC 3267: J. Sjoberg, M. Westerlund, A. Lakaniemi, Q. Xie, "Real-Time Transport Protocol (RTP) Payload Format and File Storage Format for the Adaptive Multi-Rate (AMR) and Adaptive Multi-Rate Wideband (AMR-WB) Audio Codecs." IETF, June 2002.

[58] RFC 3952: "Real-time Transport Protocol (RTP) Payload Format for internet Low Bit Rate Codec (iLBC) Speech," by A. Duric, S. Andersen. IETF, December 2004.

The RTCP Extended Reports (RTCP XR)[59] provides additional quality information. In particular, the VoIP Quality report is especially of interest in VoIP networks. An endpoint or Gateway can collect these VoIP quality reports of actual calls and log the information.

Typical Service Features

Besides the basic call completion described in the previous section, most VoIP service offerings include many of the services described in this section. Detailed call flows for many of these services are described in the SIP Service Examples document.[60]

Calling Line Identification

Calling line identification, or Caller ID as it is sometimes known, is a simple service feature that can be provided for incoming calls. A SIP identity mechanism such as the P-Asserted-Identity header field can be used to display the calling party number on a display on a SIP phone or adapter. Alternatively, if an Identity[61] header field is present and validated, the From header identity can be displayed as an authenticated identity.

Forwarding

Call forwarding can be easily implemented in a SIP proxy server in a routing table. When incoming INVITE requests are received, the forwarding tables can be used to send the call to another telephone number or SIP phone. It is also possible to implement a forwarding service in a SIP phone or adapter. However, typically it is performed in the network so that the service is always available, even if the SIP phone or adapter is disconnected from the network.

Find Me/Follow Me

Once the proxy server implements simple call forwarding tables, it is easy to extend this service to multiple phone numbers or URIs. This can implement

---

[59] RFC 3611: "RTP Control Protocol Extended Reports (RTCP XR)," by T. Friedman, Ed., R. Caceres, Ed., A. Clark. November 2003.

[60] Johnston, A. and R. Sparks, "Session Initiation Protocol Service Examples." IETF Internet Draft, Work in progress.

[61] Peterson, J., and C. Jennings, "Enhancements for Authenticated Identity Management in the Session Initiation Protocol (SIP)." draft-ietf-sip-identity-03 (work in progress), September 2004.

a "hunt group" or ACD (Automatic Call Distributor) functionality. The searching can be performed in sequence or in parallel. The caller could either just hear ringing or hear a recorded announcement saying that the called party is being located.

Voicemail

A voicemail service can be implemented using call forwarding on no answer or busy logic in the proxy server along with a voicemail server. A voicemail server answers incoming INVITEs, plays prompts, records messages, and provides message waiting indications. The voicemail platform selects the proper voicemail box using either the Request-URI[62] generated by the proxy or perhaps using the Diversion header field[63] (note that Diversion is not a normative SIP standard). The message waiting indication can be accomplished using SIP Events[64] and the Message Waiting Indicator event package.[65] It is also common for VoIP systems to implement unified messaging systems in which messages can be retrieved over email and the web. A typical voicemail call flow is shown in Figure 2.3.

DTMF

The ability to send Dual Tone Multi-Frequency (DTMF) signals is a requirement for many PSTN services such as calling card, voicemail, pagers, and Interactive Voice Response (IVR) systems. While some SIP VoIP systems transport DTMF using INFO[66] messages, this method has actually never been standardized by the IETF. A number of approaches are possible:

- In-band delivery. If a non-compressed codec such as G.711 is used, DTMF tones can be transported in-band without problems.
- Telephone Events RTP packets. [67] For real-time synchronized DTMF tones, sending telephone events RTP packets, sometimes

---

[62] RFC 3087: Campbell, B. and R. Sparks, "Control of Service Context using SIP Request-URI." IETF, April 2001.

[63] "Diversion Indication in SIP," by S. Levy, J.R. Yang, and B. Byerly. IETF Internet-Draft, August 2004, Work in progress.

[64] RFC 3265: Roach, A., "Session Initiation Protocol (SIP)-Specific Event Notification." IETF, June 2002.

[65] RFC 3842: Mahy, R., "A Message Summary and Message Waiting Indication Event Package for the Session Initiation Protocol (SIP)." IETF, August 2004.

[66] RFC 2976: "The SIP INFO Method," by S. Donovan. IETF, October 2000.

[67] RFC 2833: "RTP Payload for DTMF Digits, Telephony Tones and Telephony Signals," by H. Schuzrinne and S. Petrack. IETF, May 2000.

also known as RFC 2833 tones. This payload type in the RTP must be negotiated during the offer/answer exchange. An example offer/answer exchange that allows Telephone Events transport of DTMF is shown in Table 2.3. Many SIP phones and adapters can only send Telephone Events, although most SIP-PSTN gateways can both send and receive Telephone Events.

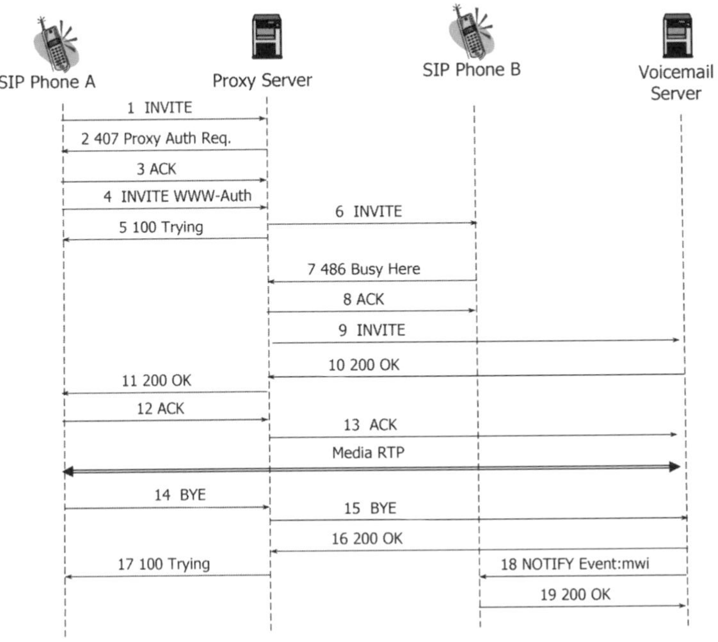

Figure 2.3 – Voicemail call flow

- KPML—Key Press Markup Language.[68] Instead of carrying tones and pre-ascribing meaning to them, this approach uses the SIP Events framework (SUBSCRIBE and NOTIFY) to define virtual "keys" which can be pressed. A companion protocol uses the REFER method to help applications learn they should subscribe to these key events, as outlined in the Application Interaction Framework document.[69]

[68] Burger, E., "A Session Initiation Protocol (SIP) Event Package for Key Press Stimulus (KPML)." draft-ietf-sipping-kpml-07 (work in progress), December 2004.

[69] "A Framework for Application Interaction in the Session Initiation Protocol (SIP)," by J. Rosenberg. IETF Internet-Draft, October 2004, Work in progress.

Fax

Facsimile transport is more of a business requirement than a consumer VoIP requirement. Again, if uncompressed codecs such as G.711 are used, fax will work. Otherwise, the T.38 fax over IP standard is used. Example call flows have been described by Li and Mule.[70]

Table 2.3 – Telephone events Offer/Answer exchange

Offer

```
v=0
o=alice 2890844526 2890844526 IN IP4 host.atlanta.com
s=
c=IN IP4 host.atlanta.com
t=0 0
m=audio 49170 RTP/AVP 0 97 98
a=rtpmap:0 PCMU/8000
a=rtpmap:97 iLBC/8000
a=rtpmap:98 telephone-event/8000
```

Answer

```
v=0
o=bob 2808844564 2808844564 IN IP4 host.biloxi.com
s=
c=IN IP4 host.biloxi.com
t=0 0
m=audio 49172 RTP/AVP 97 98
a=rtpmap:97 iLBC/8000
a=rtpmap:98 telephone-event/8000
```

Transfer

Call transfer is a very common operation. Basic unattended transfer or "blind transfer" is achieved using the REFER[71] method. The telephone number or URI of the target is included in a Refer-To header field. A more complex service is attended transfer.[72] This call flow, shown in Figure 2.4,

---

[70] J. Li and J. Mule, "SIP T.38 Call Flow Examples and Best Current Practices." IETF Internet-Draft, October 2001, Work in progress.

[71] RFC 3515: Sparks, R., "The Session Initiation Protocol (SIP) Refer Method." IETF, April 2003.

[72] "Session Initiation Protocol Call Control—Transfer," by R. Sparks, A. Johnston, and D. Petrie. IETF Internet-Draft, October 2004, Work in progress.

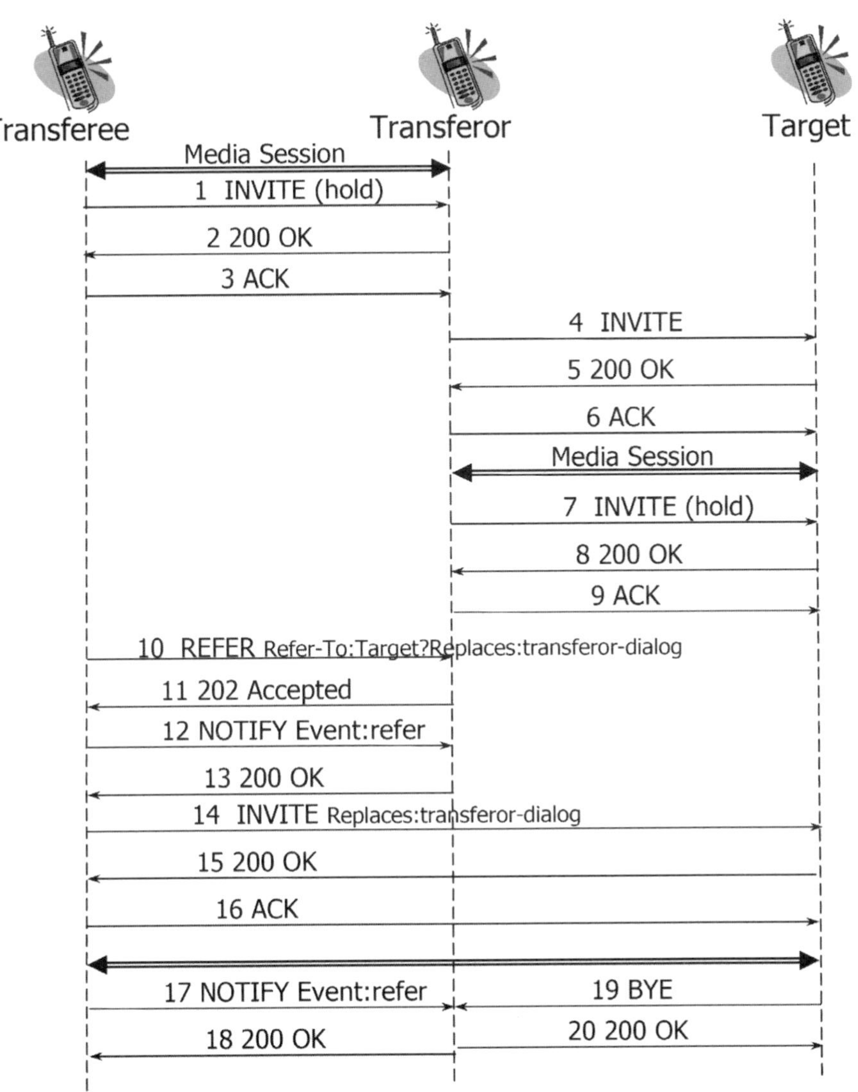

Figure 2.4 – Attended transfer using REFER and Replaces

is when the Transferor has sessions with both the Transfer Target and the Transferee. The Transferor then sends a REFER to the Transferee with a URI which resolves directly to the Transfer Target. In addition, a

Replaces[73] header field containing the dialog identifier of the session between the Transferor and the Target is escaped into the Refer-To URI. As a result, the Transferee generates an INVITE with a Replaces header field which causes this new session between the Transferee and the Target to "replace" the session between the Target and the Transferor, completing the transfer.

There is also another class of transfer services, sometimes known as "semi-attended transfer" which begins as an attended transfer but turn into an unattended transfer. However, there are race conditions associated with many of these call flows, as described by Sparks, Johnston, and Petrie.[72]

Call Park and Pickup

Call park and pickup services can also be implemented using REFER and Replaces. A call park can be a transfer to a media server which acts as a "Call Park Server." To pickup this call, an INVITE with Replaces can be sent to retrieve the call.

Automatic Callback

Automatic callback can be implemented using simple phone presence. If a call fails due to a busy signal, the calling phone can subscribe to the presence of the busy SIP phone. When the state of the SIP phone changes from busy to available, a notification will be sent, and the calling SIP phone can alert the user or automatically dial the user again.

Web Page Configuration

Many VoIP services provide a web page for user self-provisioning. In addition, the web portal can be used for call logging, call control, and unified messaging. Features and services can be invoked from the web page. Directory services and click-to-dial can be implemented as well.

Quality of Service Issues

Though quality of service (QoS) is technically not part of SIP for VoIP, questions on quality of service is often raised when considering VoIP. (The authors have actually wondered where people who have raised the QoS issue for VoIP were getting their insight from, since they were mostly not

[73] RFC 3891: "The Session Initiation Protocol (SIP) 'Replaces' Header," by R. Mahy, B. Biggs, R. Dean. IETF, September 2004.

users of VoIP themselves and could not be reached on some published VoIP address).

Public VoIP services are a fast-growing industry, though none of the large public VoIP service providers we know of has any QoS guarantees. The lack of QoS guarantees in public VoIP services is for a simple reason: VoIP service providers don't control the network where their customers may be. This may change, however, as DSL and cable Internet service providers are starting to offer VoIP as well. VoIP bundled with Internet access may have some QoS guarantees, but these can only be valid on the network of the access provider and are thus of very limited value.

VoIP is essentially a broadband Internet-enabled service and users who experience voice quality issues can safely apply several rules:

1. In case of voice clipping due to network congestion, just increase the bandwidth. ADSL and cable subscribers should have at least 150 kb/s uplink speed for each simultaneous voice call in their small office or home (SOHO) network.
2. Doing email or file transfers during a VoIP call will mostly severely impact the voice quality on links that have speeds below roughly 1 Mb/s. Even web browsing can interfere with VoIP on bandwidth-starved access links, since many web pages carry large amounts of data, such as animated commercials. Homes and small offices with lower speed Internet access may request Differentiated Services for VoIP from the Internet access provider and also apply local policy that protects VoIP on the access link from data. However, before spending money on expensive QoS service guarantees and special network gear for QoS, we recommend keeping in mind the maxim uttered by Dr. Lixia Zhang from UCLA:

QoS Does Not Create Bandwidth

We would like to add that adequate bandwidth is the best guarantee for QoS for VoIP.

It is the authors' experience in deploying commercial VoIP services that call quality issues can arise in both the local area network and in the access link between the local area network and the Internet. Quality issues on the core Internet backbone are so rare as to be negligible. QoS can be addressed in those parts of the network where there are problems, resulting in high end-to-end quality. Some common approaches to assure QoS in the LAN and on the access link include the following:

- **Use of switched Ethernet LANs:** Providing 100 Mb/s Ethernet ports to the desktop will practically eliminate any QoS issues on the LAN for VoIP, even if video is used as well.
- **Avoiding congested wireless LANs:** WLANs that are not 'oversubscribed' will support good quality VoIP, but congested wireless LANs (WLANs) will produce both VPN disconnects and poor VoIP QoS. Operators of WLANs must have an adequate density of WLAN access points for acceptable VoIP.

Packet marking of Differentiated Services bits:[74] This allows prioritization for voice packets to be applied in routers in the access network and in the IP backbone. This section will cover briefly some quality of service issues. The topic is a large one, but a few points will be made.

It is the authors' experience in deploying commercial VoIP services that call quality issues may arise in both the local area network and in the access link between the local area network and the Internet. Quality issues on the core Internet backbone are so rare as to be negligible. As a result, instead of the more difficult end-to-end QoS problem, QoS can be addressed in parts of the network, resulting in high end-to-end quality. Some common approaches to provide QoS in the LAN and access link include the following:

- **Packet marking of Differentiated Services bits.** This allows some prioritization to be applied in routers and the access link. Many SIP phones and clients can be configured to set particular Differentiated Services bits.
- **Packet length.** If the VoIP IP network is being shared with data applications, the network can be configured to ensure that large data packets are not generated. As VoIP media packets will typically be less than 500 bytes, these packets can have significant latency introduced if mixed in with large (e.g., 1500 bytes) data packets over a slow access link. Local policy enforcement and various techniques on slow access links can segment long data packets and limit the throughput of data packets so as not to interfere with voice.

---

[74] RFC 2475: "An Architecture for Differentiated Service," by S. Blake, D. Black, M. Carlson, E. Davies, Z. Wang, W. Weiss. IETF, December 1999.

Having used VoIP for many years both in the corporate office, at home and on travel, we caution users to always check if just providing adequate bandwidth is not less costly and less complex than deploying QoS.

- **Use of Internet codecs.** ITU-T voice codecs designed and developed for circuit switched networks perform poorly under packet loss. Loss rates of 1% can cause observable deterioration in quality. However, a new generation of voice codecs has been designed and developed for the Internet. These codecs can handle high loss rates, some up to 10% and higher without loss in perceived quality. The freeware Internet Low Bit rate Codec (iLBC)[75,.58] is an example of this class of codec, standardized as per RFC 3951 and RFC 3952. Last but not least, compressed codecs such as the iLBC can provide usable VoIP even on occasional dial-up Internet access links, though this may not always work, especially in dial-up links that are run at less than 40 kb/s.
- **Real-time monitoring of actual VoIP calls in a network.** Test calls and network simulators have limited use in finding and fixing real end user QoS problems due to the highly "bursty" nature of both the packet flows and the resulting error burst performance. An approach that allows real-time monitoring of actual VoIP calls is described in the SIP Performance Report event package.[76] This event package allows RTCP XR reports, which include such useful metrics as simulated MOS scores, to be collected by the VoIP service provider. The information can be published to a collector using the PUBLISH method.[77] Alternatively, a collector can SUBSCRIBE to a particular UAs quality reports. This gives a VoIP service provider useful quality reports on actual VoIP calls.

SIP-based VoIP Implementations

There are so many SIP-based VoIP products and services on the market, that finding the most suitable for a particular network or business requires some comparison shopping. The most well known sources on SIP VoIP implementations are given here.

---

[75] See http://www.ilbcfreeware.org/

[76] A. Johnston, H. Sinnreich, A. Clark, and A. Pendleton, "SIP Service Quality Reporting Event." IETF Internet-Draft, October 2004, Work in progress.

[77] RFC 3903: "Session Initiation Protocol (SIP) Extension for Event State Publication," A. Nemi. IETF, October 2004.

Arguably, many of the SIP implementations support more than just VoIP, but since the majority are focused on VoIP and SIP VoIP is also the most mature part of SIP applications, we will list these sources here, under the umbrella of SIP VoIP.

Commercial Sources for SIP Products and Services

- Pulver.com maintains a list of many existing SIP products at http://www.pulver.com/products/sip/. Most of the products on the Pulver web site are also shown at the VON conferences, see http://www.pulver.com/conference/index.html.
- The International SIP Forum keeps an updated catalog of SIP products at http://www.sipforum.org/.
- The SIP Products and Services Directory at the SIP Center http://www.sipcenter.com/sip.nsf/index is an excellent resource, not only for SIP products, but also for technical information about SIP and related topics, such as wireless and broadband.

Open Source SIP Applications

The saying that "some of the best things in life are for free" applies also to the open source SIP resources.

- Vovida is the original organization for free SIP software, among other open source code. Most key software components for SIP can be found at Vovida at http://vovida.org/
- The SIP Foundry has an impressive list of SIP modules that can be packaged by developers into various applications for VoIP. See http://www.sipfoundry.org/
- The open source PBX from Pingtel is based on the experience from developing the leading edge Pingtel SIP phones and servers. See: http://www.pingtel.com/solutions/products.jsp
- There are several open sources for specific SIP products, such as SIP Soft Phone at http://siphon.sourceforge.net/index.html

Example of Commercial SIP VoIP Service: MCI Advantage

We will provide here an example for a public, commercial VoIP service, MCI Advantage, better known to us, since the authors have contributed to its early development. MCI has been the first large carrier to our knowledge to announce a SIP-based VoIP service early in 2003, after which most other large carriers have followed suit.

MCI Advantage as shown in the diagram in Figure 2.5 is a hosted SIP service, targeted for small and medium enterprises that prefer a carrier hosted IP voice service. The SIP-based services provide many features that are detailed at the web site http://business.mci.com/index.htm

Essentially, small business customers need only to plug into their IP network SIP phones selected from a portfolio of SIP phones, tested for full interoperability by MCI. Existing telephony key systems or PBXs can also be connected as shown in the right side of Figure 2.5.

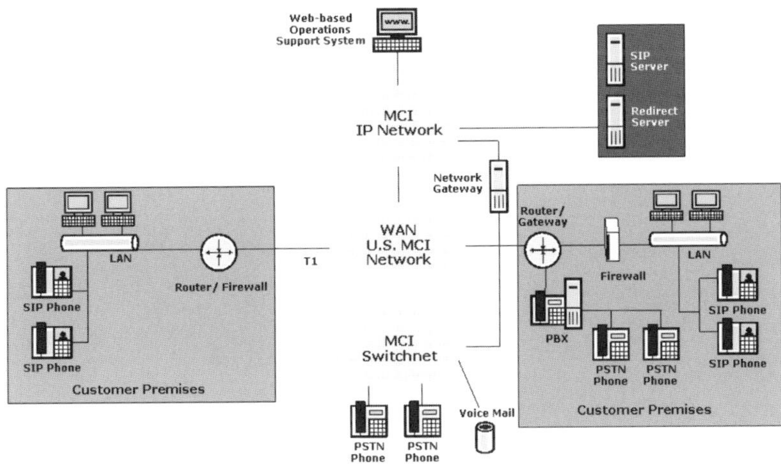

Figure 2.5 – MCI Advantage diagram

The Windows Messenger is also available as a soft phone, IM and video UA as shown in Figure 2.6.

Figure 2.6 – Microsoft Windows Messenger UA in MCI Advantage

Users have thus the choice of desktop SIP adapters, SIP phones, the PC softphone or to keep existing PBX phones during the migration phase to VoIP.

The authors have used the MCI VoIP capability deployed initially for internal use, since 2000, both using SIP desktop phones in the office and at home and using a laptop PC while on travel in many places across the world. This use has convinced us of the superior quality and functionality of VoIP when compared to legacy telephony. Maybe the excellent global MCI IP network has biased our judgment!

Free SIP VoIP Services

There are also a number of free VoIP services based on SIP. The word "free" should not mislead the reader that there is a business model best known to the "free" service provider that can assure a financially sustainable service. Here are some of such SIP services at the time of this writing:

- The Pulver FWD (Free World Dialup) service (founded in 1995) provides free registration and free SIP-SIP call routing at http://www.fwd.pulver.com. Related paid services provide PSTN gateway service and there are also a number of SIP phones and PC soft clients available that work with the FWD service.
- The iptel.org offers free registration and SIP-SIP call routing at http://www.iptel.org.
- SIPphone.com provides free SIP-SIP call routing with the purchase of a SIP adapter. Free soft phones can be downloaded directly form the site.

Summary

The basic architecture, elements, and features in a SIP VoIP service have been described. SIP-based VoIP can support all PBX and Centrex call features known from legacy circuit switched telephony. SIP VoIP is mature and deployed in many products and services.

Chapter 3

The Universe Beyond VoIP

Introduction

Paradoxically enough, when having to make a long distance or international phone call, most people think even at the time of this writing of the telephone network first. They probably think of the mobile phone second and only early experimenters and network savvy users will know to make long distance and international phone calls using the Internet. It is therefore interesting to explore a short summary comparing the legacy telephone network with what is marketed at present as voice over IP (VoIP) and what VoIP really means in the context of the Internet.

The Short History of VoIP

Voice over Internet Protocol (VoIP) was preceded by the conventional time division multiplex (TDM), public circuit switched telephone network (PSTN) that as of this writing still dominates the voice traffic. The telephone networks shown in Figure 3.1 use the central control of the Intelligent Network.[1]

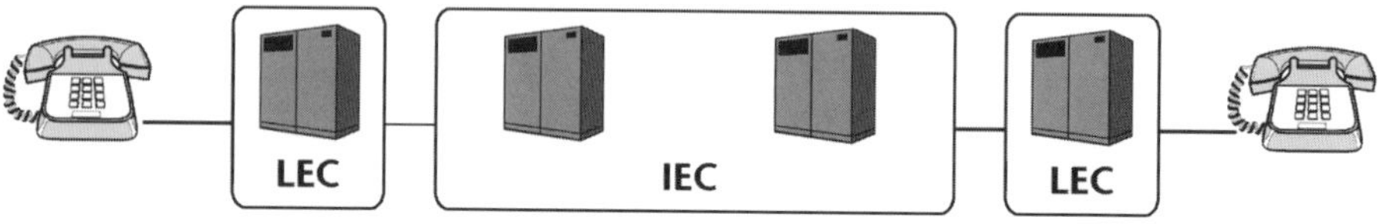

Legend
LEC: Local Exchange Carrier (local phone company)
IEC: Inter-exchange Carrier (long distance phone company)

Figure 3.1 – Conventional circuit switched telephone network model

Innovators however quickly discovered that the long distance (IEC) and global part of the circuit switched telephone network can be bypassed, by using the Internet. Since long distance and international phone calls could be transported at less cost using the Internet in the middle, the first phase of VoIP was commercially launched and led to the model in Figure 3.2. This model based on the lower cost of VoIP is also called arbitrage.

Arbitrage refers to a telephony business model that avoids the artificial high rates charged for traditional long distance and international telephony.

[1] The Intelligent Network has proven not to be a good idea, as first noted by D. Isenberg in his paper "Rise of the Stupid Network." The paper can be found at http://www.hyperorg.com/misc/stupidnet.html.

Such rates are supported by government protected tariffs and by government regulations.

> To quote a well known magazine, "the market has a dim view of the long-distance business" (*Barrons*, 7/19/2004). This is due besides oversupply also to the well known limitation of the telephone system, (and not the long distance part alone):
>
> 1. The telephone network has been designed and optimized for one single application: Voice telephony.
> 2. A byproduct of the focus on voice has made telecom networks perennially starved for bandwidth that is required for data. Later attempts to accommodate 'data', such as ISDN and BISDN could not change this bandwidth penury.
> 3. All new services and applications require the upgrade of the network, since control is 'in the network'. This is also referred to as the "Intelligent Network." The Intelligent Network concept has been proven to be a formidable obstacle for innovation.
>
> By contrast, the Internet is replacing the telephone network because:
>
> 1. The Internet has been designed to support any application and any type of communications,
> 2. Bandwidth hungry computers have made the Internet core a "very broadband" network.
> 3. The end-to-end (e2e) control principle of the Internet places new applications and services in the endpoints. This has also been articulated as the Internet is a "dumb network." The dumb network has been proven to be the true home for innovation.

Initial VoIP implementations were run over private IP networks due to the perception promoted mostly by the circuit switched industry that the "Internet does not have quality of service (QoS)." Private IP networks, however, have among other drawbacks that they do not have the geographical reach of the Internet and cannot be economically justified for one single application like VoIP. After a costly reality check, many arbitrage networks moved therefore from private IP networks to the public Internet.

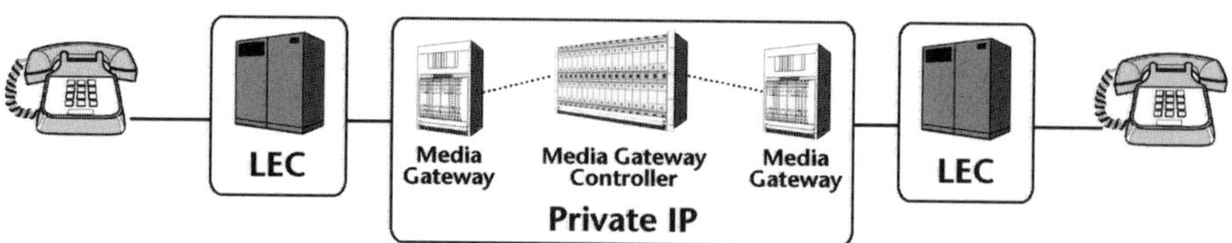

Figure 3.2 – VoIP version 00: Arbitrage for long distance and international calls

The arbitrage model for VoIP shown in Figure 3.2 uses media gateways to convert voice between the PCM format of the PSTN and the IP packet format. The main features of this model are:

- The VoIP network is essentially private and may have proprietary technologies,
- There is no IP interconnect to any other VoIP network,
- The media gateways have mostly central control: Media gateway (MG) controller,
- The MG emulates the control of the long distance switches of the PSTN,
- The end users are not aware of IP, except for the lower rates they may pay,
- There is considerable controversy and uncertainty about taxing and regulation for this VoIP model.

The arbitrage VoIP model has fast eroding profitability for its operators since they can compete only on price.

New services are however the key requirement for new revenue. An economic study by IDC[2] states that "unless VoIP providers can offer compelling new services, IP telephony will become nothing more than price arbitrage."

The LD and international arbitrage model have produced countless access charge disputes between LD and LECs. There are also many issues related to regulation and taxation that are however beyond the scope of this book. The authors believe the arbitrage telephony model does not qualify as true VoIP.

---

[2] Readers are encouraged to get up-to-date telecom market forecasts, for example the Gartner *Forecast: Telecommunications Market Take, 4Q004* and other similar reports from other sources, such as IDC Market Analysis *US Landline 2004-2008 Forecast*.

The increased penetration of broadband in the consumer market and the widespread deployment of IP networks in the enterprise have enabled the next model for VoIP, where end users can actually use IP devices for telephony as shown in Figure 3.3.

Broadband users have a choice of using adapters to connect traditional analog phones in the home to their local IP network, to use the PC or laptop as a phone or to use dedicated SIP phones as shown in Figure 3.3.

Notice the implementation of the IP-PSTN gateways in Figure 3.2 using a central controller for the media gateways. Such a central controller is also called a softswitch and can control special "slave" type of media gateways and IP phones also called "terminals." The control protocols deployed by the softswitch are of the master-slave type. The most widely deployed master-slave protocols are SGCP, MCGP (RFC3435) and MEGACO/H.248 (RFC3525 and RFC3054).

The softswitch concept is an attempt to model the PSTN switch voice services over IP technology.

- The intelligence in the endpoints and the possible applications are ignored,
- The end user gets only PSTN-like voice service, but no IP applications,
- The end user has no control or choice of VoIP service providers.

In the case of peering between softswitches within the network of a single service provider or between service providers, SIP is the preferred protocol and this is commonly referred to as SIP trunking. A softswitch network with SIP trunking does not however support SIP telephony devices, instant messaging, presence, etc.

Teresa Hastings from MCI has made the case that IP-PSTN gateway service may have a rather short life cycle as shown in Figure 3.3b, since with the proliferation of broadband Internet access, the need to use the PSTN at all will rapidly diminish as users can have more opportunities for end-to-end Internet communications with all the resulting advantages.

The IP-PSTN gateway service can act as a replacement for both local and long distance PSTN telephone services and most so called VoIP service providers (VISP) are based on this model at the time of this writing.

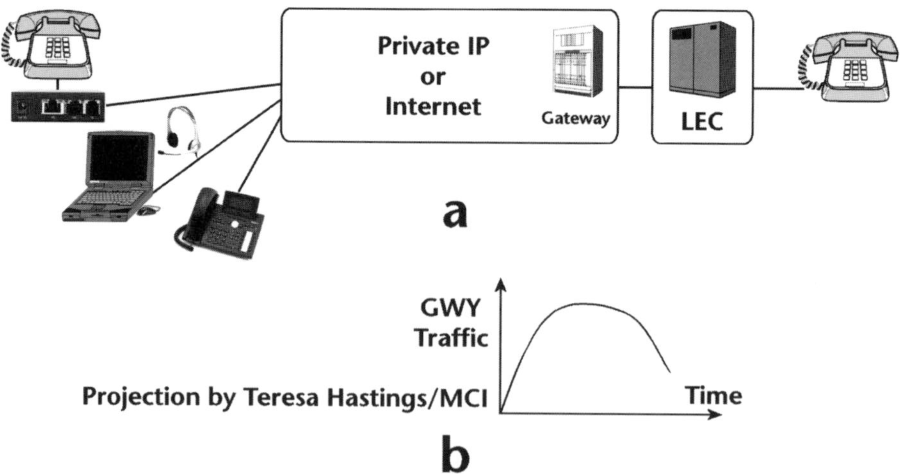

Figure 3.3 – VoIP version 01: Gateway service to the PSTN.
a) Network diagram; b) The lifecycle for gateway service

This service model has some of the same drawbacks as the arbitrage model:

- Users still get the PSTN telephony experience only,
- Only telephone numbers can be used,
- No IP communications are possible (presence, IM, multimedia, etc.).

Similar to the arbitrage telephony model, gateway services raise countless access charge disputes between LD and LECs and there are also many issues related to regulation and taxation. The authors believe the IP-PSTN telephony model does not qualify as true VoIP either.

A few advantages of VoIP however are already manifesting:

- Some VoIP providers offer to users the free choice of phone numbers in any calling area served by that provider (practically in all or most are codes in the US for example). The choice of local area codes by users is however not permitted by regulators in some other countries. The reader may however note that in principle, such a capability could also be provided by PSTN number portability, though at some higher cost.
- Calls within the IP network of the same VoIP operator are usually free.

- Video phones are supported, but only within the IP network of the same VoIP operator. The 100's of kb/s bandwidth required for acceptable video telephony is not possible on the PSTN.

Just like in the previous model, the VoIP network has no direct VoIP connectivity to any other network. This leads to the anomaly shown in Figure 3.4.

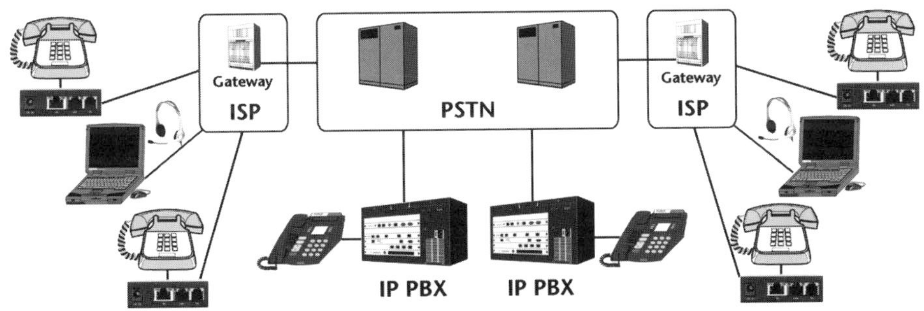

Figure 3.4 – VoIP islands

In this version users at both ends are connected to IP networks, in most cases over the public Internet, but the only way to communicate between the VoIP islands is via the PSTN. The VoIP islands in Figure 3.4 can be either VISP networks or enterprise IP networks.

- IP islands can support internal IP-IP VoIP calls,
- IP islands must use the PSTN for off-net calls,
- IP endpoints on different islands can communicate only using the PSTN with all the limitations, expense and regulatory issues that result form touching the PSTN.

The fact that IP endpoints like PC/laptops and SIP phones on different VoIP islands must use the PSTN to communicate is very bizarre as mentioned, but sadly enough reflect the status of most VoIP networks at the beginning of 2005. We assume that no direct IP connectivity is allowed for off-net calls because the VISP operators consider IP-IP calling a business threat, in the sense that it circumvents their PSTN gateway service for which they can charge by usage.

In our opinion, all three VoIP models shown here are essentially a form of reselling PSTN service since the only off-net calls allowed are two and from the PSTN. Since PSTN resources (including telephone numbers) are used, we will state here the following controversial position for the VoIP community:

So-called VoIP services that provide only PSTN phone numbers and connectivity only to the PSTN may in our opinion justifiably be taxed and regulated as applicable to any other PSTN service. The fact that some VoIP technology is part of the internal plumbing, not visible to the end user is not a distinctive service feature to qualify for special regulatory treatment.

Direct IP-IP connectivity for VoIP is also a major threat to the whole legacy telephony industry. Indeed, *if users can make direct IP-IP phone calls for everything, including emergency calls, who needs the traditional phone services?*

The magnitude of the disruption by VoIP on the telecom industry can be judged by the following indicators[3]:

- Fixed voice services market in 2004: Over $400 billion (endangered revenue)
- Mobile services, mostly voice: $480 billion (endangered revenue)
- Fixed Internet/PublicIP access service: Over $70 billion (this revenue will increase).

Users having Internet access can have however telephony service that is essentially part of the Internet service, at little or no extra cost. In other words, the fixed services voice market, to the degree that it has not migrated to mobile voice may be absorbed totally or mostly as part of the Internet access services.

With the advent of 4G wireless networks, mobile voice may also be absorbed to a large degree as part of wireless broadband internet access services.

The above numbers show a potential of shrinkage of up to 90% in our opinion of present fixed line and mobile telecommunications services due to the Internet. Such a huge disruption of the legacy telecommunications industry will however not come without protracted legal, regulatory and competitive battles.

[3] As stated in footnote 2 of this chapter, readers are encouraged to get up-to-date telecom market forecasts from such organizations as Gartner and IDC. Though we acknowledge the valuable numbers about the present telecom market in such reports, we believe the Internet will essentially absorb most present telecom services.

We noted previously that the only present *on-net capability* of VoIP networks that cannot be supported be the PSTN is broadband video telephony.

The above summary descriptions of the various VoIP services are in marked contrast to the sheer endless capabilities of Internet communications.

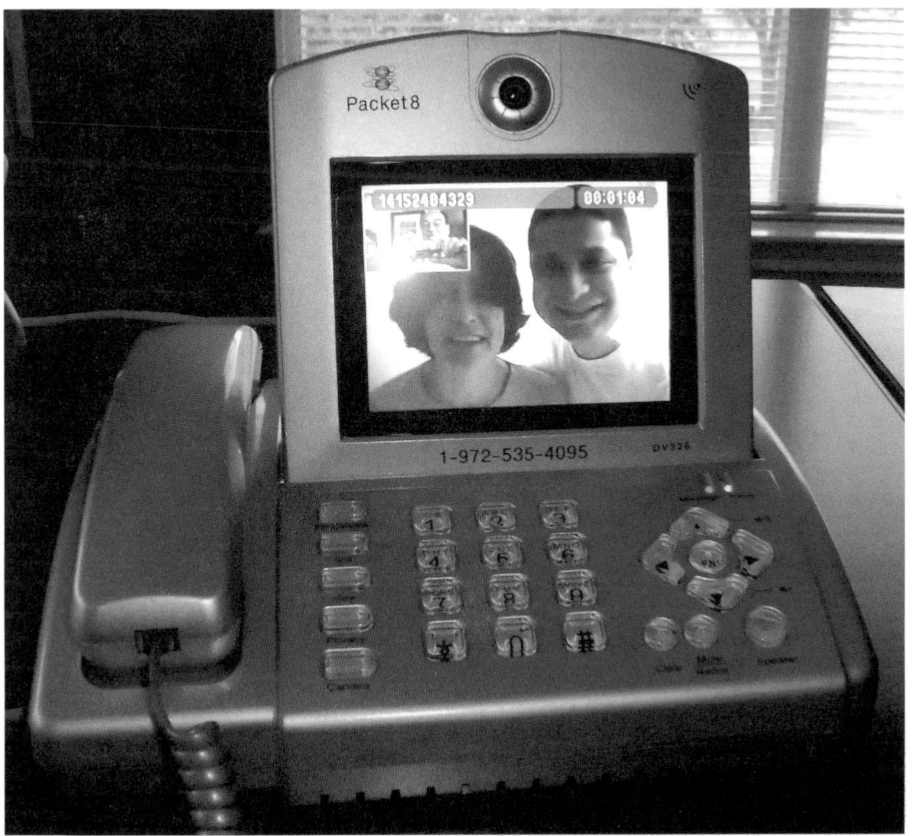

Figure 3.5 – IP video telephony using the model 326 SIP video phone from Packet8

VoIP is Only One of Many Internet Applications Enabled by SIP

SIP is at present the dominant VoIP protocol because of the rich portfolio of communication services enabled over the Internet that extend far beyond telephony.

- Voice is just another Internet application (though sometimes more equal than other applications in the model of telephony centric thinking),
- *SIP Presence* enables context aware communications. SIP Presence may well be the dial tone of the 21st century,
- The SIP presence and events architecture enables the integration of communications and applications,
- Consistent handling of all media: Instant messaging (IM), voice, video, games,
- Conferencing and collaboration using all media types,
- SIP-enabled contact centers for customer support,
- Global connectivity using Internet DNS and ENUM services,
- Global mobility and the enabling of the so-called *fixed-mobile convergence,*
- SIP security with SIP identity as a core component,
- NAT and firewall traversal,
- Meeting regulatory requirements better than the PSTN,
- Going back to the peer-to-peer roots: P2P SIP,
- Last but not least: What has not yet been invented. Here, the flexibility and extensibility of SIP is probably one of its main assets, in spite of the complexity that comes from multiple extensions to SIP. RFC 3427 specifies the change process for SIP so as to maintain the architectural integrity required for interoperability over the Internet.

> The above capabilities of Internet communications are a good reference guide for purchasing VoIP services or equipment:
>
> - Don't buy any VoIP service that does not support Internet addressing (URLs),
> - Any service, solution or design that does not support SIP presence and IM is technically obsolete.

Even when considering telephony alone, the importance of presence cannot be overstated to avoid wasting time with unsuccessful call attempts (don't call when I am not there) and for polite and sensitive telephony etiquette (don't call me when I am busy, use IM when I am in a quiet place or in another conference). An example of a SIP phone that features presence is shown in Figure 3.6.

The above capabilities of SIP beyond VoIP will be described in the chapters that follow.

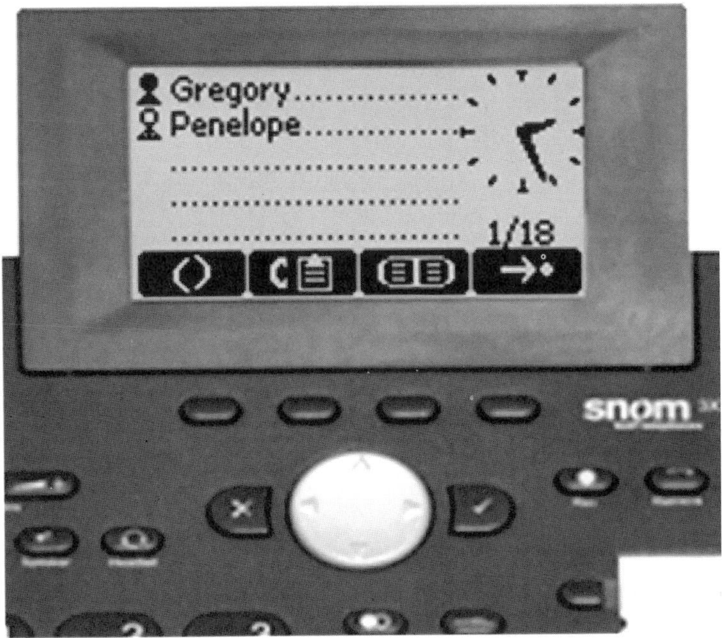

Figure 3.6 – SIP phone with display of presence
(Photo of snom 360 courtesy of snom Technology, AG.)

Summary

The so called VoIP services have progressed from the arbitrage model to the IP-PSTN gateway service model, but mostly are still an emulation of legacy circuit switched telephony, since:

- Direct IP-IP calling between VoIP providers is usually not possible at present,
- User do not get any exposure to the rich capabilities of Internet communications,
- Presence and IM is not provided in VoIP services that only emulate the PSTN or the PBX.

Chapter 4

Application Examples for SIP Location and Emergency Services

Introduction

SIP is a general approach for creating, modifying and terminating sessions between applications over the Internet. Most work to date has been dedicated to the specific application area of real-time communications, such as telephony, instant messaging, voice and video, but this does not limit the use of SIP for other applications. SIP also provides location information of users (or their applications) and thus can also act as a rendezvous protocol.

SIP is also particularly well suited as a presence protocol and this is due to both the rendezvous function and the intrinsic property of the SIP event notifications. The initial applications of the SIP events architecture was focused on communications applications, such as automatic call-back services, message waiting indicators, presence for instant messaging and PSTN to Internet interworking based on call state events.

The communication of events based on the SUBSCRIBE and NOTIFY model can however be extended to any type of application and has found numerous useful applications in the marketplace as we will show here.

Table 4.1 – New Services Based on SIP

Service	Description
Multimedia (Chapter 1)	Rich multimedia communications that include instant text messaging (M), interactive text, SMS, voice and video sessions. The choice of media and the negotiation of the codec types.
Presence (Chapter 5)	The publication of presence information and subscriptions to receive notification about presence. Various presence attributes and data formats. The managing and filtering of presence information for privacy depending who the watchers of presence are.
Events (Chapter 5)	The registration of users, call state, message waiting and watcher information for presence can be best handled using the SIP events architecture.

Table 4.1 *(continued)*

Service	Description
Conferencing/ collaboration (Chapter 6)	SIP was developed initially for multimedia conferencing on the Internet and is now the basis of all leading commercial conferencing and collaboration products in industry and academia.
Integration of comm's and applications (This chapter)	SIP events can support notifications for any type of business or other applications and can in turn trigger processes based on communication events, such as presence or dialog state.
Global connectivity, ENUM (Chapter 7)	The sheer countless VoIP and IM islands, such as PBXs, enterprise and public VoIP services can be connected on a global basis using URLs and the Internet DNS and in particular, using ENUM for telephone number-based addressing.
Mobility (Chapter 9)	The IP Multimedia System in 3G wireless networks is based on SIP. Beyond that, SIP application level mobility can support user mobility, terminal mobility and session mobility.
Customer care (Chapter 11)	The voice-only telephony call centers are migrating to contact centers that mix presence, information and IM with voice for superior customer satisfaction and high network efficiency.
Secure communications (Chapter 12)	Secure SIP signaling, identity and encryption can prevent nuisances such as telemarketing, spam and also the illegal intercept of communications.
NAT and firewall traversal (Chapter 13)	Network Address Translators (NAT) can be a significant obstacle for many Internet applications. A well designed approach for SIP can however assure the traversal of NAT and firewalls consistent with flexibility for new services, security and local policies.

Table 4.1 *(continued)*

Service	Description
User choice and preferences (Chapters 1 and 2)	SIP caller preference and the indication of user capabilities (RFC 3841 and RFC 3840) can tailor the session to best fit the choice of users. Moreover, just like on the Web, SIP can support simultaneous user accounts with several service providers.
Lowest cost of communications	Internet-centric communications are based on standards compliant software running on commodity server machines in the client-server mode (CS SIP) or even only in the user devices in the peer-to-peer mode (P2P SIP). Once developed, SIP services offer not only the richest communications, but also at the lowest cost compared to other alternatives, such as the legacy telecom networks, the PBX or 2G mobile networks. SIP-based communications do not necessarily require dedicated network infrastructure on the Internet.

The SIP Ecologic System

SIP is not just a protocol, but an ecologic system by itself since it depends on other protocols, such as SDP and RTP and has generated new protocols such as SIMPLE, XCON and XCAP.

Figure 4.1 shows the ecologic system around SIP.[1]

The various protocols shown here, are in part explained in this book, but may also require consulting the vast list of Internet standards.

Reading Map for SIP and Applications

As of this writing there are 69 RFCs about SIP and its applications. The numbers and titles of the SIP RFCs can be found at the IETF web site http://www.rfc-editor.org/rfcsearch.html

[1] "SIP—are we there yet?" by Henning Schulzrinne and Kundan Singh. VON SIP Summit, Jan 17, 2005.

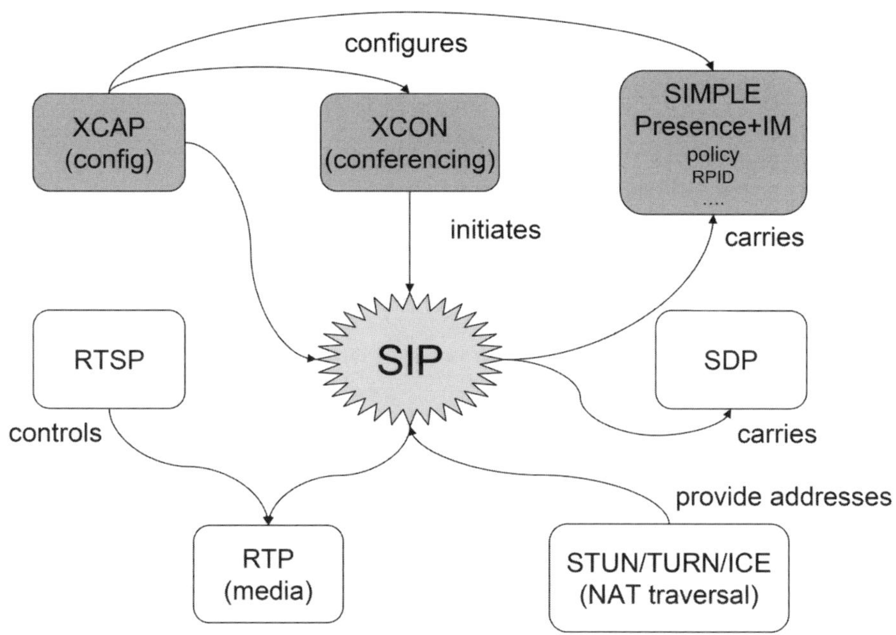

Figure 4.1 – The ecologic system of SIP

The working groups relevant to SIP can be found at the following URL: http://ietf.org/html.charters/wg-dir.html

The IETF working groups related to SIP are:

SIP:	Session Initiation Protocol
SIPPING:	Session Initiation Proposal Investigation
SIMPLE:	SIP for Instant Messaging Leveraging Extensions
XCON:	Centralized Conferencing
IPTEL:	IP Telephony
SPIRITS:	Service in the PSTN/IN Requesting InTernet Service

There are at present 447 Internet Drafts under consideration by the SIP related working groups. The various Internet Drafts can be found at http://search.ietf.org/cgi-bin/htsearch.

Location Applications and Emergency Calls

Location, location, location

Location information (LI) is extremely valuable for various commercial and emergency applications, for example:

- A flower delivery service has a SIP URI sip:getflowers.com. Using the LI provided by the caller (automatically), the call can be routed to the nearest GetFlowers flower shop for delivery.
- A call from a mobile phone to an information service will be routed to the nearest local office so as to provide the caller with directions to the nearest restaurant, hospital or any other place.
- Emergency calls are however the most important application at present and we will show further below how location is used to route emergency calls on the Internet to the nearest dispatcher for police, fire or ambulance.

Figure 4.2 shows two demo applications using location.

Location Generators

There are several technologies available as sources for Location Information,[2] such as:

GPS: The Global Positioning System (GPS) information is generally only available where there is a clear view of a large swath of the sky. It is accurate to tens of feet. Chips for GPS can be included in various mobile devices, such as phones and PDAs.

DHCP: The device obtains location information provided by its DHCP server, when logging on and getting an IP address. This also includes getting the location from a nearby Wi-Fi access point.

Location beacons: A short range wireless beacon, e.g., using BlueTooth or infrared, announces its location to mobile devices in the vicinity.

Subscriber information: A carrier has address information reflecting the service location for its subscribers.

Manual configuration: A user manually enters civil or geospatial information into a mobile or stationary device.

---

[2] "Emergency Services for Internet Telephony Systems," by H. Schulzrinne, et al. Internet Draft, IETF, July 2004. Accessible at http://www.cs.columbia.edu/sip/draft/emergency-arch/draft-schulzrinne-sipping-emergency-arch-01.html.

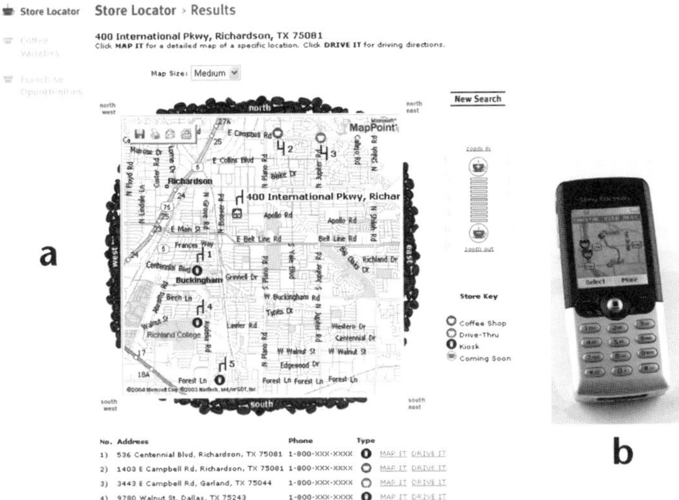

Figure 4.2 – Location applications for mobile devices; a) Locating lunch places near an office using Microsoft Maplink on a laptop and b) displaying location on a mobile phone[3]

In some cases a device, such as a mobile phone may have more than one source of LI: The mobile phone can have a GPS chip set, while the mobile phone network may also inform the phone of its location. In such an instance it makes probably good sense to convey both LOs to the Emergency Control Center (ECC) where the judgment can be made which LO is more accurate and discard the other one, so as to avoid confusion when forwarding the call for providing emergency assistance.

Geographic Location and Privacy

As we have mentioned in the previous section, there are a wealth of emerging technologies available at present to determine the geographic location of an object that we will call here the 'target'.

Communicating the location of the target to various applications and using the location for emergency calls make location a core capability for various commercial services and also for emergency services.

The location of a target is however a very sensitive piece of information and the issues regarding the protection of location information have been clarified in great detail in the Geographic Location and Privacy (Geopriv)

[3] See ESRI GIS and Mapping Software at http://www.esri.com/industries/locationservices/

working group in the IETF (see http://ietf.org/html.charters/geopriv-charter.html). The requirements for geographic location and privacy have been published in RFC 3693.[4]

The four primary entities in Geopriv are shown in Figure 4.3. They are as follows:

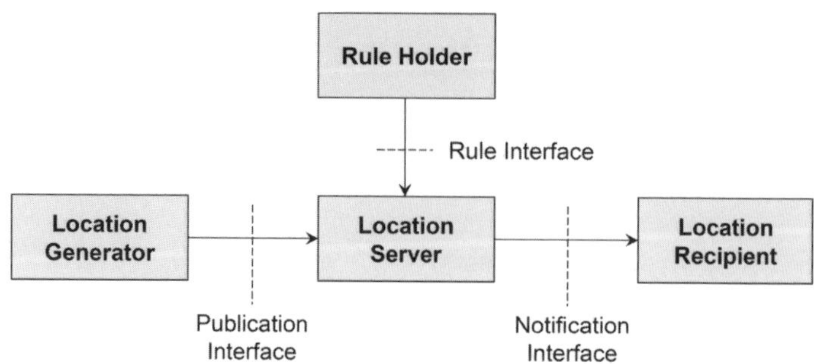

Figure 4.3 – Primary entities for geographic location and privacy

- The location generator determines the location of the target and creates location objects (LO) that describe that location.
- The location server receives the LOs and also receives subscriptions from various location recipients.
- The location recipient may render these LOs to a user or some receiving application.
- The rule holder is the repository for privacy rules for filtering and distributing LOs for specific targets. A rule maker (not shown) populates the rule holder with rules.

The communications between the entities have to be authenticated and protected.

An important definition in Geopriv is that of a *Using Protocol*, that is a protocol that uses (reads or modifies) the LOs.

- SIP is one using protocol, since it may base routing decisions on location and privacy considerations. SIP is well suited for emergency services.
- SIMPLE presence is another using protocol that can convey extremely rich location information and usage rules for all applications that use presence.

---

[4] RFC 3693: "Geopriv Requirements," by J. Cuellar, et al. IETF, February 2004.

A location event package using SIP has been defined in an Internet Draft by Mahy.[5]

Types of Location Information

There are several types of location information: Geospatial, civic, postal and cell tower identity and antenna sector.

Geospatial Location includes longitude, latitude and altitude. Global Positioning Systems (GPS) can provide longitude and latitude only.

Geographic location, for example, inserted into a SIP header could be as follows[6]:

```
Location: ;lat=38.89868 ;long=-77.03723 ;alt=15 ;alt-unit=m
;lares=0.000122 ;lores=0.000122
;hno=600 ;lmk="White House" ;mcn="Washington"
;stn="Pennsylvania" ;sts="Ave" ;sta="DC";privacy=dnf
```

Civic Location contains the street address, floor and suite/apartment in a building. DHCP servers can be configured to provide Civic Addresses.[7] The civic address format differs from country to country (US and Canadian address formats differ for example) and the various national formats will be registered with IANA. In the United States the data fields have been established by the National Emergency Number Association (NENA).

Postal location may differ from the civic location due to the use of mailboxes and P.O.B. type of addresses. The name of a post office may for example be different from the name of a community.

Cell Tower/Sector is information available from the mobile phone network and can represent a polygon shaped area. This information is not fine grained at all and should not be confused with exact location information available in some mobile phone networks derived from triangulation within a cell and antenna sector.

---

[5] "A Location Event Package using the Session Initiation Protocol (SIP)," by R. Mahy. Internet Draft, IETF, January 2005. Work in progress.

[6] "Emergency Services for Internet Telephony based on the Session Initiation Protocol (SIP)," by H. Schulzrinne. Internet Draft, IETF, June 2003, expired.

[7] RFC 3825: "Dynamic Host Configuration Protocol Option for Coordinate-based Location Configuration Information," by J. Polk, J. Schnizlein, M. Linsner, July 2004.

Presence and Location Information

Location Objects (LO) can be carried across the Internet by extending the Presence Information Data Format (PIDF) as described by J. Peterson.[8] The strict privacy requirements to which the PIDF was designed matches very well the requirements for geographic location privacy.

PIDF already has some useful data elements for Geopriv:

- 'contact' provides a URI where the presentity can be reached,
- 'timestamp' for when the PIDF document was created,
- 'status' for such information as OPEN or CLOSED
- 'id' to uniquely identify a segment of the presence information so it can be tracked over time.

The PIDF has been extended for Location and Usage Rules.

- 'geopriv' for location and usage rules
  - 'location-info' element based on the Geography Markup Language (GML) 3.0 defined by the Open Geospatial Consortium.[9] The Geography Markup Language is an XML grammar written in XML schema for the modeling, transport and storage of geographic information.
  - 'usage rules' data element to meet the policy requirements of Geopriv by the Rule Maker entity.
- 'method' is optional and specifies how the location was discovered or derived, for example:

```
<method>gps</method>
```

- 'provided by' is also optional and describes the organization that supplied this location information.

We reproduce[10] an example of an XML segment within a PIDF document that describes the civic location and the usage rules. The civic location in this example is 123 Broadway, New York, NY 10027 USA and usage rules specify that retransmission is allowed. The expiration date and time is also given.

---

[8] "A Presence-based GEOPRIV Location Object Format," by J. Peterson. Internet Draft, IETF, May 2004.

[9] OpenGIS, "Open Geography Markup Language (GML) Implementation Specification," OGC 02-023r4, January 2003. http://www.opengis.org/techno/implementation.htm

[10] "Requirements for Session Initiation Protocol Location Conveyance," by J. Polk, et al. Internet Draft, IETF, July 2004, work in progress.

```
<?xml version="1.0" encoding="UTF-8"?>
 <presence xmlns="urn:ietf:params:xml:ns:pidf"
  xmlns:gp="urn:ietf:params:xml:ns:pidf:geopriv10"
  xmlns:cl=" urn:ietf:params:xml:ns:pidf:geopriv10:civilLoc"
  entity="pres:geotarget@example.com">
 <tuple id="sg89ae">
 <status>
  <gp:geopriv>
   <gp:location-info>
    <cl:civilAddress>
     <cl:country>US</cl:country>
     <cl:A1>New York</cl:A1>
     <cl:A3>New York</cl:A3>
     <cl:A6>Broadway</cl:A6>
     <cl:HNO>123</cl:HNO>
     <cl:LOC>Suite 75</cl:LOC>
     <cl:PC>10027-0401</cl:PC>
    </cl:civilAddress>
   </gp:location-info>
   <gp:usage-rules>
    <gp:retransmission-allowed>yes</gp:retransmission-allowed>
    <gp:retention-expiry>2003-06-23T04:57:29Z</gp:retention-
     expiry>
   </gp:usage-rules>
  </gp:geopriv>
 </status>
 <timestamp>2003-06-22T20:57:29Z</timestamp>
 </tuple>
</presence>
```


Presence information in PIDF documents can be carried securely in various protocols, such as SMTP, HTTP or SIP using the MIME type registered for PIDF:

'application/cpim-pidf+xml

A large body of work deals with using LI with SIP for emergency services in an analog manner to the telephone system but delivered over the Internet.

Emergency Services Using Internet Communication

Making emergency calls for help, such as 911 in USA and directing them to the police, fire department or ambulance service is one of the most valuable features of the public telephone network. While the Internet features rich technology that can potentially make emergency calls much more effective, the problems associated with emergency calls over the internet present however significant challenges as well. We will explore here these challenges and current emerging solutions. There is a wealth of proposals for providing emergency services over the internet and good document to start with is "Emergency Services for Internet Telephony" by H. Schulzrinne and also to review the references listed there.[11]

Problem Space for Emergency Call Routing

It is not easy to determine the location of a caller on the Internet. Consider an extreme example where a nomadic user with a laptop PC at a wireless LAN (WLAN) hotspot in Japan using a VPN tunnel to the corporate network in Sweden. An emergency call placed from the laptop may actually land in the private network in Sweden. It is therefore imperative:

1. UA must know its location using any of the options available, and
2. SIP call routing must be capable of routing the call to the correct PSAP and the PSAP must be able to route the call to the correct ECC.

Determining the location has been described in the previous section, so we will explore here item 2: SIP call routing for emergency calls.

Emergency calls have to reach first the ECC that is responsible for handling the call. For this, some database lookup has to map the civic address or the geographic coordinates known to the device to the right ECC. There are roughly 6,000 ECCs in North America and probably three times more in the rest of the world. ECCs cover a geographic area in the shape of some irregular polygon.

---

[11] "Emergency Services for Internet Telephony Systems," by H. Schulzrinne, et al. Internet Draft, IETF, July 2004. http://www.cs.columbia.edu/sip/draft/emergency-arch/draft-schulzrinne-sipping-emergency-arch-01.html. The new IETF Working Group Emergency Context Resolution with Internet Technologies (ECRIT) has just been formed to develop these standards.

Table 4.2 – Emergency Call Terminology

Term	Definition
Emergency call taker	The person who answers the emergency call, usually in an emergency call center.
Emergency control center (ECC)	Facilities used to accept and handle emergency calls from the PSAP and route the calls to police, fire and ambulance services.
Emergency service routing proxy (ESRP)	SIP proxy that routes emergency calls to the appropriate ECC.
Public safety answering point (PSAP)	Physical location where emergency calls are received. PSAPs are under the responsibility of a public authority.
User stationary device	User agent with a stable location, such as an Internet kiosk, public phone or home PC.
Nomadic Device (User)	User agent that is connected temporarily to the network in various locations, such as a laptop computer.
Mobile Device (User)	May change the location and network attachment during an emergency call.

The ECC will answer the call and forward it to the appropriate responder for assistance to the caller. The various responders have their own service boundaries (police, fire, ambulance) that may be different from the ECC.

If the location is available as a civic address, the database used is the Master Street Address Guide (MSAG). The MSAG is also useful to resolve inconsistencies in writing addresses, such as '1st St.' instead of 'First Street'.

DNS-Based Emergency Call Routing

The Domain Name System (DNS) is especially well suited to support the *location database* function for SIP emergency call routing.[12] An Internet

[12] "Emergency Call Information in the Domain Name System," by B. Rosen. Internet Draft, IETF, July 2004.

Authority for Assigned Numbers and Addresses registry for civic addresses has been proposed.[13]

The Dynamic DNS Delegation System (DDDS)[14] can hold a hierarchy of civic locations. Here is an example of such a hierarchy that starts with the top level domain (TLD) sos.arpa and goes all the way to locate a cubicle (234-5) in the high rise building on 123 Main Street in Pittsburg, Allegheny County in Pennsylvania, USA:

```
                                              sos.arpa
                                           us.sos.arpa
                                        pa.us.sos.arpa
                             allegheny. pa.us.sos.arpa
                  pittsburg. allegheny. pa.us.sos.arpa
            main. pittsburg. allegheny. pa.us.sos.arpa
       123. main. pittsburg. allegheny. pa.us.sos.arpa
234-5. 123. main. pittsburg. allegheny. pa.us.sos.arpa
```

Output from the respective DNS queries are NAPTR records which may either produce the end result or point to new DNS entries for further lookups.

The NAPTR records contain service fields for all registered emergency services. Emergency SOS Services can be as follows:

- ECC
- Fire
- Rescue
- Marine
- Police
- Mountain

NAPTR records provide the contact URI for XML location documents for so called 'subdomains' or 'polygon documents' for that particular service.

Examples of Location Documents

The Subdomain Document can be used by SIP proxies for call routing. The schema for the subdomain document is shown here:

---

[13] "Dynamic Host Configuration Protocol (DHCPv4 and DHCPv6) Option for Civic Addresses Configuration Information," by H.Schulzrinne. Internet Draft, IETF, February 2005.

[14] RFC 3403: "Dynamic Delegation Discovery System (DDDS) Part Three: The Domain Name System (DNS) Database," by M. Mealling. IETF, October 2002.

```
<?xml version="1.0" encoding="UTF-8"?>
<xs:schema xmlns:xs="http://www.w3.org/2001/XMLSchema"
   targetNamespace="urn:ietf:params:xml:ns:sos-subdomain"
   xmlns:sos-sd="urn:ietf:params:xml:ns:sos-sd"
   elementFormDefault="qualified">
  <xs:element name="sos-subdomain">
    <xs:complexType>
      <xs:list type="xs:anyURI" minOccurs="0"/>
    </xs:complexType>
  </xs:element>
</xs:schema>
```

The Polygon Document can be used in the ECC to route the call to the correct emergency response unit. The polygon subdomain schema is shown here:

```
<?xml version="1.0" encoding="UTF-8"?>
 <xs:schema xmlns:xs="http://www.w3.org/2001/XMLSchema"
    targetNamespace="urn:ietf:params:xml:ns:sos-boundary"
  xmlns:gml="http://www.opengis.net/gml"
  xmlns:sos-boundary="urn:ietf:params:xml:ns:sos-boundary"
    elementFormDefault="qualified"
    attributeFormDefault="unqualified">
  <xs:import namespace="http://www.opengis.net/gml"
     schemaLocation="feature.xsd"/>
  <xs:import namespace="http://www.opengis.net/gml"
     schemaLocation="geometryPrimitives.xsd"/>
  <xs:complexType name="boundary">
   <!--xs:restriction base="gml:AbstractFeatureType"-->
    <xs:sequence>
     <xs:sequence>
      <xs:element ref="gml:boundedBy" minOccurs="0"/>
     </xs:sequence>
     <xs:sequence>
      <xs:element ref="gml:extentOf"/>
     </xs:sequence>
    </xs:sequence>
   <!--/xs:restriction-->
  </xs:complexType>
 </xs:schema>
```

The schema for the boundary document is based on the Geography Markup Language defined by the OpenGIS consortium.[15]

Using SIP to Convey Location Information

As mentioned, SIP can be a 'using protocol' for carrying and using the LO in accordance with the requirements of Geopriv. Two groups of SIP methods (UA-UA and UA-proxy) are suitable to carry the LO:

1. SIP methods for UA-to-UA to convey LI:
   INVITE,
   UPDATE,
   MESSAGE,
   PUBLISH.
2. Methods for UA-to-Proxy to convey LI:
   INVITE,
   UPDATE,
   MESSAGE.

Figure 4.4 illustrates the basic UA-to-UA call flow where INVITE is used to carry the LO in the form of geographic location.

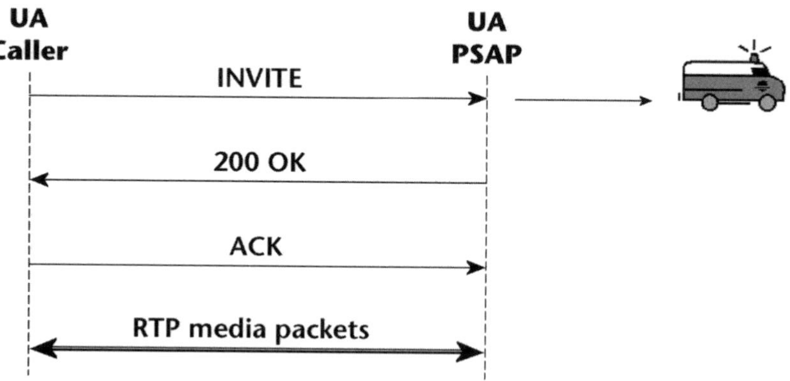

Figure 4.4 – UA-UA call flow with location information in INVITE

An example how UA-to-UA INVITE (message M1) may look is shown here.[16] Note the geographic location specifies the coordinates (for North

[15] OpenGIS, "Open Geography Markup Language (GML) Implementation Specification," OGC 02-023r4, January 2003. http://www.opengis.org/techno/implementation.htm

[16] "Requirements for Session Initiation Protocol Location Conveyance," by J. Polk, et al. Internet Draft, IETF, July 2004, work in progress.

and West), the method of obtaining them (DHCP) and also the usage rules (no retransmission is allowed and expiration date and time have to be provided).

```
INVITE sip:bob@biloxi.example.com SIP/2.0
Via: SIP/2.0/TCP pc33.atlanta.example.com
  ;branch=z9hG4bK74bf9
Max-Forwards: 70
From: Alice <sip:alice@atlanta.example.com>;tag=9fxced76sl
To: Bob <sip:bob@biloxi.example.com>
Call-ID: 3848276298220188511@atlanta.example.com
CSeq: 31862 INVITE
Contact: <sip:alice@atlanta.example.com>
Content-Type: multipart/mixed; boundary=boundary1
Content-Length: ...

  --boundary1

Content-Type: application/sdp
v=0
o=alice 2890844526 2890844526 IN IP4 atlanta.example.com
c=IN IP4 10.1.3.33
t=0 0
m=audio 49172 RTP/AVP 0 4 8
a=rtpmap:0 PCMU/8000

  --boundary1

Content-Type: application/cpim-pidf+xml
  <?xml version="1.0" encoding="UTF-8"?>
    <presence xmlns="urn:ietf:params:xml:ns:pidf"
     xmlns:gp="urn:ietf:params:xml:ns:pidf:geopriv10"
     xmlns:gml="urn:opengis:specification:gml:schema-
     xsd:feature:v3.0"
     entity="pres:alice@atlanta.example.com">
    <tuple id="sg89ae">
     <timestamp>2004-07-11T08:57:29Z</timestamp>
     <status>
```

```
<gp:geopriv>
 <gp:location-info>
  <gml:location>
   <gml:Point gml:id="point96" srsName="epsg:4326">
    <gml:coordinates>41.87891N 87.63649W</gml:coordinates>
   </gml:Point>
   </gml:location>
  <method>dhcp</method>
 </gp:location-info>
 <gp:usage-rules>
  <gp:retransmission-allowed>no</gp:retransmission-allowed>
  <gp:retention-expiry>2004-07-13T14:57:29Z</gp:retention-
     expiry>
 </gp:usage-rules>
</gp:geopriv>
</status>
</tuple>
</presence>

--boundary1--
```

SIP Proxy Routing with Location Information in INVITE

- The UA must have the LI available and include the LO as a Presence Information Data Format (PIDF) document in the body of the message.
- The location object (LO) has to be protected using hop by hop Transport Level Security (TLS). TLS is invoked by using SIP secure (SIPS) as shown in the example below. The call must be routed however even if some hops do not have TLS protection.
- The UA must not use end-to-end S/MIME security since the routing SIP proxies would not have access to the LI required for proper routing.

SIP proxies have to distinguish an emergency call and handle it appropriately The proxy has to look in the message body for the location information to route the call.

Figure 4.5 shows a simple call flow example on how a proxy may route an emergency call to an emergency control center (ECC).

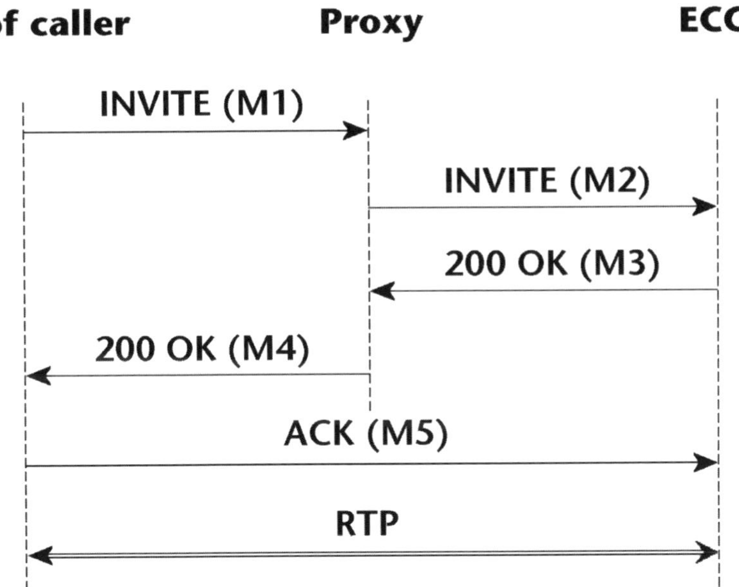

Figure 4.5 – SIP proxy routing with location in INVITE

In the example shown in Figure 4.5 we assume the first proxy understands the 'sos' request URI in message M1. Note also the SIPS in the request URI in the first line.

```
INVITE sips:sos@atlanta.example.com SIP/2.0
Via: SIP/2.0/TLS pc33.atlanta.example.com;branch=z9hG4bK74bf9
Max-Forwards: 70
From: Alice <sips:alice@atlanta.example.com>;tag=9fxced76sl
To: <sips:sos@atlanta.example.com>
Call-ID: 3848276298220188511@atlanta.example.com
CSeq: 31862 INVITE
Contact: <sips:alice@atlanta.example.com>
Content-Type: multipart/mixed; boundary=boundary1
Content-Length: ...

  --boundary1

Content-Type: application/sdp
v=0
o=alice 2890844526 2890844526 IN IP4 atlanta.example.com
c=IN IP4 10.1.3.33
```

```
t=0 0
m=audio 49172 RTP/AVP 0 4 8
a=rtpmap:0 PCMU/8000

 --boundary1
```

Once the Proxy receives M1 and recognizes it as an emergency INVITE Request, this proxy knows to look into the message body for a location body part to determine the location of the UAC in order to match the location to an ECC. Once this look-up occurs, the message is sent directly to the ECC (in message M2).

For message M2 in Figure 4.5, the proxy has determined where to send the message. Note also the location information is sent using the message format for common presence and instant messaging (CPIM) information (RFC 3862), encoded as specified in RFC 3863 using the Presence and IM Data Format (PIDF) and XML (application/cpim-pidf+XML).

Note the civic address is the office number 60606 on the Floor 1 of the Sears Tower on 233 South Wacker Drive in Chicago, Illinois. This address was determined using the DHCP method from a mobile device of the T-mobile.com network.

```
INVITE sips:sos@192.168.10.20 SIP/2.0
Via: SIP/2.0/TLS proxy.atlanta.example.com;branch=z9hG4bK873
Via: SIP/2.0/TLS pc33.atlanta.example.com;branch=z9hG4bK74bf9
Max-Forwards: 69
From: Alice <sips:alice@atlanta.example.com>;tag=9fxced76sl
To: <sips:sos@atlanta.example.com>
Call-ID: 3848276298220188511@atlanta.example.com
CSeq: 31862 INVITE
Contact: <sips:alice@atlanta.example.com>
Content-Type: multipart/mixed; boundary=boundary1
Content-Length: ...

 --boundary1

 Content-Type: application/sdp
 v=0
 o=alice 2890844526 2890844526 IN IP4 atlanta.example.com
 c=IN IP4 10.1.3.33
 t=0 0
 m=audio 49172 RTP/AVP 0 4 8
```

```
a=rtpmap:0 PCMU/8000

 --boundary1

 Content-type: application/cpim-pidf+xml
 <?xml version="1.0" encoding="UTF-8"?>
  <presence xmlns="urn:ietf:params:xml:ns:pidf"
    xmlns:gp="urn:ietf:params:xml:ns:pidf:geopriv10"
    xmlns:gml="urn:opengis:specification:gml:schema-
        xsd:feature:v3.0"
    entity="pres:alice@atlanta.example.com">
   <tuple id="sg89ae">
    <timestamp>2004-07-11T08:57:29Z</timestamp>
    <status>
    <gp:geopriv>
     <gp:location-info>
      <cl:civilAddress>
       <cl:country>US</cl:country>
       <cl:A1>Illinois</cl:A1>
       <cl:A3>Chicago</cl:A3>
       <cl:HNO>233</cl:HNO>
       <cl:PRD>South</cl:PRD>
       <cl:A6>Wacker</cl:A6>
       <cl:STS>Drive</cl:STS>
       <cl:PC>60606</cl:PC>
       <cl:LMK>Sears Tower</cl:LMK>
       <cl:FLR>1</cl:FLR>
      <cl:civilAddress>
      <method>dhcp</method>
      <method>802.11</method>
      <provided-by>www.t-mobile.com</provided-by/>
     </gp:location-info>
     <gp:usage-rules>
      <gp:retransmission-allowed>no</gp:retransmission-allowed>
      <gp:retention-expiry>2004-07-13T14:57:29Z</gp:retention-
           expiry>
     </gp:usage-rules>
    </gp:geopriv>
    </status>
   </tuple>
   </presence>
--boundary1--
```

Conclusions

Location information can enable useful applications and must be provided for Internet communications. Location information can be made available using various technologies with various degrees of accuracy.

Location information is however very sensitive data and has to be protected using the Geopriv requirements.

Emergency call routing on the Internet is not trivial, but mechanisms such as the DNS can be used to support protocols such as SIP and SIMPLE for Presence to route emergency calls. The location objects used in emergency call routing are standardized XML documents to convey the location.

Chapter 5

Context Aware Communications

Presence, Events and Instant Messaging

Introduction

The immense popularity of instant messaging, especially when combined with VoIP, video, whiteboard, etc., may give us some pause and ask ourselves, what is it about these services that make them so special?

No significant extra cost and multimedia are certainly part of the attraction, but a closer examination will reveal the vastly increased efficiency and time savings provided by the new communication feature of presence. The conveyance of presence is not possible in legacy phone systems and as a result, callers may waste much time trying to reach someone, only to end up speaking to voicemail and generating annoyance to the calling party who has to listen to the voicemail and try to call back (and risk ending up on voicemail in turn). Even when calls are successful in reaching the callee, the caller may discover the call was at an inappropriate time, since the called party was working, engaged in some other activity or just not in good mood to talk.

There are numerous studies and presentations on the usefulness of presence and instant messaging for enhancing productivity in the workplace and also their usefulness in private life.

It turns out that along with basic presence, other information can be conveyed, such as location, free/busy, disposition, etc. as we will show here. Events that happen in business applications and communications (my co-worker is talking to an important customer) can also be interpreted as presence and represented as "contacts." Any event of interest can be subscribed to for notification using the presence technology. Presence and events are thus very suitable technologies to integrate communication and applications.

Presence is More Useful than Dial Tone and Phone Numbers

We will show here why presence and events are not only complete new Internet communication services, but also why presence and events are more useful than listening for dial tone and looking up phone numbers. In a way, presence may well be the dial tone of the 21st century.

Interestingly enough, wireless communications are among the first to be enhanced using presence-based services, such as "push-to-talk." Figure 5.1 shows an early prototype menu for a mobile phone display based on presence. The caller needs to select only the name of a party and by pressing the select button can see if presence information is available. A second press will reveal the presence information itself, such as available to talk or even the desire to chat.

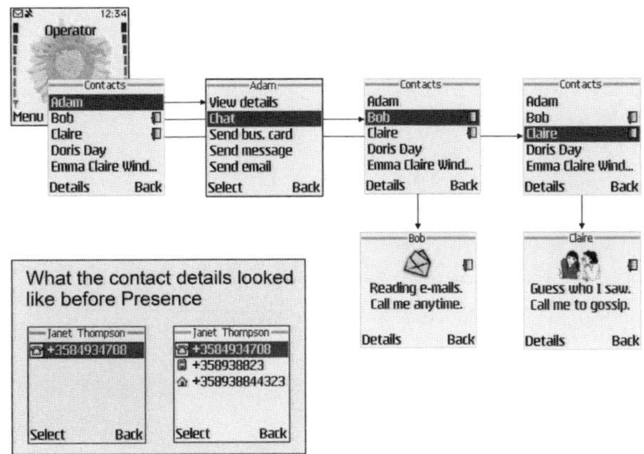

Figure 5.1 – Screen shots for mobile phone display of presence-based menu
(Courtesy Nokia.)

The legacy user interface (bottom left) that can display the phone book with several entries for a person (home, office, mobile) is not very helpful. How can the caller know which number to call so as to avoid being sent to voicemail? The caller has no indication even if a phone number is still in service.

Personal Communications

Rich and successful interaction between individuals and their environment, at work or in private life is a continuing challenge. Humans evolve from children to adults by coping with this challenge. The Internet is fortunately providing us with a set of powerful tools to interact with people, applications and entertainment across the world.

Context aware communications take into account[1] the following:

- The human context, such as
  - Not connected

---

[1] "The Future of Enterprise Communications," by H. Schulzrinne, et al. Columbia University and Sipquest, Sept. 2003.

    - Activity: Active, inactive.
    - Idle since,
    - Busy or reachable by certain people only,
    - Time: From-until,
    - Relationship (for alternate contact): family, associate, supervisor,
    - Private environment,
    - Place where silence is required,
    - Driving,
    - Location.
- Diversity of resources
    - Broadband connected computer and/or SIP phones,
    - Mobile 2G phone,
    - Analog phone/fax in a hotel,
    - Access to a computer at an Internet cafe or kiosk.
- Applications and events
    - Start communications from a desktop personal productivity application,
    - Initiate communications from some event: Financial, inventory, health/biometrics.
    - Alert me that a customer executive has joined a conference.

Table 5.1 gives an overview of Internet applications and communications.[2]

Table 5.1 – Internet Applications and Communications

Delivery Mode		Synchronous	Asynchronous
Pull	HTTP FTP SOAP	Data retrieval File download Remote procedure call	Peer-to-peer file sharing
Push	*SIP, SIMPLE* RTP RTSP	*Presence and IM* *Event notification* *Session setup* Streaming media	email

[2] "Rich Presence and Location," by H. Schulzrinne. VON Spring 2004.

The items in the table shown in *italic* are part of SIP-based communications and will be discussed in the following section.

It is interesting to note that many or most presence indications could be derived automatically. Table 5.2 shows some samples.

Table 5.2 – Presence indications and source

Presence Indication	Source
On the phone	Automatic, from phone
Mobile phone is on the air	2G/3G network gateway to IP
Away	Automatic, from security system
Appointment	Calendar
Holiday	Calendar
Meal	Calendar
Meeting	Calendar
Driving	
In-transit	
Travel	Calendar
Vacation	Calendar
Busy	Manual setting
Permanent absent	Left company

The rich presence information and its data format are developed as an Internet standard.[3]

Integration of Communications with Business Applications

The events architecture, when combined with presence and IM may have an enormous impact on business applications. The basic idea[4] is to

1. Make various business applications appear as "buddies" on the contact list and invoke these applications from the IM graphical users interface, and

---

[3] "RPID: Rich Presence Extensions to the Presence Information Data Format (PIDF)," by H. Schulzrinne, et. al. Internet Draft, IETF, March 2004.

[4] "Instant Messaging Applications: Leveraging the Power of Presence for Business Value." White paper by IM Logic, 2004. http://imlogic.com/

2. Use the presence technology to alert the user when important information is conveyed by various business applications.
3. Integrate with desktop applications.

An example of integrating presence with desktop applications is Microsoft Office 2003 where word processing, graphics, spreadsheet and the personal calendar are real-time communication enabled by showing for example the presence of the author of a document. If for example someone is reading email, by clicking on the presence icon of the sender a multimedia conversation using IM, voice, video and data collaboration can be initiated.

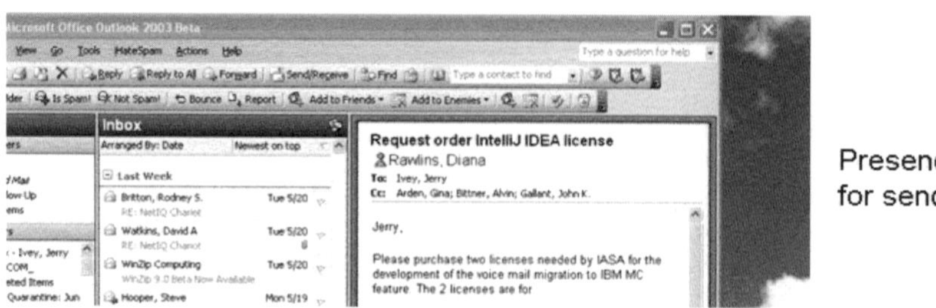

Figure 5.2 – Using the presence icon of the email sender to initiate an IM, audio and video call in the Microsoft Office 2003 desktop suite

Here are some examples of business scenarios with events, presence and IM:

- A stock trader receives and IM query from a customer about a stock of interest. The trader can immediately reply with a link to a web page with more information and get back an order for buying or selling that stock. Note that this IM exchange can be 'multiplexed' with other activities that both the customer and the trader are pursuing at the time and this scenario requires no voice communications.
- A corporate controller notices an important international wire transfer and contacts the responsible bank using IM for more information. This is also happening in real time, without having the controller interrupt any other work or conference they may be in.
- Changes in travel arrangements from an airline or travel office show up as an IM on the screen of the user. Again, silent interaction by the user with the travel agent is possible.
- Significant changes or (no changes) in inventory can alert planners and purchase agents to take appropriate actions.

Integration of Personal Communications with Applications

The technique of making significant events or applications as your "buddies" in the contact list for presence and events can also lead to significant applications for personal use, such as:

- Access weather information from the contact list and publish weather events,
- Reminder of anniversaries generated from a calendar application,
- Notifications of interesting movies and show times,
- Contacts to help with homework, taxes, etc.

Presence with SIP

SIP is a natural tool for enabling presence-based applications. The heart of SIP is providing rendezvous—allowing us to reach Alan using a well-known name (Address of Record) without knowing ahead of time where or how that he is connected to the network. This rendezvous function, by itself, provides a basic form of presence. If Alan does not have any points of contact registered against his AOR, attempts to reach him might return "Temporarily Unavailable." If he does have registered contacts, then he might be available for communication.

This simple presence function is insufficient to enable the kind of context-aware communication we describe in this chapter. Alan's service provider might send all attempts to reach him when he has no registered contacts off to some unified messaging system. Having registered contacts does not imply that Alan is available to communicate right now–he may be in the middle of some other conversation. By itself, rendezvous does not tell us much about how likely we are to actually communicate in real-time with Alan before we try. However, the spark of presence in rendezvous is enough to build on. A few extensions to SIP allow us to get exactly the information we are looking for.

The Basic Mechanics: SIP Events

The first extension, defined by RFC 3265,[5] allows a SIP element to subscribe to "events" at some other SIP element. This allows a client endpoint to subscribe to, for instance, changes in Alan's presence, as shown in Figure 5.3.

---

[5] RFC 3265: "Session Initiation Protocol (SIP)-Specific Event Notification," by A. B. Roach. IETF, June 2002.

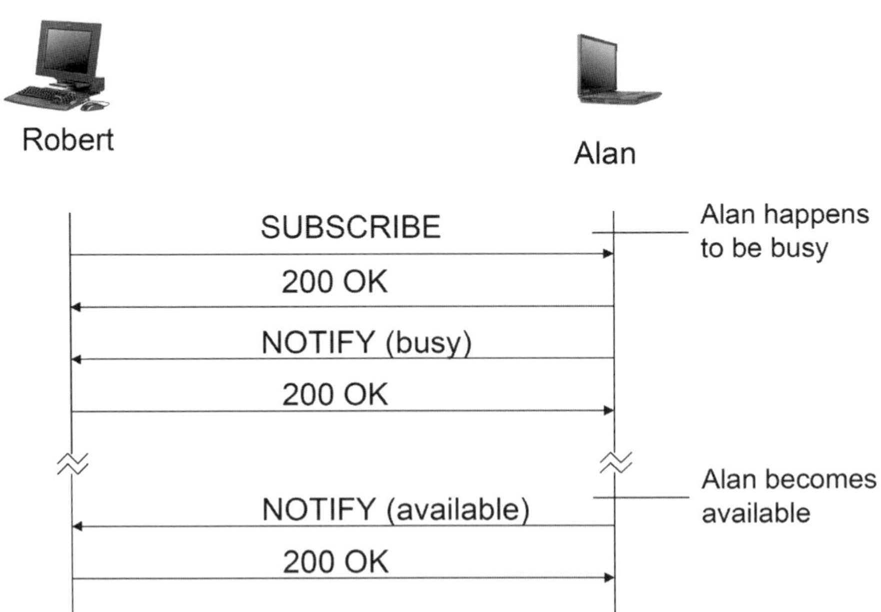

Figure 5.3 – A Basic SIP Events Presence Subscription

This extension adds two methods to SIP, SUBSCRIBE and NOTIFY. A successful SUBSCRIBE request creates a subscription to changes in some specific data. All subscriptions have these key properties:

- A subscription is for a specific "event" declared by the Event: header field in the SUBSCRIBE message. That event value identifies a standardized event package within the SIP Events framework. The package for "Event: presence" is defined by RFC 3856.[6]
- A new subscription starts with notification of the current state
- A notification will be sent each time the state changes
- A subscription has a finite duration, measured in seconds. If the subscription is not refreshed before that duration passes, it expires. This duration is negotiated during the initial SUBSCRIBE request
- Either side can terminate the subscription at any time. This particular termination is explicitly signaled. In Figure 5.3, Robert

[6] RFC 3856: "A Presence Event Package for the Session Initiation Protocol (SIP)," by J. Rosenberg. IETF, August 2004.

could unsubscribe, or Alan could send a notification indicating that the subscription is terminated.

Presence as a Peer-to-Peer or a Hosted Service

The SIP Events framework and the Presence package defined for it allow a variety of presence architectures to be deployed. At one extreme is a pure peer-to-peer structure where each endpoint subscribes directly to the endpoint of each peer on its contact list, as shown in Figure 5.4.

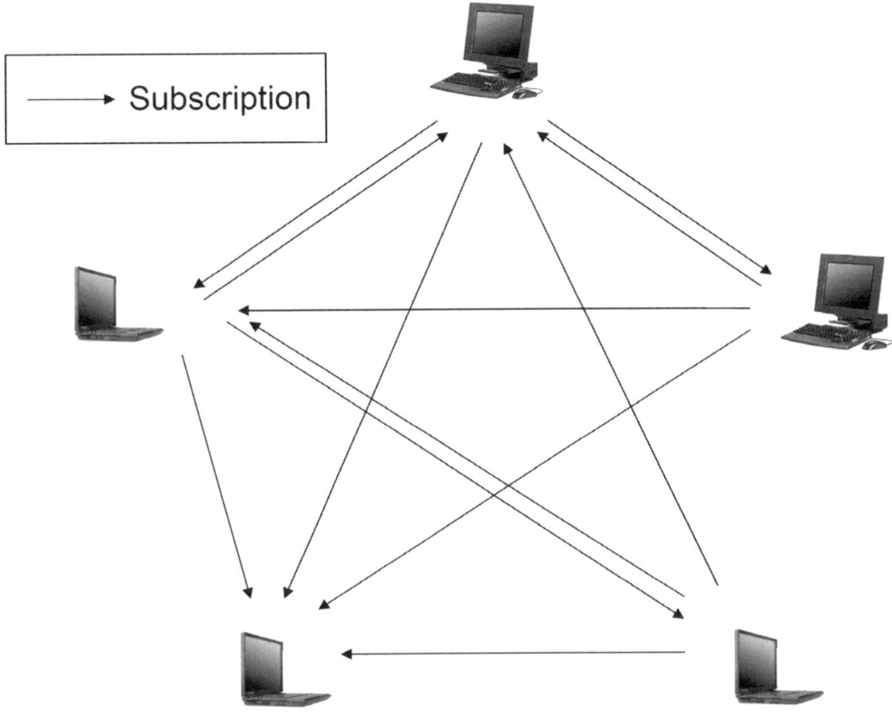

Figure 5.4 – A Peer-to-Peer network of subscriptions

The other extreme hosts presence at a centralized server, which acts as a presence agent for each of the endpoints as shown in Figure 5.5 (for the same set of subscriptions).

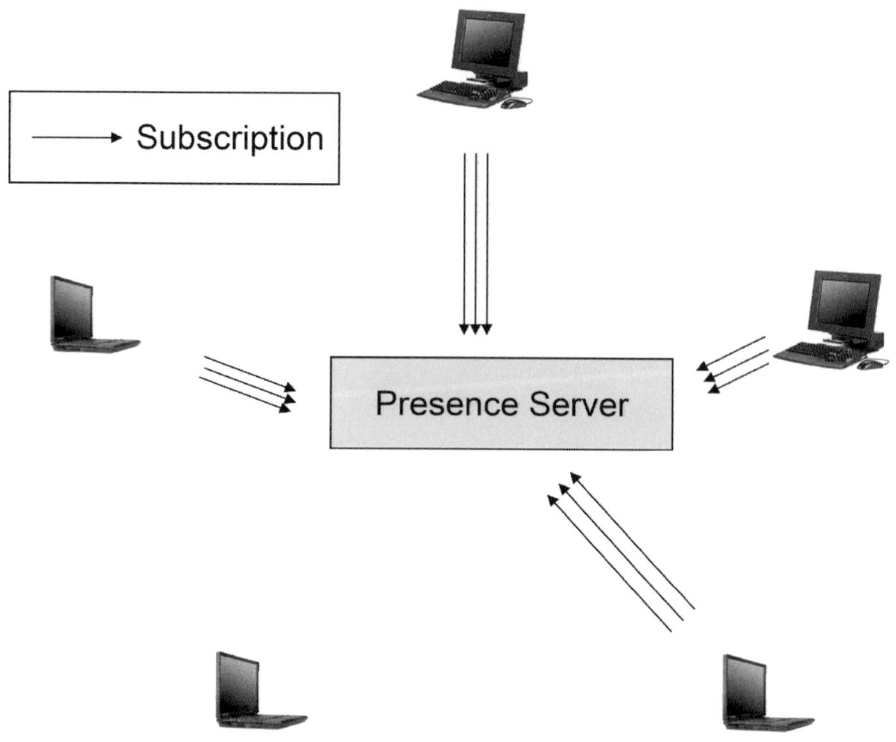

Figure 5.5 – Subscriptions through a centralized service

Individual service providers may chose to deploy one of these extremes, or a blend between them as shown in Figure 5.6. Since different systems will make a range of choices, that figure provides a useful model of the presence architecture on the Internet as a whole. One of the strengths of SIMPLE presence is that a subscribing endpoint does not need to know which architectural style is in use for a given subscription—it behaves exactly the same in either case.

The labels in Figure 5.6 are terms from the standards.[7] They are elucidated in Table 5.3.

[7] RFC 2778: "A Model for Presence and Instant Messaging," by M. Day, J. Rosenberg, H. Sugano. IETF, February 2000.

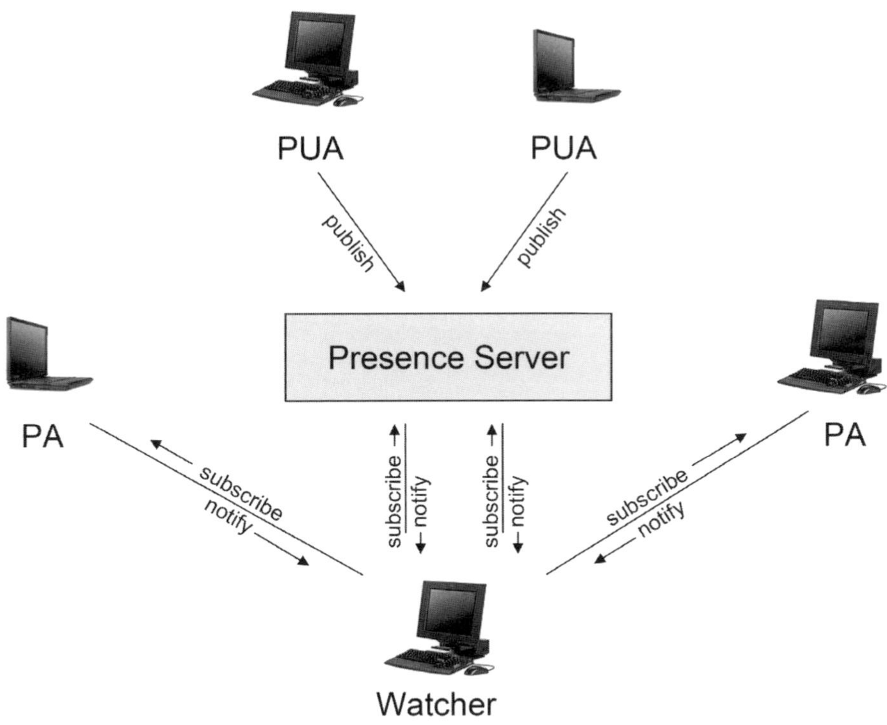

Figure 5.6 – The general presence architecture

Rendezvous Makes the Connection for Presence

The model in Figure 5.6 does not explain how a watcher finds the PA that has the presence information it is interested in. This is done using the same rendezvous mechanism SIP provides to get calls to the right endpoints. To subscribe to Alan, we send a SUBSCRIBE request to his well-known Address-of-Record: sip:ajohnston@mci.com. SIP's standard routing rules will take this request to the rendezvous service at mci.com, which will either proxy or redirect the request to Alan's presence server. Likewise, some other service provider choosing a more peer-to-peer model for subscriptions would proxy or redirect the request directly to the endpoint registered to handle subscriptions for a given AOR. Figure 5.7 shows where the elements in Figure 5.6 fit in a typical SIP infrastructure.

Table 5.3 – Explanation of Terms

Term	Also Called	Description
Watcher	Subscriber	A watcher is an endpoint that subscribes to presence changes.
Presentity		A person that has presence that can be described. This term was formed by running together the words presence and entity. While the standards were written expecting presentities to be people, applications have been discovered where the presentities are automata.
Presence Agent (PA)	Notifier	A PA serves presence subscriptions for a resource. A presentity can use one of its own endpoints as a PA, or use a centralized Presence Server for that task. A PA will often be referred to as a notifier.
Presence User Agent (PUA)	Publisher	A PUA is a program that knows the current presence description for a presentity. An endpoint acting as a PA is also acting as a PUA. When a presentity uses a centralized Presence Server for a PA, the PUA provides the current presence information to that presence server, usually through the SIP PUBLISH extension.

Cooperating service providers or enterprises can leverage this rendezvous mechanism to allow access to the presence of each other's users as shown in Figure 5.8. Here, each domain's presence server acts as a presence agent for users in the other domain. Each server maintains a single shared subscription to a user in the other domain whenever there is one or more local watchers subscribing to that user's presence.

Presence beyond "Busy"

Presence brings a new and powerful dimension to real-time communications. Without presence, most telephony calls are made blind. The caller has very little knowledge ahead of time how likely the call is to actually reach its intended target. Many calls in systems without presence go to voicemail. Other calls unintentionally interrupt people already engaged in other activities, such as a heated argument. This could adversely affect the mood of the called party, leading to a less-than-successful call experience.

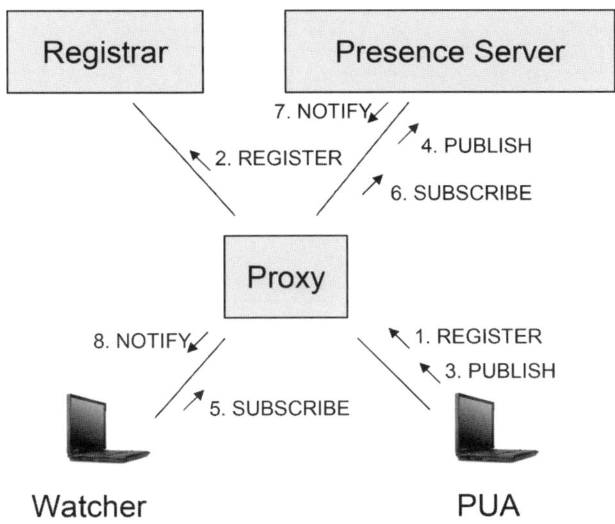

Figure 5.7 – Presence Components in a SIP Infrastructure

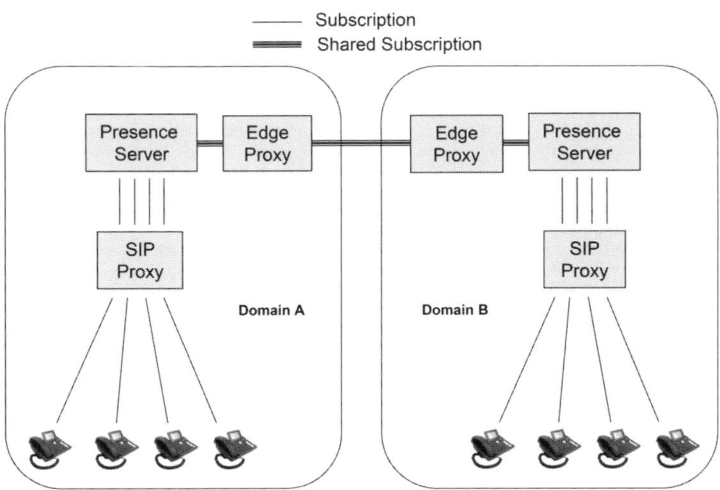

Figure 5.8 – Sharing Subscriptions across Domains

Presence brings context to these communication attempts. With the most basic of presence systems, the caller has enough extra knowledge to call only when the target is available—avoiding voicemail and the inevitable game of phone-tag.

One bit of information (available vs. not available) is enough to dramatically change the way communication systems are used. The effect of more bits can be quite profound.

The SIMPLE protocol suite builds on the IMPP base standard presence document format[8] to provide many useful pieces of information that can be used to choose when to attempt to communicate. The Rich Presence Extensions to the Presence Information Data Format (RPID) allows users to describe the context in which communication with them will occur in great detail. Table 5.4 shows some of the additional information an RPID document can convey.

Table 5.4 – A Sample of Information Described by RPID Documents

Type of Information	Examples
Activity	away, meal, meeting, driving
Mood	happy, angry, bored, excited, sad
Place-Type	car, library, office, outdoors, restaurant
Privacy	audio, video, text (will be private vs. seen by others)
Relationship	family, assistant (used when the contact will likely reach someone other than the presentity)
User-Input	active (meaning the user recently provided some kind of input), idle

We might choose to wait to call a person until they are not driving a car. If we are going to ask a favor, we may choose not to call while a person is angry. Automata can provide some of these values (a calendar program can indicate that someone is in a meeting), while others must be set directly by the person being described.

RPID documents are represented in XML. Each RPID document describes the presence of a single person by revealing the various ways that person is willing to communicate. In the example presence document shown in

[8] RFC 3863: "Presence Information Data Format (PIDF)," by H. Sugano, S. Fujimoto, G. Klyne, A. Bateman, W. Carr, J. Peterson. IETF, August 2004.

Table 5.5, Alice is happy, but in a conference call. She's not available for voice communications, but we can send her an instant message.

Table 5.5 – A Rich Presence Document

```
<?xml version="1.0" encoding="UTF-8"?>
<presence xmlns="urn:ietf:params:xml:ns:pidf"
    xmlns:rp="urn:ietf:params:xml:ns:pidf:status:rpid-status"
    xmlns:p="urn:ietf:params:xml:ns:pidf:person"
    xmlns:sc="urn:ietf:params:xml:ns:pidf:status:servcaps"
    entity="sip:alice@example.com">
  <p:person>
   <status>
    <rp:mood> <rp:happy/> </rp:mood>
    <rp:activities>
     <rp:activity>on-the-phone</rp:activity>
     <rp:activity>meeting</rp:activity>
    </rp:activities>
   </status>
  </p:person>
  <tuple id="2309nd23">
   <status>
    <basic>closed</basic>
   </status>
   <contact>sip:alices-desk-phone-gruu@example.com</contact>
  </tuple>
  <tuple id="3929342">
   <status>
    <basic>open</basic>
    <contact>sip:alices-pc@example.com</contact>
    <sc:servcaps>
     <sc:methods>
      <sc:method>MESSAGE</sc:method>
     </sc:methods>
    </sc:servcaps>
   </status>
  </tuple>
</presence>
```

The most important part of a presence document is the collection of "tuples" it contains. Each of these tuples represents a way to communicate. Each tuple can independently be open or closed. Open tuples are available for communication right now. Closed tuples are not. A tuple will contain one contact in the form of a URI. This URI can be of any scheme, but will typically reflect a scheme that can be used for real-time communication like sip: or tel:.

A presence document can contain a single <person> element with information that describes the person independent of the ways to communicate. Information like mood or location, is best expressed in this element.

Each tuple can be marked up with the capabilities available at that contact. The <servcaps> element[9] describes what SIP methods a contact supports (assuming the URI in the contact is sip:), what type of media that contact supports (audio, video, etc.), and even whether the contact will reach a human or an automaton.

Tuples can also be marked with their geographic location. This information might be derived from triangulation by a radio access network, or it could be self reported by a device containing a GPS receiver. This information enables many interesting new applications. For instance, it allows us to choose to contact someone who is closest to us, or to a specific location, like a bank or grocery store. Of course, exposing this kind of information has far-reaching privacy implications, so secure mechanisms to control access to presence documents are very important.

Table 5.6 shows an example where the contact is a SIP mobile phone that reports its location. In this document, Alice associates her contact with a device, states that the device is mobile, and describes where it is. The location information is conveyed using the presence-based GEOPRIV location object format.[10] In addition to stating location, this format allows Alice to express how private she would like recipients to keep this information.

As these two examples show, presence documents have many optional elements. Two presence documents can appear to be very different structurally.

[9] "User Agent Capability Extension to Presence Information Data Format (PIDF)," by M. Lonnfors, K. Kiss. Internet Draft, IETF, October 2004.

[10] "A Presence-based GEOPRIV Location Object Format," by J. Peterson. Internet Draft, IETF, September 2004.

Table 5.6 – Presence for a Mobile SIP Phone Reporting Location

```
<?xml version="1.0" encoding="UTF-8"?>
 <presence xmlns="urn:ietf:params:xml:ns:pidf"
  xmlns:gp="urn:ietf:params:xml:ns:pidf:geopriv10"
  xmlns:gml="urn:opengis:specification:gml:schema-xsd:feature:v3.0"
  xmlns:d="urn:ietf:params:xml:ns:pidf:device"
  xmlns:dc="urn:ietf:params:xml:ns:pidf:status:devcaps"
  entity="sip:alice@example.com">
  <tuple id="ndao38sne">
   <contact>sip:alicephone@example.com</contact>
   <d:device-id>mac:8asd7d7d70</d:device-id>
  </tuple>
  <d:device device-id="mac:8asd7d7d70">
  <status>
   <gp:geopriv>
    <gp:location-info>
     <gml:location>
      <gml:Point gml:id="point1" srsName="epsg:4326">
       <gml:coordinates>39:09:00N 84:04:00W</gml:coordinates>
      </gml:Point>
     </gml:location>
    </gp:location-info>
    <gp:usage-rules>
     <gp:retransmission-allowed>no</gp:retransmission-allowed>
     <gp:retention-expiry>2005-01-01T12:05:29Z</gp:retention-
      expiry>
    </gp:usage-rules>
   </gp:geopriv>
   <dc:devcaps>
    <dc:mobility>
     <dc:supported>
      <dc:mobile/>
     </dc:supported>
    </dc:mobility>
   </dc:devcaps>
  </status>
  <timestamp>2005-01-01T00:05:29Z</timestamp>
  </d:device>
 </presence>
```

All presence documents created by SIMPLE conformant systems will follow the Presence Data Model[11] shown in Figure 5.9. In this model, all points of contact for communication are modeled as services. Services may be associated with a device, and more than one service may share a device. The model also allows a presence document to optionally describe the person's state in addition to the state of the services and devices.

The concepts of person and device in the model are natural. Service requires a little more explanation. The model asserts that any means of communication that can be represented by a contact is a means being offered as "service." A person may have one or more telephone, instant messaging, SMS, video-conferencing, receptionist, or email services for example. These services may or may not involve a third-party service provider.

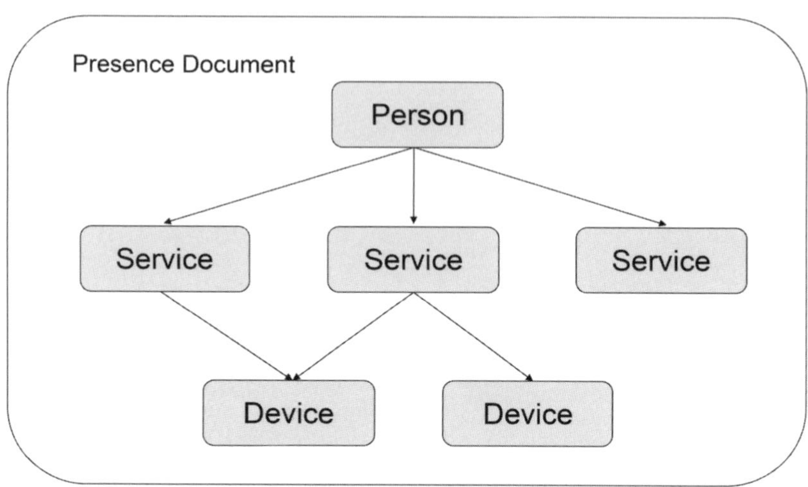

Figure 5.9 – The Presence Data Model

This model allows watchers to infer even more information about the availability of the presentity, in terms of how likely using any given service is to succeed. If Alice left her cell phone at home (which we might be able to tell from very different location data reported for the person and the mobile device in the model), we can infer that attempts to call or SMS her on that device are not as likely to be as immediately useful as sending an instant message to the service running on the PC right next to her.

---

11 "A Data Model for Presence," by J. Rosenberg. Internet Draft, IETF, October 2004.

Publishing Presence

Once a PUA has constructed a presence document, it needs to provide it to the PA or presence server that will be handling subscriptions for it. This is done with the SIP PUBLISH request.[12] Figure 5.10 shows a simple PUBLISH transaction.

The key items to note in this transaction are:

- The state being published is identified by the combination of the Request URI (sip:alice@example.com) and the Event header field (presence)
- The published state (in this case, the presence document) will expire, and that expiry is negotiated by the PUA and the presence server during the PUBLISH transaction. In this case, the PUA asked for the server to hold this presence document for an hour. The server agreed to hold it, but only for 5 minutes. The PUA must refresh this state before it expires if it wishes the server to continue to hold it.
- The server returned a SIP-ETag value in its response. This value can be used later to see if some other PUA has modified the document.

Often, a person will have more than one PUA contributing presence information to a presence server. Alice, for example, has a PC at home, and a PC at work, both publishing her availability to enter into an instant messaging conversation. The presence server must do something sensible with these multiple, potentially conflicting data sources. One popular approach is "last publish wins"—a published document simply overwrites any document that was previously received. This could lead to watchers seeing a strobing presence value, flashing availability from on to off as the publishing automata alternately publish what each believes is right. The SIP-ETag mechanism lets these automata discover that this is happening, so that this strobing can be avoided.

After a PUA receives a SIP-ETag, it can include it in future publication requests, asking that the publish fail if the resource has changed since it last published (i.e. the resource's current SIP-ETag is different from what this PUA currently holds). Figure 5.11 shows this in action. Once PUA1 discovers that it is arguing with PUA2, it will stop aggravating the situation and ask its user to resolve the conflict.

---

[12] RFC 3903: "Session Initiation Protocol (SIP) Extension for Event State Publication," by A. Niemi. IETF, October 2004.

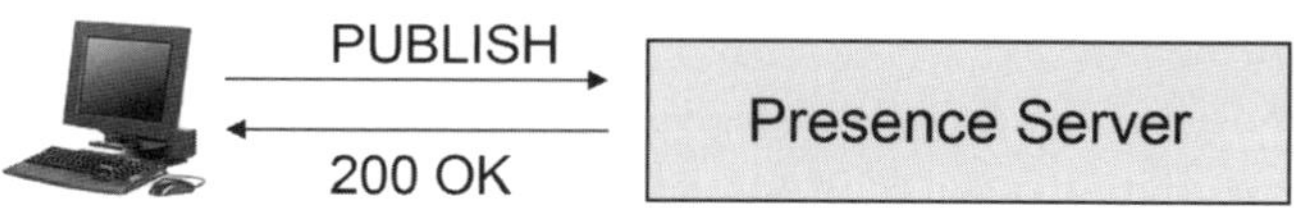


```
PUBLISH sip:alice@example.com SIP/2.0
Via: SIP/2.0/TCP pua.example.com;branch=z9hG4bK83nfi84
To: <sip:alice@example.com>
From: <sip:alice@example.com>;tag=387nd90dh234
Call-ID: af3240rajwdfi3@example.com
CSeq: 28823 PUBLISH
Max-Forwards: 70
Event: presence
Expires: 3600
Content-Type: application/pidf+xml
Content-Length: 306

<?xml version="1.0" encoding="UTF-8"?>
<presence xmlns="urn:ietf:params:xml:ns:pidf"
        entity="sip:alice@example.com">
 <tuple id="h73892hris">
  <status>
   <basic>open</basic>
   </status>
   <contact>sip:alices-desk-phone@example.com</contact>
 </tuple>
</presence>
```

```
SIP/2.0 200 OK
Via: SIP/2.0/TCP pua.example.com;branch=z9hG4bK83nfi84
To: <sip:alice@example.com>;tag=n4398dh3s
From: <sip:alice@example.com>;tag=387nd90dh234
Call-ID: af3240rajwdfi3@example.com
CSeq: 28823 PUBLISH
Expires: 300
SIP-ETag: asdiufhe78y23
Content-Length: 0
```

Figure 5.10 – A SIP PUBLISH transaction

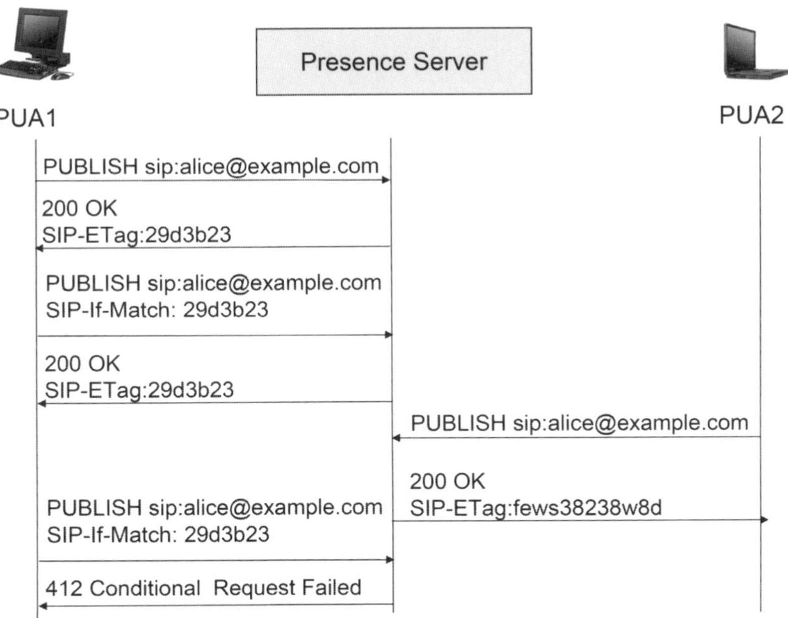

Figure 5.11 – Conflicting PUAs

The SIP-ETag mechanism can also be used to save bandwidth. The second PUBLISH in Figure 5.11 is a refresh publication. It doesn't change the presence document–it just asks the presence server to hold onto the document it already has for a little while longer. Because the server already has the document, it would be wasteful to send it again in that PUBLISH request. To avoid that waste, PUBLISH requests that have a matching SIP-If-Match header field and no body are defined to refresh the state the server already holds.

Detailed Presence Subscriptions

Now that we have the basic presence architecture, the form of presence documents, and the basic publication mechanism in hand, we can look more closely at the mechanics of a presence subscription. Though a few detailed examples, we'll explore

- How subscriptions are created.
- How subscriptions (which inherently expire) are extended, or refreshed.
- Why subscriptions must receive an immediate NOTIFY.
- How subscriptions are terminated.

A subscription is created by a successful (200 class) response to a SUBSCRIBE request, or by the arrival of an initial NOTIFY. The watcher requests a duration for the subscription using the Expires header field in the SUBSCRIBE request. The notifier chooses the actual duration, always less than what was requested, and lets the watcher know through the Subscription-State header field in the first NOTIFY it sends. Figure 5.12 shows a subscription created, then allowed to expire. The example messages show only those parts of the message important to the example—there are required header fields present, but not shown.

In message F1, the watcher requests a presence subscription for an hour. In F2, the notifier lets the watcher know that it has a subscription, but only for 5 minutes. Three-and-a-half minutes into the subscription, the PA receives a new document from the presentity, and notifies the watcher with the change in message F3, which notes that only 90 seconds remain in this subscription. When 5 minutes have passed, the watcher has not extended the subscription, so the notifier sends the NOTIFY in F4 whose Subscription-State header field shows that the subscription ended because it timed-out.

All of the messages that are part of a single subscription occur in the same SIP dialog. Typically, the message that creates a subscription creates the dialog that contains it, and the message that terminates the subscription also terminates the dialog. (The exceptions occur when more than one subscription, or other dialog usage, share a common dialog–a practice that is strongly discouraged by the IETF). In Figure 5.12, all of the messages between the watcher and the PA are contained in one dialog. The PUBLISH requests between the PA and the PUA are not part of that (or any other) dialog.

A watcher can request to extend, or refresh, a subscription by issuing another SUBSCRIBE request inside the subscription's dialog before the subscription expires. In Figure 5.13, the watcher asks for an hour-long subscription but only gets 5 minutes. A minute before that subscription expires, the watcher asks to extend the subscription by an hour, but again gets only 5 minutes. The watcher lets the subscription expire after that interval. Note that the total subscription duration was nine minutes, not 10. The expiration negotiated by a refresh subscription starts from the time of the refresh, not the time of the original expiration.

A watcher can terminate a subscription before it expires by unsubscribing. This is accomplished by sending a new SUBSCRIBE request inside the subscription's dialog, but requesting an expiration time of zero. The notifier must issue a final notify noting that the subscription has been terminated.

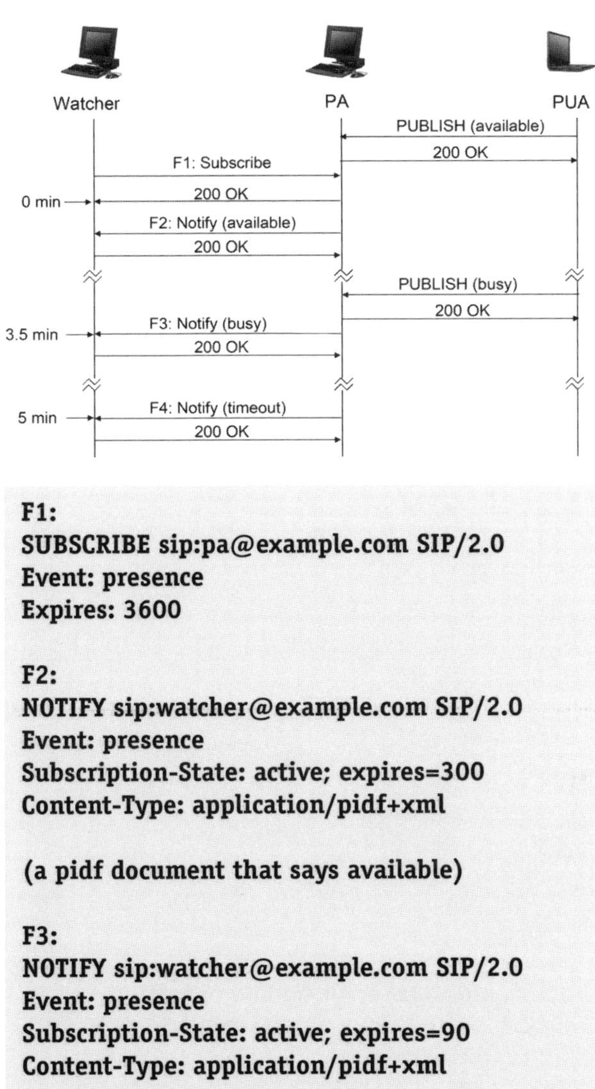


```
F1:
SUBSCRIBE sip:pa@example.com SIP/2.0
Event: presence
Expires: 3600

F2:
NOTIFY sip:watcher@example.com SIP/2.0
Event: presence
Subscription-State: active; expires=300
Content-Type: application/pidf+xml

(a pidf document that says available)

F3:
NOTIFY sip:watcher@example.com SIP/2.0
Event: presence
Subscription-State: active; expires=90
Content-Type: application/pidf+xml

(a pidf document that says busy)

F4:
NOTIFY sip:watcher@example.com SIP/2.0
Event: presence
Subscription-State: terminated;reason=timeout
```

Figure 5.12 – Lifetime of a simple presence subscription

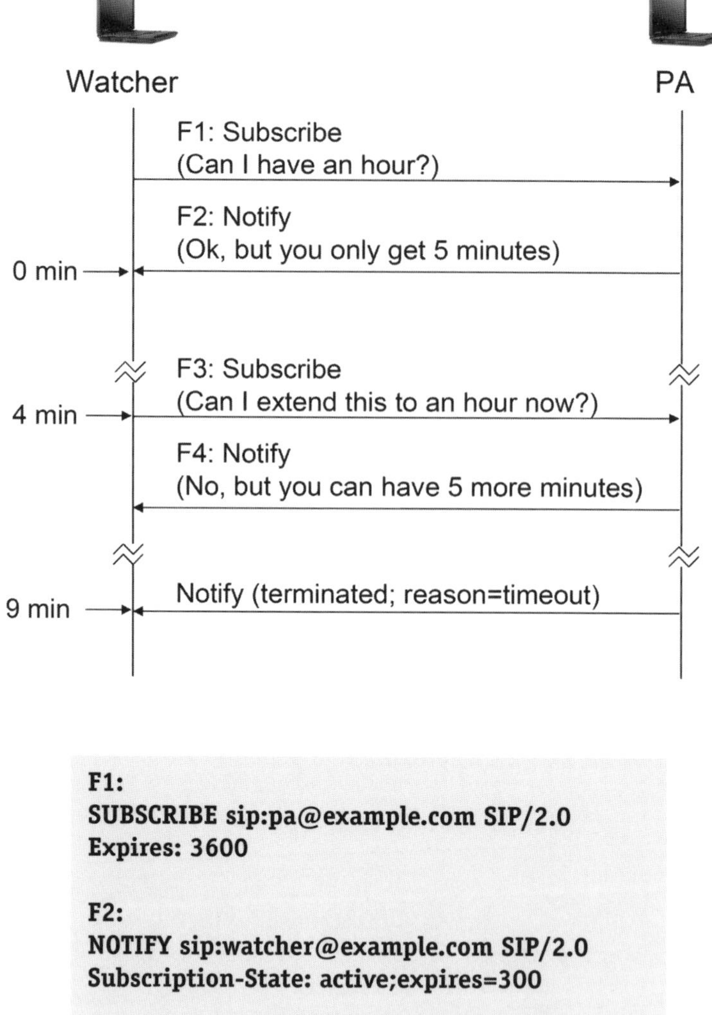


```
F1:
SUBSCRIBE sip:pa@example.com SIP/2.0
Expires: 3600

F2:
NOTIFY sip:watcher@example.com SIP/2.0
Subscription-State: active;expires=300

F3:
SUBSCRIBE sip:pa@example.com SIP/2.0
Expires: 3600

F4:
NOTIFY sip:watcher@example.com SIP/2.0
Subscription-State: active;expires=300
```

Figure 5.13 – Refreshing a Subscription

Typically, it will claim a reason of timeout since the remaining time of 0 seconds just expired. This same mechanism can be used to fetch, or poll, the current presence for someone without really creating a subscription. An initial subscribe with a requested duration of zero seconds will stimulate a single NOTIFY from the notifier with the desired state.

A watcher can also terminate a subscription by returning certain error responses to any NOTIFY messages it receives. A 481 is most effective, but should be used with caution if any other dialog usages were sharing the dialog with the subscription (the dialog and all of its current usages will be destroyed).[13] This method of terminating subscriptions is particularly useful at the beginning of a subscription when the initial SUBSCRIBE can fork.

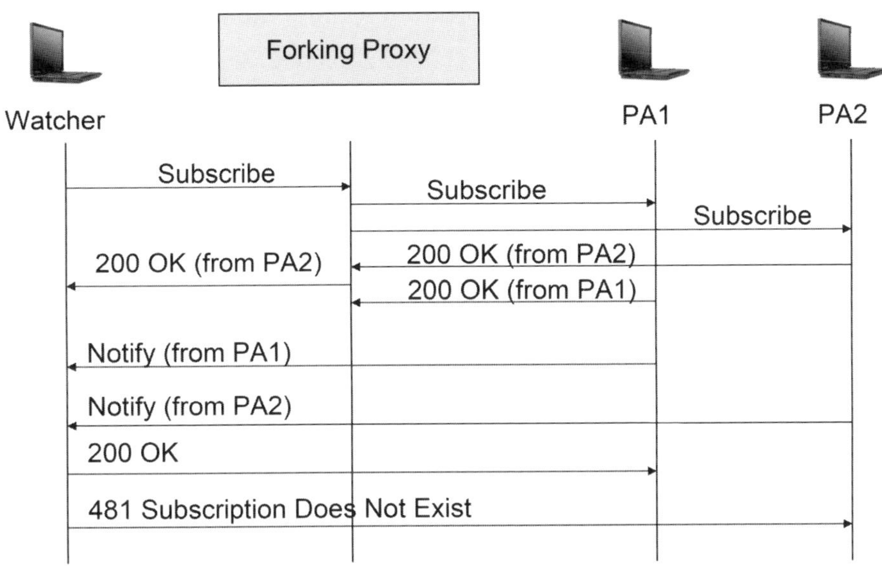

Figure 5.14 – Initial Subscribe Requests can Fork

Figure 5.14 shows a SUBSCRIBE request that forks to two PAs. RFC 3261[14] requires the forking proxy to return the first 200 OK response it

[13] "Multiple Dialog Usages in the Session Initiation Protocol," by R. Sparks. Internet Draft, IETF, July 2004.

[14] RFC 3261: "SIP: Session Initiation Protocol," by J. Rosenberg, H. Schulzrinne, G. Camarillo, A. Johnston, J. Peterson, R. Sparks, M. Handley, E. Schooler. IETF, June 2002.

sees to a non-invite request and silently drop any that arrive after that. With only the SUBSCRIBE request and response, there is no way for the watcher to know that PA1 thinks it has established a subscription, because the 200 OK from PA2 happened to arrive first at the proxy. This is particularly bad if PA1 has the state that the watcher is really interested in. As a workaround to this problem, all notifiers are required to send a NOTIFY immediately after accepting any SUBSCRIBE request (be it an initial or refresh request). This lets the watcher discover all of the notifiers that accepted its subscription.

The watcher will be able to tell these notifications apart by looking at their dialog identifiers. Each notifier will have provided a distinct remote-tag. The presence event package, RFC 3856, requires that a watcher only accept one branch of a forked subscribe and immediately terminate all others, so the watcher in Figure 5.14 chooses to keep the subscription it has with PA1 and terminate the subscription with PA2 by rejecting its initial NOTIFY request.

Notifiers can also terminate subscriptions before they expire. They may choose to do so because they are about to go down, or because the access permissions to the presence document have changed and the watcher no longer has the authority see that data. To accomplish this, the notifier will send a NOTIFY request containing a Subscription-State header field indicating terminated with one of the reasons from Table 5.7.

Granting Permission to Subscribe

Our discussion and examples so far in this chapter have assumed that the watcher has permission to subscribe to the presentity's presence. Without this authorization, subscriptions will either be rejected, or placed into a pending state. We'll discuss now what watchers will see as permissions change, how presentities discover that permissions are needed, what permissions a presentity can grant, and how a presentity gets those permissions to a presence server.

Table 5.7 – Server Reasons for Terminating a Subscription

Reason	Sent when	Subsequent actions
deactivated	The server needs to terminate this particular subscription, but replacing it with another would work. One server in a cluster could use this to move a subscription to another cluster member.	The watcher should immediately attempt a new subscription to the resource
probation	The server needs to get rid of this subscription, and needs time before the watcher tries again. A server might issue this when it knows it will be some time before it obtains authorization, or if an entire cluster is going to go down for a few minutes.	The watcher should attempt a new subscription later. If the Subscription-State header field includes a retry-after parameter, the watcher should wait at least that long before trying a new subscription.
rejected	Authorization policy has changed and this watcher no longer has permission to subscribe to this resource.	None. Watcher software should not attempt to subscribe again automatically.
timeout	The subscription expired without being refreshed.	None
giveup	Authorization can't be obtained right now, and the server wants to shed the load this subscription is costing it.	The watcher should try again later. If the Subscription-State header includes a retry-after parameter, the watcher should wait at least that long before trying a new subscribe
noresource	The resource for this subscription has been permanently deleted.	None. Attempts to resubscribe would result in a 404 Not Found.

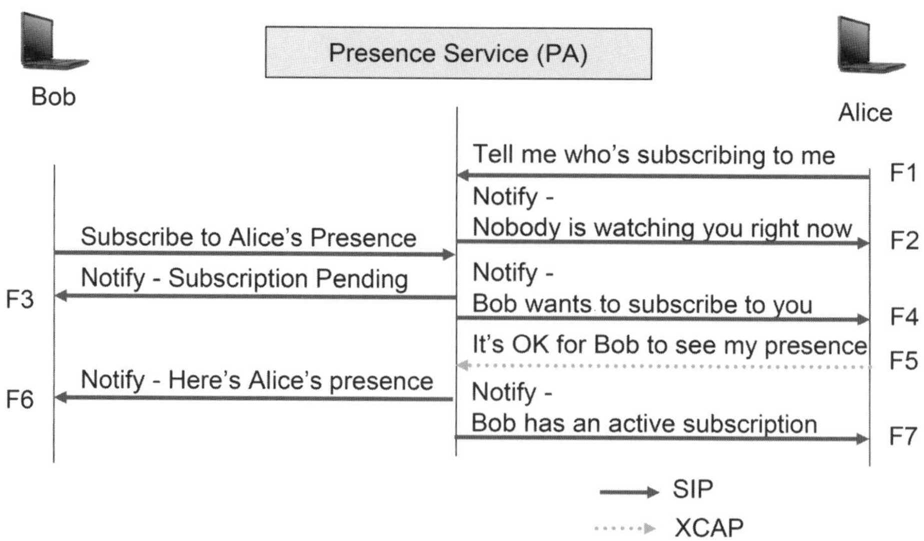

Figure 5.15 – Using Watcher Info and XCAP to Manage Presence Permissions

Figure 5.15 shows Bob subscribing to Alice's presence, which she serves from a central presence server. Before Bob subscribed, Alice had asked the presence server to tell her when new subscriptions for her presence arrive. She does this using SIP Events, but she subscribes to a new event: "presence.winfo". Winfo,[15] or watcher information, is a summary of all current subscriptions to the presence event for any given resource. The essential parts of her presence.winfo subscription request are:

```
(Excerpts from F1):
SUBSCRIBE sip:alice@example.com SIP/2.0
Event: presence.winfo
To: <sip:alice@example.com>
From:
<sip:alice@example.com>;tag=23asd392
Accept: application/watcherinfo+xml
```

---

[15] RFC 3857: "A Watcher Information Event Template-Package for the Session Initiation Protocol (SIP)," by J. Rosenberg. IETF, August 2004.

Here, Alice requests that the server tell her about anyone watching her presence information by sending her documents in the "application/watcherinfo+xml" format defined in RFC 3858.[16] The immediate notify she receives will contain the following:

```
(Excerpts from F2):
NOTIFY sip:alice-pua@example.com SIP/2.0
Event: presence-winfo
Content-Type: application/watcherinfo+xml

<?xml version="1.0"?>
<watcherinfo xmlns="urn:ietf:params:xml:ns:watcherinfo"
     version="0" state="full">
 <watcher-list resource="sip:alice@example.com" package="presence">
 </watcher-list>
</watcherinfo>
```

The empty <watcher-list> element lets Alice know that no-one is currently subscribed to her presence. The <watcherinfo> element has two important attributes, version and state. These are used to allow future watcher information notifications to contain only what's changed in the watcher list, instead of sending the entire watcher list each time.

In this example, the presence server doesn't know whether Bob has permission to see Alice's presence when he attempts to subscribe. The notification Bob receives in F3 will indicate that his subscription has been accepted, but he will not receive presence information pending authorization from Alice.

```
(Excerpts from F3):
NOTIFY sip:bobs-watching-ua@example.com SIP/2.0
Event: presence
Subscription-State: pending;expires=600
```

Now that a presence subscription has arrived for Alice, the presence server notifies her, sending the NOTIFY in F4 inside her presence.winfo subscription. The state attribute of the <watcherinfo> element lets Alice know

---

[16] RFC 3858: "An Extensible Markup Language (XML) Based Format for Watcher Information," by J. Rosenberg. IETF, August 2004.

that this is an update to the watcher information document she previously received as opposed to replacing that document entirely. The version is only one higher than the last version she saw, so she knows she hasn't missed any information. (If she did, she'd need to ask the server to send the full document again by refreshing her subscription.) This particular addition lets Alice know that Bob attempted to subscribe, and currently holds a pending subscription:

```
 (Excerpts from F4):
NOTIFY sip:alice-pua@example.com SIP/2.0
Event: presence-winfo
Content-Type: application/watcherinfo+xml

<?xml version="1.0"?>
<watcherinfo xmlns="urn:ietf:params:xml:ns:watcherinfo"
     version="1" state="partial">
 <watcher-list resource="sip:alice@example.com" pack-
age="presence">
    <watcher status="pending"
          id="djfwier230sdfj3"
          event="subscribe">
      sip:bob@example.org
    </watcher>
 </watcher-list>
</watcherinfo>
```

Alice's PUA will now alert Alice in some way, perhaps by popping up a dialog box, or issuing a distinctive noise and making an entry in an address book flash. Alice has a range of choices in what kind of permissions to grant Bob. For now, she just gives him full access by adding a presence rule using the XML Configuration Access Protocol (XCAP[17]) in message F5. XCAP requests are simply HTTP requests against resources like presence rules with standardized formats and semantics.

[17] "The Extensible Markup Language (XML) Configuration Access Protocol (XCAP)," by J. Rosenberg. Internet Draft, IETF, November 2004.

```
(Excerpts from F5):
PUT http://xcap.example.com/xcap-root/pres-rules/users/alice HTTP/1.1
Content-Type: application/auth-policy+xml

<?xml version=“1.0” encoding=“UTF-8”?>
<cr:ruleset xmlns:cr=“urn:ietf:params:xml:ns:common-policy”
    xmlns:pr=“urn:ietf:params:xml:ns:pres-rules”>
 <cr:rule id=“fjieiownx93”>
 <cr:conditions>
  <cr:identity>
  <cr:id>bob@example.com</cr:id>          <-- This part matches Bob
  </cr:identity>
 </cr:conditions>
 <cr:actions>
  <pr:sub-handling>allow</pr:sub-handling>      <-- This lets him subscribe
 </cr:actions>
 <cr:transformations>
  <pr:provide-person>true</pr:provide-person>   <-- This lets him see everything
  <pr;provide-services><pr:all-services/></pr:provide-services>   <-- This lets him see everything
  <pr:provide-devices><pr:all-devices/></pr:provide-devices>      <-- This lets him see everything
 </cr:transformations>
 </cr:rule>
</cr:ruleset>
```

Once the presence server has this rule, it makes Bob's pending subscription active, sending Bob Alice's presence information in F6. Note that three minutes of his five-minute subscription have passed.

```
(Excerpts from F6):
NOTIFY sip:bobs-watching-ua@example.com SIP/2.0
Event: presence
Subscription-State: active;expires=120
Content-Type: application/pidf+xml

(Alice's current full presence document)
```

The server will also let Alice know that the state of Bob's subscription has changed by updating her watcher information with message F7. It's possible that Alice could have made her XCAP assertion from a different device, so it is necessary to report this as a change in watcher information. The server has chosen to include some optional information in this notification about how long Bob's subscription has been held, and when it is scheduled to expire.

```
(Excerpts from F7):
NOTIFY sip:alice-pua@example.com SIP/2.0
Event: presence-winfo
Content-Type: application/watcherinfo+xml

<?xml version="1.0"?>
<watcherinfo xmlns="urn:ietf:params:xml:ns:watcherinfo"
     version="2" state="partial">
 <watcher-list resource="sip:alice@example.com" package="presence">
    <watcher status="active"
         id="djfwier230sdfj3"
         event="approved"
         duration-subcribed=180
         expiration=120>
     sip:bob@example.org
    </watcher>
 </watcher-list>
</watcherinfo>
```

Our examples have touched on several states a subscription can enter. Table 5.8 lists all possible subscription states and their meaning. The "waiting" status that can be reported in watcher information subscriptions is particularly interesting. It exists to address the case where Bob and Alice are never on-line at the same time. Figure 5.16 shows how authorization can be obtained in this "ships passing in the night" scenario.

Table 5.8 – Subscription States

Subscription-State header field value for presence subscriptions	Status parameter of watcher elements for presence watcher information subscriptions	Meaning
Active	active	A subscription is in effect and is authorized. Presence data is being supplied
Pending	pending	A subscription is in effect, but authorization has not yet been obtained. No presence data is being supplied
Terminated	terminated	A subscription has come to an end for one of the reasons in Table 5.7.
Waiting	waiting	A watcher has tried to subscribe in the past. Authorization for that watcher has not yet been obtained. The watcher currently has no subscription in effect.

The watcher information event package is special in the SIP Events framework. It is an event template that can be applied to any other event. The IETF currently defines several events that can be subscribed to: presence, registration events, message summaries, the results of a referred action, the current state of dialogs, and more. The subscribers to any of these can be monitored by watching that event's watcher information. Watcher information for presence is, itself, an event, so it is well-defined to monitor who's watching that by subscribing to presence.winfo.winfo, but such recursion is not generally useful and almost all service providers will reject such a request by policy. The vast majority of expected uses of the winfo template assume that only the person in charge of the resource (the presentity in the case of presence) should have access to the watcher information. Most services set this policy directly and don't allow their users to affect it without their assistance.

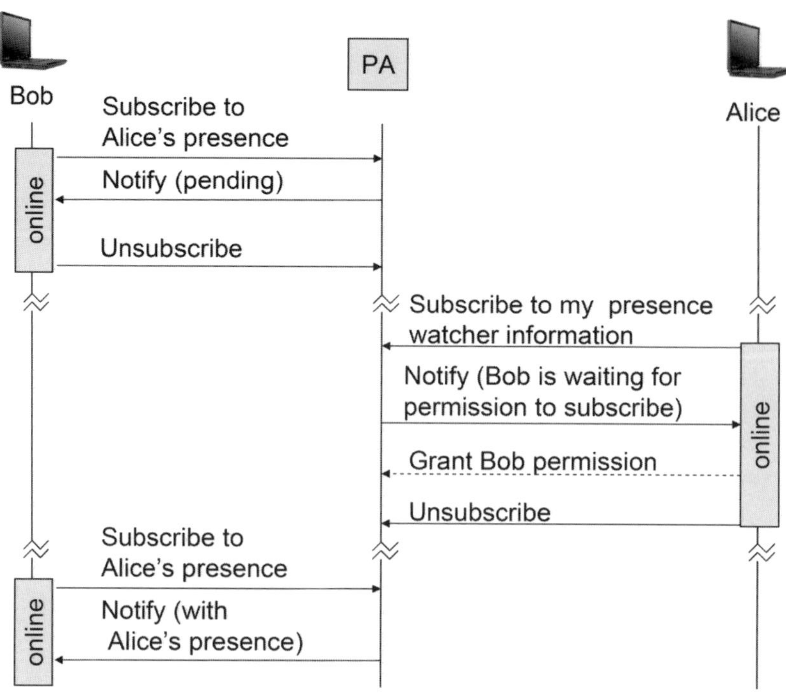

Figure 5.16 – Obtaining authorization without being online at the same time

Beyond White-lists—Controlling Access to Presence Data

Early presence systems granted access to presence data with very basic tools. Originally, there were white-lists. People placed on the white-list were allowed to see presence. Others were not. Sometimes this white-list was simply the buddy list. Alice could see Bob's presence if and only if Bob could see Alice's. Black-lists were rapidly added to the toolkit to prevent having to repeatedly ask the user for permission when the answer was previously no. These simple tools were sufficient to allow presence systems to attain considerable popularity, but their users quickly discovered they wanted to say more complex things. Alice only wants to share her presence with co-workers when she's actually at work. Bob wants customers to see that he's busy, but co-workers to know that he's in a staff meeting. Carol wants to let Alice know where she is, but doesn't want Bob to know what city she's in, much less whether she left her cell phone at home today. To achieve these goals, users resorted to such wild gyrations as maintaining multiple identities at each service.

SIMPLE systems give users the ability to state these intricate policies by providing presence rules.[18] Each rule is a statement, expressed in XML, containing three parts:

- Conditions which determine to whom the rule applies.
- An action instructing the presence system whether to allow access to presence when the conditions match.
- Transformations of the presence information before it is exposed to people matching the conditions.

Figure 5.17 shows a simple presence rule that gives permission to subscribe to bob@example.com, and allows him to see all any available person, device or service-tuple elements. It does not provide access to the finer detailed attributes a presence document can contain.

```
<?xml version="1.0" encoding="UTF-8"?>
<cr:ruleset xmlns:cr="urn:ietf:params:xml:ns:common-policy"
    xmlns:pr="urn:ietf:params:xml:ns:pres-rules">
 <cr:rule id="fjieiownx93">
 <cr:conditions>
  <cr:identity>
  <cr:id>bob@example.com</cr:id>
  </cr:identity>
 </cr:conditions>
 <cr:actions>
  <pr:sub-handling>allow</pr:sub-handling>
 </cr:actions>
 <cr:transformations>
  <pr:provide-person>true</pr:provide-person>
  <pr;provide-services><pr:all-services/></pr:provide-services>
  <pr:provide-devices><pr:all-devices/></pr:provide-devices>
 </cr:transformations>
 </cr:rule>
</cr:ruleset>
```

Figure 5.17 – A Basic Presence Rule

[18] "Presence Authorization Rules," by J. Rosenberg. Internet Draft, IETF, October 2004.

A user maintains his presence rules at a presence service using XCAP. Rules are placed into the XCAP resource tree under the pres-rules application usage for that user. We discuss the details of that management elsewhere. For now, it is enough to note that the presentity uses HTTP to PUT rules on an XCAP server all at once or one at a time. As one would expect, a GET allows the rules to be read. And the user can receive notification when someone else changes the rules.

Controlling when a Rule Applies

The <conditions> element of a presence rule can test against the identity of the subscriber, and the current sphere, such as work or home, of the presentity. It can also limit the validity of the rule to a certain period of time.

The identity used in a condition can match a specific person, an entire domain, or an entire domain except for some explicitly listed specific people. A rule that grants permissions to alice@example.com and bob@example.com would contain this identity element:

```
<identity>
  <id>alice@example.com</id>
  <id>bob@example.com</id>
</identity>
```

A rule that granted permissions to everyone in example.com except carol@example.com, contains the following:

```
<identity>
 <domain>example.com</domain>
  <except>carol</except>
</identity>
```

A presence server will, of course, have to carefully verify the identity of any subscriber in order to apply these presence rules using any of the standardized techniques available to it.

People often wish to provide different kinds of presence information, and allow a different set of subscribers, depending on whether they are at work or at home. SIMPLE captures this notion in a concept named "sphere." Someone tells a presence server about his current sphere using the <sphere> element inside the <person> element of an RPID presence document.

Presence rules will depend on the current value of sphere when a sphere element appears inside the conditions. For example, Carol could have two rules, one that allows Alice and Bob to subscribe as long as Carol is at work, and another that lets only Alice subscribe when Carol is at home.

Conditions matching the "work" sphere

```
<conditions>
<sphere>work</sphere>
<identity>
<id>alice@example.com</id>
<id>bob@example.com</id>
</identity>
</conditions>
```

Conditions matching the "home" sphere

```
<conditions>
<sphere>home</sphere>
<identity>
<id>alice@example.com</id>
</identity>
</conditions>
```

The standards define two common values for sphere, work and home, but allow a presentity to use an arbitrary string as well. This allows users to customize their rulesets to fit their individual situations. It might make sense for Bob to define and use a "soccer" sphere for when he is coaching, and Alice to use a "screaming-metal" sphere while her band is on stage.

A rule may also declare a specific period of validity. This is particularly useful when Alice wants to allow Bob to subscribe, but only during a particular afternoon meeting, and she isn't sure if she'll be online (or remember) to revoke Bob's permissions at the end of the day. Such a condition is stated with a validity element:

```
<validity>
 <from>2004-12-15T12:00:00.000-05:00</from>
 <to>2004-12-15T18:00:00.000-05:00</to>
</validity>
```

Controlling Subscriptions when a Rule Applies

Once the conditions on a rule match for a given subscription attempt, the actions clause determines whether a presence system will accept a subscription. The <actions> element contain a single <sub-handling> element with one of the following values as described in Table 5.9:

Table 5.9 – Possible values for <sub-handling> element

Value	Meaning
block	Reject the subscription attempt.
confirm	Place the subscription in the pending state and seek approval from the presentity.
polite-block	Accept the subscription, but provide a service-specific presence document indicating the presentity is not available for communication and is otherwise non-informative.
allow	Accept the subscription and share presence information as constrained by the transformations of this rule.

A presence system can hold a large number of rules. Any given subscription may match the conditions of several rules. Whenever this happens, the subscription is treated using the most liberal of the matching rules. If one rule blocks and another rule allows, the subscription will be allowed.

Controlling the Information that is Exposed

If a subscription is allowed, the transformations portion of a presence rule controls what parts of a presence document actually get sent to the subscriber. Consistent with the general principles behind the common-policy format[19] shared with the GEOPRIV protocols, these transformations default to exposing nothing. The presentity explicitly allows different parts of a presence document to be seen by including "provide" clauses in the transformation section of a presence rule.

At a course level, the transformations control whether to provide the information in the person, service, or device sections of a presence document, as described in Table 5.10.

[19] "A Document Format for Expressing Privacy Preferences," by H. Schulzrinne, J. Morris, H. Tschofenig, J. Cueller, J. Polk, J. Rosenberg. Internet Draft, IETF, October 2004.

Table 5.10 – Transformation elements, values and effects

Transformation element	Values	Effect
<provide-person>	true or false	The <person> element is exposed only if this transformation element is set to true
<provide-services>	<all-services/>	All service tuples are exposed
	<uri-scheme>scheme</uri-scheme>	Only tuples with a contact URI using the named scheme (like sip) are exposed
	<uri>specific-uri</uri>	Only tuples with a contact exactly matching the provided specific-uri are exposed
<provide-devices>	<all-devices/>	All devices elements are exposed
	<device-id>id</device-id>	Only devices matching the provided id are exposed

Finer control over the attributes appearing in the exposed person, service, or device elements is also available. Several of these transformations have a simple boolean value—the element they name is exposed only if the value of the transformation is true. These transformation elements and presence attributes are listed in Table 5.11:

A special binary provide transformation, provide-unknown-attribute allows a presentity to control exposure of presence document elements not defined in RPID (such as a custom non-standard element, or an element belonging to a standardized extension). This transformation element has a mandatory attribute named "name" which identifies the element the transformation controls.

Table 5.11 – Transformation elements and the presence attributes over which they control exposure

Transformation element	Controls exposure of presence attribute
<provide-activity>	**<activities>**
<provide-mood>	**<mood>**
<provide-class>	**<class>**
<provide-place-type>	**<place-type>**
<provide-privacy>	**<privacy>**
<provide-relationship>	**<relationship>**
<provide-sphere>	**<sphere>**
<provide-status-icon>	**<status-icon>**
<provide-timezone>	**<timezone>**

For example, if Alice wanted to ensure that the watcher matching this rule did not get to see any <secret-message> elements in her current presence document, she would include a transformation of:

<provide-unknown-element name="secret-message">false</provide-unknown-element>

A final transformation element controls how the user-input element of a presence document is exposed, as described in Table 5.12.

Class versus Sphere

We've seen that a <person> in a presence document can be marked up to show the current <sphere>. This represents where the presentity currently is and/or what the presentity is doing. Sphere can be arbitrary, but the standards provide two common values, home and work. The important thing to remember about sphere is that it describes something current about the presentity, and can be used in conditions of rules to select what rules fire based on that current value.

Table 5.12 – Transformation element values and their effects on how the user-input element of presence document is exposed

<provide-user-input> element value	Effect
False	<user-input> is not exposed
Bare	<user-input> is exposed, but only active or idle is shown, no threshold or idle since information is included
Thresholds	<user-input> is exposed, and the idle-threshold is given, if present. No idle since information is included.
Full	All <user-input> information is exposed

<class>, on the other hand, is a tool that allows a presentity to group similar elements in a presence document, like service tuples, together to make transformations easier. Class values tend to describe the watchers, not the presentity. Typical values might represent "soccer parents," "band members," or "stuff I only let Alice see" (the actual values wouldn't have spaces). This is not the only use of class, but is likely to be the most common. Another example use would be a class of "things I'll expose only on holidays." A rule might have a condition based on identity and transformations that expose a class only to that identity:

Conditions: **Is this Alice subscribing?**

Actions: **Allow the subscription**

Transformations: **Include anything in class "stuff I let only Alice see"**

Classes will frequently also include "people I work with," which leads to confusion between class and sphere. To keep them straight, remember that sphere focuses on the presentity. Class focuses on grouping elements for different consumption by different watchers.

Working with Lists

Presence naturally involves many lists. A user will have lists of people to whom to subscribe, lists of people who are allowed to subscribe, perhaps even lists of people who have tried to call, but got voicemail. The SIMPLE protocols provide a format to represent these lists in a standard way, and, using XCAP, maintain them at a service provider.

The XCAP list usage[20] can be used to represent any list of resources, where a resource is identified by a URI. A user keeps all of her resource lists in a single XML <resource-lists> document. Each <list> in that document will have a unique name, and a list can contain other lists. Lists contain entries. Each <entry> element is identified by a uri, and may be marked-up with a display name. Alice (and her services) might maintain the lists contained in Figure 5.18. She keeps her buddy-list here. Example.com's voicemail service gives her a list of waiting messages, and she has configured her web browser to keep her bookmarks here.

Of course, Alice doesn't know any XML. She uses a graphical interface that presents the list as a tree and lets her edit it using intuitive actions as shown in Figure 5.19.

Like presence rules, resource lists are maintained at an XCAP server, under the resource-lists application usage for each user. XCAPs ability to let the user edit the list, and notice when someone else changes the list, solves the problem of moving buddy lists between multiple clients and keeping them up-to-date. Figure 5.20 shows Alice adding a buddy from her work computer. Her home computer is on at the time, and has subscribed to changes in her buddy list. So when she gets home, the new friend she added will already be on her home computer's display. If Alice's list were large, her server also has the choice of notifying her home computer with only the change (using an XML difference format) instead of only telling it the list changed.

---

[20] "Extensible Markup Language (XML) Formats for Representing Resource Lists," by J. Rosenberg. Internet Draft, IETF, October 2004.

```
<resource-lists xmlns="urn:ietf:params:xml:ns:resource-lists">
 <list name="presence-list">
  <display-name>My Buddies</display-name>
  <list name="Co-workers">
    <entry uri="sip:carol@example.com">
     <display-name>Carol</display-name>
    </entry>
    <entry uri="sip:techsupport@example.com">
     <display-name>Crazy Dave</display-name>
    </entry>
    <list name="irritants">
     <display-name>People who annoy me</display-name>
     <entry uri="sip:bob@example.com">
       <display-name>Bob</display-name>
      </entry>
    </list>
   </list>
   <list name="Friends">
    <entry uri="sip:frank@example.com">
     <display-name>Frank</display-name>
    </entry>
   </list>
  </list>
  <list name="voice-mail">
   <entry uri="sip:msg1282934@vxmail.example.com"/>
   <entry uri="sip:msg1283188@vxmail.example.com"/>
  </list>
  <list name="Bookmarks">
   <entry uri="http://www.example.com"/>
   <entry uri="http://www.example.com/hr/2005/holidays">
    <display-name>Holiday Schedule</display-name>
   </entry>
  </list>
</resource-lists>
```

Figure 5.18 – Alice's resource lists

Figure 5.19 – How Alice views and edits her Presence list

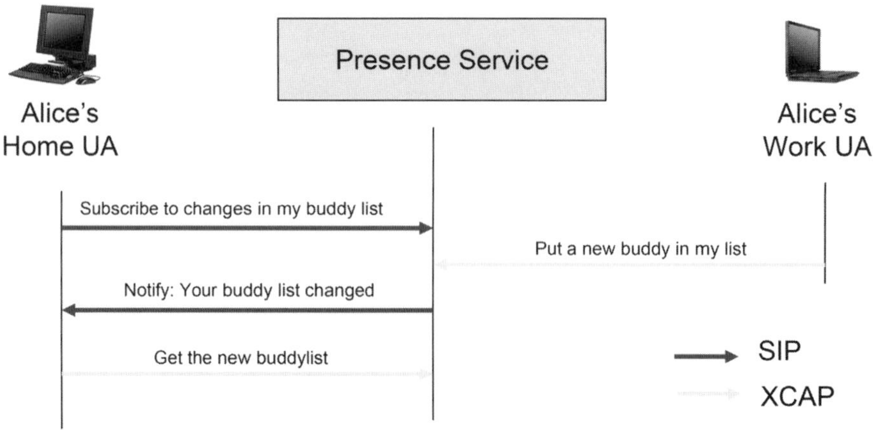

Figure 5.20 – Alice adds a buddy while at work, and her home machine picks it up

Optimizing Subscriptions using Event Lists

Baseline SIMPLE presence requires a subscription for each peer being watched. Each of these subscriptions has to be managed and refreshed individually. In many deployments, all of these subscriptions terminate on the same presence server. Concerned about overhead, the SIMPLE working group created an extension to the presence protocols to allow a single subscription to the entire list of peers being watched.[21] Figure 5.21 shows how this affects network traffic for a buddy list as small as three people. This "eventlist" subscription allows a single SUBSCRIBE to a resource that indicates a list. The event server for this list is also known as a Resource List Server, or RLS.

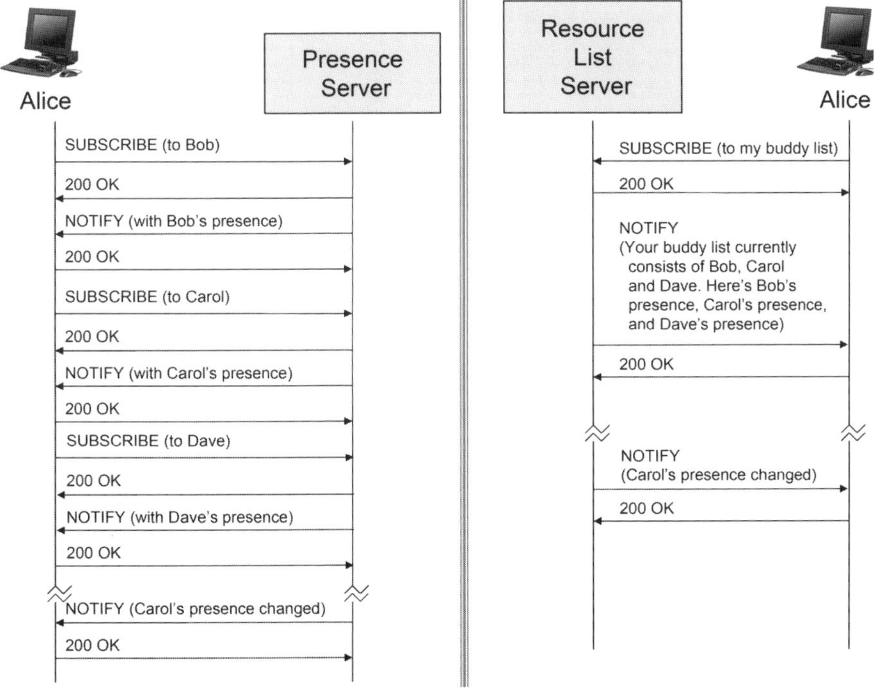

Figure 5.21 – Eventlist subscriptions have fewer (but larger) messages

[21] "A Session Initiation Protocol (SIP) Event Notification Extension for Resource Lists," by A. B. Roach, B. Campbell, J. Rosenberg. Internet Draft, IETF, October 2004.

A watcher does not need to know ahead of time if the resource it is subscribing to is a list. It only needs to indicate that it supports the eventlist extension. If the resource is a list, the server will let the watcher know by including a Require header field (indicating eventlist) in each NOTIFY. If the resource is a list, and the watcher doesn't indicate support for the eventlist extension, the server will return a 421 Extension Required response letting the watcher know it needs to support eventlist to subscribe to this resource.

While the number of messages to the RLS in Figure 5.21 is fewer than what's required for individual subscriptions, the number of bytes may be larger. The initial NOTIFY for an eventlist subscription contains a multipart-MIME document. The first part is an XML document of type application/rlmi+xml reflecting the names on the list and the state of the subscription to each name (pending, active, or terminated). The remaining parts contain a presence document for each name with an active subscription.

The rlmi+xml (resource list meta-information) contains most of the information that would be in the Subscription-State header field of NOTIFY requests in individual subscriptions. This is how Alice can discover that her subscription to Bob is pending while her subscriptions to Dave and Carol are active. The Subscription-State header field in the NOTIFY of eventlist subscriptions speaks only to the state of the subscription to the list, not the subscriptions to the elements of the list.

Like watcher information, eventlist notifications can contain full or partial state. When a single element of the list changes its presence (or changes its subscription state), only the information for that element has to be sent. A partial state notification will contain an rlmi+xml document indicating which element is changing and any new presence document for that element. This is what is happening in the second NOTIFY in Figure 5.21. There are a few changes, however, like adding or removing names from the list that require a full-state notification to be sent.

A resource list can contain sub-lists nested arbitrarily deep. The resource list meta-information contained in any full-state NOTIFY, especially the initial NOTIFY of an eventlist subscription gives the watcher the names, structure, and elements of the sub-lists.

An RLS need not have the information for each individual resource locally in order to serve a list subscription. It may issue one or more "back-end" subscriptions, using SIP events, or perhaps a proprietary protocol to obtain the presence for each element on the resource list (see Figure 5.22). There are subtle and important issues around the identity an RLS uses when making these back-end subscriptions. If the RLS subscribes as itself, it will be able to reuse any information it gets from the back-end. That is, if Bob is on both Alice and Carol's list, the RLS can serve subscriptions from both Alice and Carol keeping only one subscription to Bob's presence server. However, the RLS will only be able to show Alice and Carol what the RLS is allowed to see, and that might not be the same as what Bob allows Alice and Carol to see individually. The RLS can try to pretend to be the watcher when it makes its back-end subscription, but then it loses the ability to share subscriptions. Of course, special arrangements have to be made to allow the RLS to try to pretend to be the watcher (if it were easy to do so, any random person could subscribe pretending to be Alice).

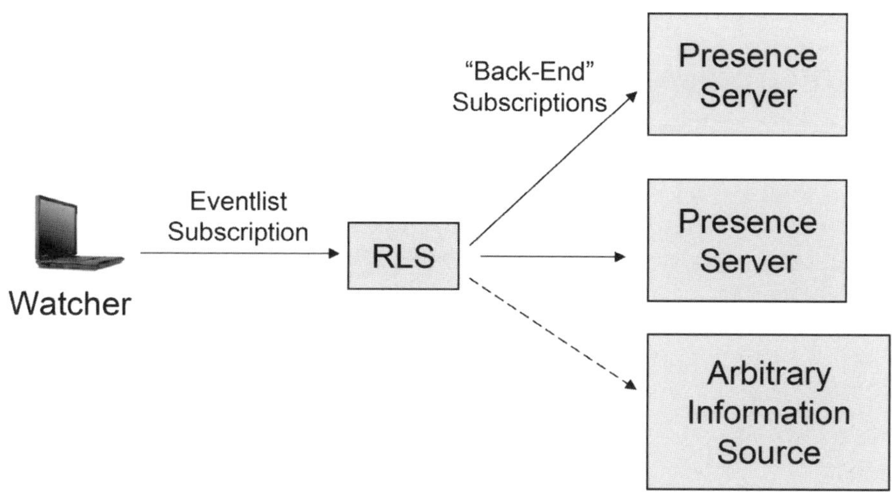

Figure 5.22 – Back-end subscriptions from an RLS

One possible use of a shared back-end subscription would be sharing presence across enterprises. If enterprise B wanted to allow anyone from enterprise A to subscribe, A's RLS could subscribe to B's RLS for everyone in B. A typical optimization would be for A to subscribe to a dynamically maintained list of only those people in B who are being watched by people in A right now. This shared subscription forces everyone in A to have the same view of a given person's presence in B. The presence rules that person provides will apply to the entire of enterprise A and can't be tailored to individuals within A.

Currently, eventlist subscriptions require an RLS to know the contents of the list before a SUBSCRIBE arrives. This list must be maintained out-of-band, perhaps using XCAP. The SIMPLE working group is investigating future extensions that would allow a list to be carried in the SUBSCRIBE message itself.

While we've focused on presence here, the eventlist extension applies equally to any event in the SIP Events framework. However, any eventlist subscription is limited to a single kind of event:

- It makes it possible to subscribe to the presence of a list of resources with one subscription.
- It makes it possible to subscribe to the dialog state of a list of resources with one subscription.
- It does not make it possible to get both presence and dialog state with one subscription.

Beyond a Single Presence Source—Composition

In addition to allowing people to describe their presence in rich detail, SIMPLE allows a presence service to obtain information about a person from several sources and compose that information into a single presence document. For instance, Bob could have several devices and agents reporting information to his presence server as shown in Figure 5.23. Bob's presence service takes the data from his various phones, his calendar, his GPS units and any other agents he wants to provide data from and creates a single, composite, presence document representing Bob.

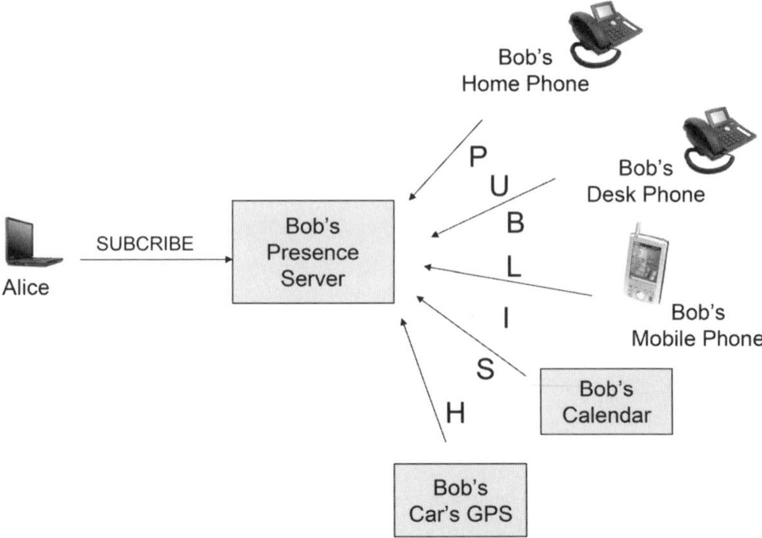

Figure 5.23 – Composition of data from several sources

There are many ways this composition can be achieved. The simplest approach is simply to copy every input into the composite document. This is sometimes referred to as composition by union, and is likely to be the primary composition policy found in deployments for some time. More complex composition functions are certainly acceptable, and even desirable. Bob's service may have custom rules to combine his calendar information into the description of his availability at each of his phones. Such functions are outside the scope of the current standards however, and will be part of what differentiates presence services from different providers.

Multimedia and Instant Messaging

We've seen here that presence can say far more than "Available." It describes the context communication can take place in and the capabilities available for communication. It can advertise that the presentity is ready for simple means of communication, like an instant messaging or a PSTN phone call, and rich multimedia including voice, video, or application sharing. Presence allows people to better decide both when and how to communicate. Once that decision is made, it's up to the Session Initiation Protocol to set up the actual communication.

Opportunities to communicate with more than simple voice can be advertised in a service tuple in a presence document by including a <servcaps> element in the tuple. This element describes the capabilities available at that service, by including one or more of audio, video, text, message or application. Setting up a session for audio and video (or any other RTP-based streaming media) is covered in other chapters. We'll discuss Instant Messaging in more detail here.

Instant messaging has caught on across the world as an important tool in people's communication toolbox. Interestingly, it was not the actual IM capability that attracted society's interest as much as the presence capabilities the early applications provided. As adoption of these tools have increased, people have realized presence is the revolution, and the discovery of the utility of instant messaging is a nice side-effect.

In SIP, there are two modes for instant messaging: a page mode, which is widely deployed, and a session mode, which is in the final stages of standardization.

Page mode messaging

Page mode messaging is like SMS. A message is sent from one party to another as a stand-alone item. There is no relationship between messages, at least from a protocol perspective, that may be sent as part of a conversation.

As with SMS, people are able to hold conversations using this tool anyway, and some applications attempt to group messages between two people into a common dialog-box (or similar display motif). Page mode messaging is realized in SIP by sending a request with a method name of MESSAGE,[22] and the contents of the message sent in the body. A page mode message can contain any mime-type (it's possible to send an html page through a SIP MESSAGE), but most deployed implementations only support plain text. Figure 5.24 shows the details of an exchange of two page mode messages between Alice and Bob. Notice that there is nothing in common in the SIP messages (Call-ID, or even the To or From tags) to let Alice or Bob's endpoints know these messages are related—such association can only be made by the humans through the content of the messages themselves. It is not possible, for example, for these endpoints to tell that if Bob and Alice are having two IM conversations about different topics at once.

Session mode messages using MSRP

Session mode messages group messages that are part of the same communication stream together. The Message Session Relay Protocol (MSRP[23]), treats message sessions very much like audio and video sessions. They are set up and terminated using SIP and described with SDP. This will facilitate treating message sessions as just another type of media in things like conference bridges. Unlike audio and video, MSRP does not use RTP. Instead, MSRP defines a set of messages that are sent between the endpoints over a TCP connection dedicated to the session. These messages are similar to SIP or HTTP messages in that they are in a text format, start with a method, have header fields, and a body. A typical MSRP session between Bob and Alice might look like the flow shown in Figure 5.25.

---

[22] RFC 3428: "Session Initiation Protocol (SIP) Extension for Instant Messaging," by B. Campbell, J. Rosenberg, H. Schulzrinne, C. Huitema, D. Gurle. IETF, December 2002.

[23] "The Message Session Relay Protocol," by B. Campbell, R. Mahy, C. Jennings. Internet Draft, IETF, October 2004.

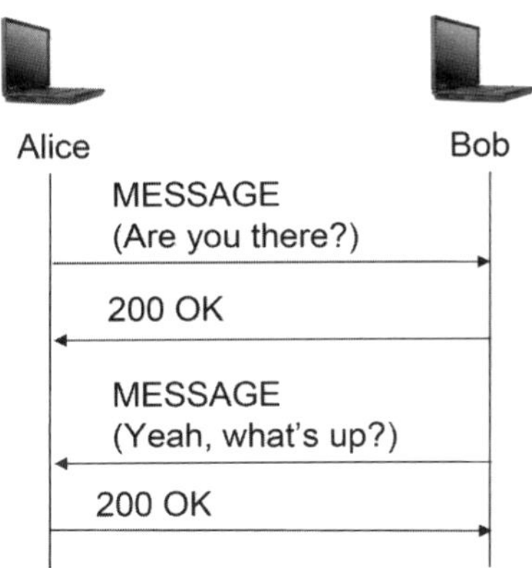


```
MESSAGE sip:bob@example.com SIP/2.0
Via: SIP/2.0/TCP aliceua.example.com;branch=z9hG4bK83n3uswdsf
To: <sip:bob@example.com>
From: <sip:alice@example.com>
Call-ID: 2309dfjw39r42nsd9fu@aliceua.example.com
CSeq: 2934 MESSAGE
Max-Forwards: 70
Contact: <sip:aliceua.example.com>
Content-Length: 16
Content-Type: text/plain

Are you there?
```

```
MESSAGE sip:alice@example.com SIP/2.0
Via: SIP/2.0/TCP bobua.example.com;branch=z9hG4bKsdfnsdie2wd
To: <sip:alice@example.com>
From: <sip:bob@example.com>
Call-ID: 89asdf3ni2wisd9fuj3@bobua.example.com
CSeq: 893829 MESSAGE
Max-Forwards: 70
Contact: <sip:bobua.example.com>
Content-Length: 18
Content-Type: text/plain

Yeah, what's up?
```

Figure 5.24 – Page mode messages

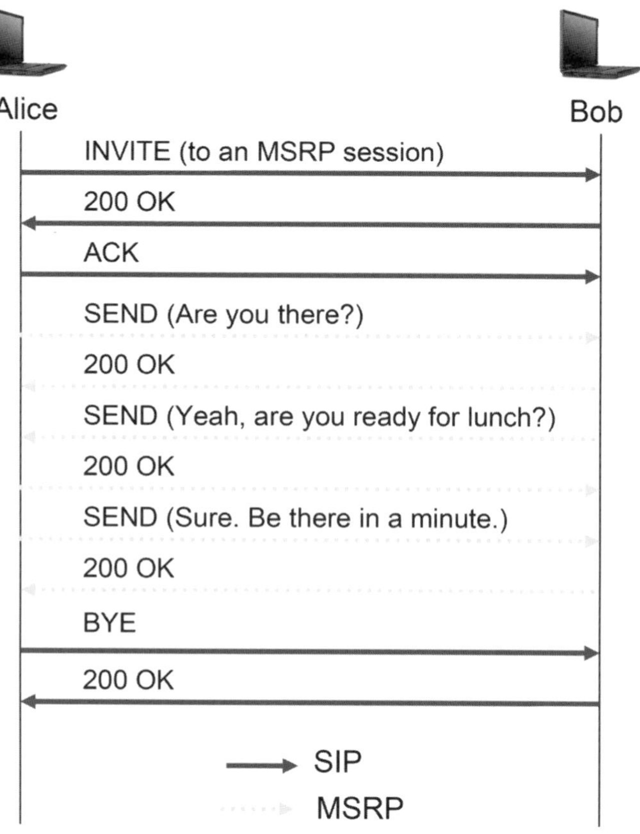

Figure 5.25 – An MSRP session between endpoints

The INVITE in this exchange contains an SDP offer with a media line (m=) indicating MSRP, an attribute line (a=) indicating the MIME types Alice is willing to accept during this session, and an attribute line letting Bob know what path to send his MSRP messages down. Similarly, Bob's 200 OK has an SDP answer with analogous content. Bob's path attribute line might look like this:

a=path:msrp://bobua.example.com:12763/kjhd37s2s2;tcp

This lets Alice's UA know to connect to port 12763 at bobua.example.com using TCP (very much like the role of the address on the "c" line and port on the "m" line play for audio and video media types). The characters after the slash following the port are an identifier specific to this session.

In MSRP, the offerer always opens the connection for the MSRP session. This convention prevents a glare-like situation where both parties are trying to establish connections to start the conversation.

Once Alice establishes the connection to bobua.example.com, she can send her first message to Bob:

```
MSRP fneied93j SEND
To-Path: msrp://bobua.example.com:12763/kjhd37s2s2;tcp
From-Path: msrp://aliceua.example.com:7654/jshA7we;tcp
Message-ID: 39023
Content-Type: text/plain

Are you there?
-------fneied93j$
```

The fneied93j on the start line is both a transaction identifier, and a boundary marker. Notice that the message ends with this string and a dollar sign following seven hyphens. MSRP elements search for this string to find the end of the message instead of using a Content-Length field like SIP. The To-Path is directly from Bob's SDP answer. The From-Path is directly from Alice's offer. This provides enough information for Bob and Alice to associate this message with the offer/answer used to set up the session. The Message-ID uniquely identifies this particular message. We'll see why this is needed in addition to the transaction identifier when we discuss relays.

Bob's UA will acknowledge the receipt of that SEND with the following 200 OK:

```
MSRP fneied93j 200 OK
To-Path: msrp://aliceua.example.com:7654/jshA7we;tcp
From-Path: msrp://bobua.example.com:12763/kjhd37s2s2;tcp
Message-ID: 39023
-------fneied93j$
```

Notice that unlike To and From in SIP, the To-Path and From-Path in the response reflect which way the message is going.

The rest of the SENDs in Figure 5.25 will look similar, but will have their own transaction and message ids.

Session mode messaging using MSRP relays

The flow illustrated in Figure 5.25 is only possible when Alice can open a TCP connection directly to Bob. Many times, NATs or firewalls will prevent that from happening. Like RTP streams for audio, MSRP sessions occur on ephemeral ports. This means an administrator can't put in a simple rule to allow MSRP sessions through a firewall. The SIMPLE working group has defined MSRP relays[24] that can be placed on such administrative boundaries to get MSRP sessions through. Enterprises deploying MSRP could place MSRP relays across their firewall, allowing MSRP traffic across the boundary without giving up control. This fits into the overall architecture similarly to an edge proxy for SIP (see Figure 5.26).

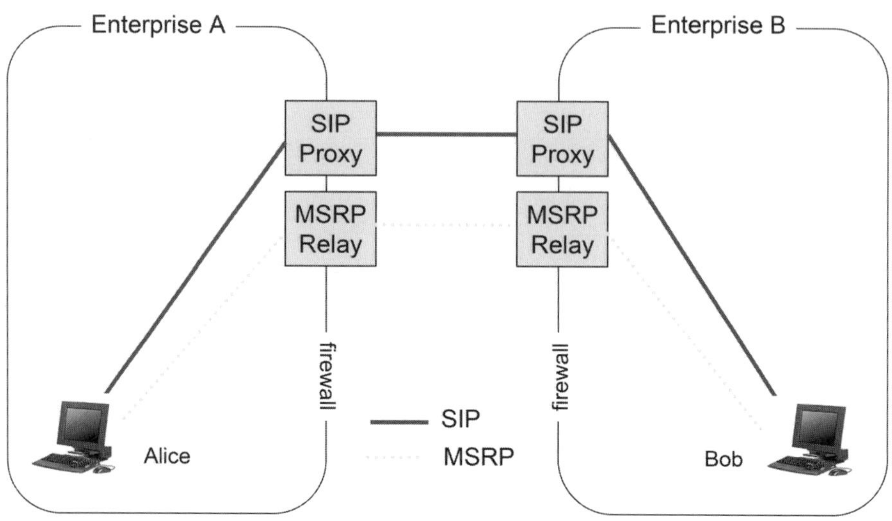

Figure 5.26 – Inter enterprise message relay session

Alice and Bob's endpoints know about their respective relays through configuration. Before starting a session, they will each connect to their relay and get permission to use them. This authorization sequence uses the MSRP AUTH request and is shown in Figure 5.27.

---

[24] "Relay Extensions for Message Sessions Relay Protocol (MSRP)," by C. Jennings, R. Mahy. Internet Draft, IETF, October 2004.

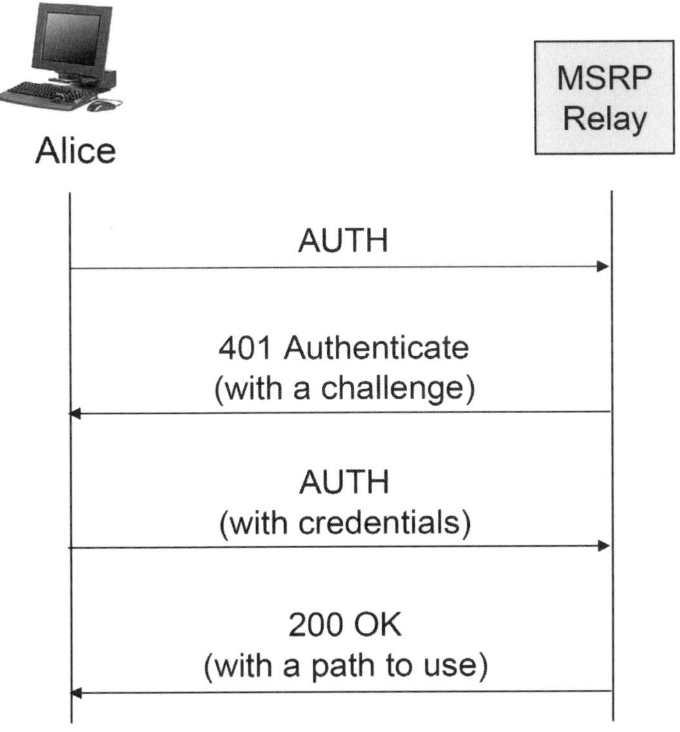

Figure 5.27 – Authorizing with an MSRP relay

This authentication handshake uses DIGEST authentication, similar to HTTP and SIP. The 401 response contains a digest challenge in an WWW-Authenticate header field. The credentials answering that challenge are carried in an Authorization header field in the subsequent AUTH request. AUTH is the *only* MSRP request that can be challenged this way.

A 200 OK response to an AUTH contains a Use-Path header field containing a sequence of MSRP URIs. This path is added to the a=path attribute of any SDP offer or answer this endpoint sends requesting MSRP. The AUTH transaction also uses the Expire header field to negotiate how long this authorization is good for (which is also how long Alice can use the path the relay returned).

Figure 5.28 shows Bob and Alice authorizing with their respective relays and starting an MSRP session through them.

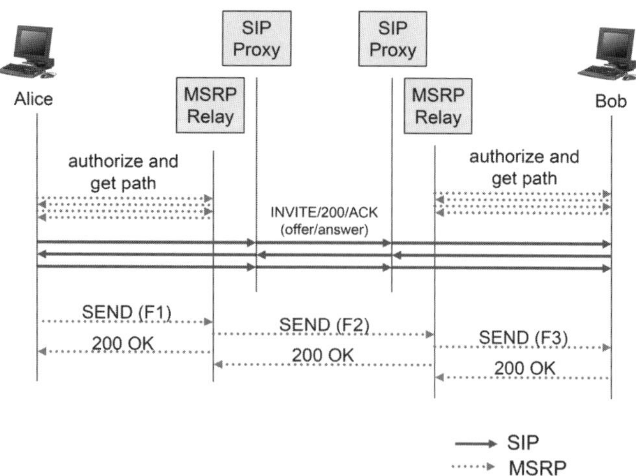

Figure 5.28 – An MSRP session using relays

Alice's relay returned the following Use-Path:

msrp:relaya.example.com:29934/we389wh;tcp.

Her INVITE to Bob contains SDP with the following:

a=path:msrp:relaya.example.com:29934/we389wh;tcp
msrp:aliceua.example.com:8192/8ehb3w;tcp

Bob's relay gave him a similar path through relayb.example.com that he includes in his SDP answer to Alice. Alice's SEND at F1 combines the information from both of these paths:

```
MSRP ahfe8823 SEND
To-Path: msrp:relaya.example.com:29934/we389wh;tcp
     msrp:relayb.example.com:15523/3dnu3a;tcp
     msrp:bobua.example.com:8322/f38wb3;tcp
From-Path: msrp:aliceua.example.com:8192/8ehb3w;tcp
Message-ID: 93932
Content-Type: text/plain

Hi Bob! When can I call you?
-------ahfe8823$
```

Note that MSRP doesn't allow line folding. The example above shows line breaks only to make the messages more readable on this page. On the wire, all values for each header field will be on one line.

The first relay responds when it receives the message (as opposed to when it delivers it downstream). An MSRP 200 OK response to a SEND request is hop-by-hop. It only lets the previous hop know the transaction was complete, not that the message successfully reached its intended final destination. The first 200 OK to F1 in Figure 5.28 appears as follows:

```
MSRP ahfe8823 200 OK
To-Path: msrp:aliceua.example.com:8192/8ehb3w;tcp
From-Path: msrp:relaya.example.com:29934/we389wh;tcp
-------ahfe8823$
```

Relay A looks at the message in F1, notes that the first To-Path URI indicates a valid MSRP session (one that was previously authorized), and builds message F2 to send to relay B. This message starts a new transaction, so it has a new transaction identifier. We see here why the transaction identifier was not also used as the message id. Notice also that the first MSRP URI from the To-Path in F1 moved to the From-Path in F2.

```
MSRP 8ewnend33 SEND
To-Path: msrp:relayb.example.com:15523/3dnu3a;tcp
      msrp:bobua.example.com:8322/f38wb3;tcp
From-Path: msrp:relaya.example.com:29934/we389wh;tcp
       msrp:aliceua.example.com:8192/8ehb3w;tcp
Message-ID: 93932
Content-Type: text/plain

Hi Bob! When can I call you?
-------8ewnend33$
```

If Relay A already has a TCP connection to relay B, it will reuse it. It only opens a new connection if none already exists. Thus, even when there are many MSRP sessions between people using relay A and others using relay B, those relays only maintain a single connection.

Furthermore, an endpoint reuses its authorized connection with a relay. This results in a minimal number of connections throughout the network, and is why each MSRP URI in the path carries a session identifier. The session identifier in the first URI in the To-Path header field of a received request lets the element know which session the message belongs to when there are several sessions in progress over the same connection.

The second relay in Figure 5.28 forwards F2 in a similar way. Bob ultimately receives:

```
MSRP edwu38wb3 SEND
To-Path: msrp:bobua.example.com:8322/f38wb3;tcp
From-Path: msrp:relayb.example.com:15523/3dnu3a;tcp
        msrp:relaya.example.com:29934/we389wh;tcp
        msrp:aliceua.example.com:8192/8ehb3w;tcp
Message-ID: 93932
Content-Type: text/plain

Hi Bob! When can I call you?
-------edwu38wb3$
```

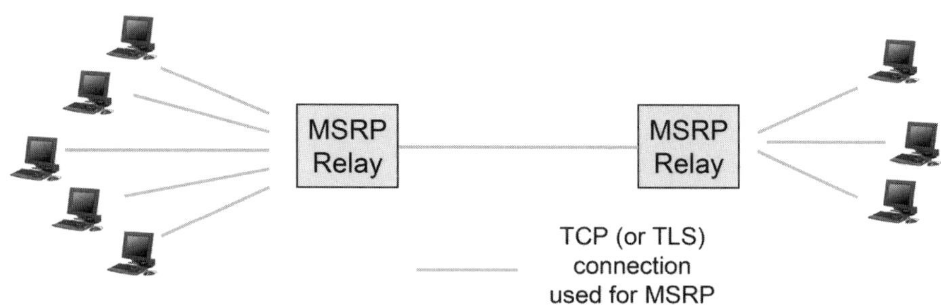

Figure 5.29 – MSRP connections are shared

Chunking messages

As Figure 5.29 shows, relays share a single connection. When Carol sends Dave a very large message (the canonical example used in discussing the protocol in the SIMPLE working group was a copy of "The Lord of the Rings"), we don't want Alice's message to Bob to wait for all Carol's bits to go through the pipe. MSRP allows relays (or even endpoints) to break up messages into "chunks" so that each connection can be shared fairly. Carol's multi-megabyte message could be broken into a series of one-kilobyte chunks. Alice's message to Bob would then only need to wait for one of those small chunks to go by.

We'll use a contrived example to show how this works. In Figure 5.30 Alice sends a short message to Bob using a single relay. The relay breaks this message into two chunks.

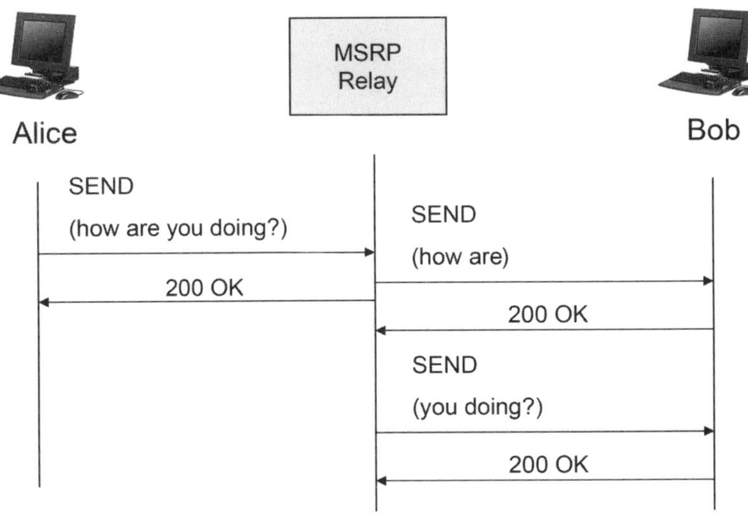

Figure 5.30 – MSRP Relays can break messages into chunks

Alice's original SEND contains her entire message:

```
MSRP 349dcnewx SEND
To-Path: msrp:relay.example.com:29934/eewts73;tcp
      msrp:bobua.example.com:8322/323aae;tcp
From-Path: msrp:aliceua.example.com:8192/hhewi388;tcp
Message-ID: 88273
Content-Type: text/plain

How are you doing?
-------349dcnewx$
```

The relay breaks this into two chunks. Each chunk gets sent in its own MSRP transaction.

```
MSRP djhfwi3e8s SEND
To-Path: msrp:bobua.example.com:8322/323aae;tcp
From-Path: msrp:relay.example.com:29934/eewts73;tcp
        msrp:aliceua.example.com:8192/hhewi388;tcp
Message-ID: 88273
Byte-Range: 1-8/20
Content-Type: text/plain

How are
-------djhfwi3e8s+
```

```
MSRP 7esiisdhh3 SEND
To-Path: msrp:bobua.example.com:8322/323aae;tcp
From-Path: msrp:relay.example.com:29934/eewts73;tcp
        msrp:aliceua.example.com:8192/hhewi388;tcp
Message-ID: 88273
Byte-Range: 9-20/20
Content-Type: text/plain

you doing?
-------7esiisdhh3$
```

Look closely at the terminating line of the first chunk. It ends with a "+" to let the receiver know that this message (with Message-ID: 88273) is not complete and will be continued. The Byte-Range header field lets the receiver know both how many bytes to expect for the whole message, and which bytes this particular transaction is delivering. The second chunk ends with a "$", letting the recipient know that this is the last chunk.

It is possible that the relay doesn't know how many bytes the entire message will contain. Carol can start sending her movie without saying how long it is in advance. When a relay needs to chunk this kind of stream, it can use an asterisk in the Byte-Range header field to say "I don't know what the total length is." For example, the first chunk of Carol's movie might leave the relay containing Byte-Range: 1-1024/*.

It is also possible that Carol wants to give up before her transfer is complete. She can do this by terminating her transaction with an end line (seven hyphens followed by the transaction id) ending with a "#" (Alice would have used -------349dcnewx# in our example). This tells the next hop that this message is aborted and no further chunks for this message will be sent.

Delivery Reports

In the examples shown in Figures 5.28 and 5.30, the 200 OK messages that Alice receives only tell her that her relay accepted her message. They do not say anything about whether the message was delivered to Bob's UA. That information comes in the form of a REPORT (or lack of a REPORT) from Bob.

Alice can request that the elements involved in transferring the message report success or failure. By default (which is the case for our examples), a SEND request asks for failure reports, but not success reports. So Alice can infer Bob's UA got her message since she didn't get a failure report within a certain period of time. This default behavior is not what's desired in all environments, so MSRP allows a sender to request different behavior. A SEND request can contain a Report-Success header field with a value of "yes" or "no." It can independently contain a Report-Failure header field containing a value of "yes," "no," or "partial." Lack of a Report-Success header field is the same as including a Report-Success value of no. Lack of a Report-Failure header field is the same as including a Report-Failure value of yes.

If Report-Success is yes, Bob's UA will send an MSRP REPORT request to Alice when the entire message is received. Had Alice requested a success report in Figure 5.30, then after both chunks arrived, Bob would issue:

```
MSRP cweihdwn3 REPORT
To-Path: msrp:relay.example.com:29934/eewts73;tcp
      msrp:aliceua.example.com:8192/hhewi388;tcp

From-Path: msrp:bobua.example.com:8322/323aae;tcp
Message-ID: 88273
Status: 000 200 OK
-------cweihdwn3$
```

The Status header field lets Alice know that the entire message arrived successfully. Only the ultimate receiving endpoint will issue a REPORT indicating success.

If Report-Failure is "yes" (which it is by default), or "partial," then any relay in the path could send a REPORT back to Alice. This will happen when a SEND to the next hop fails. When Report-Failure is set to partial, a relay will generate a REPORT only when it gets a non-200 OK response to the SEND. When Report-Failure is "yes," the relay will also start a timer when it issues the SEND, and send a failure report if no response arrives before the timer expires. These reports are sent back to the originating endpoint, not to the previous hop. A relay is not required to do anything about a report it receives other than forward it. Any recovery of a message based on a failure report is entirely the sending endpoint's responsibility.

In Figure 5.30, if the second chunk failed to make it to Bob, the relay would eventually timeout on the transaction and send a REPORT to Alice letting her know that bytes 9-20 of message 88273 failed to deliver (see the MSRP specs for the exact syntax of such a REPORT request). Alice's UA could choose to issue a new SEND transaction containing only that chunk, or just tell Alice that the message didn't make it.

To reduce the transaction processing load on networks with relays, any SEND transaction with a Report-Failure value of "no" goes silently unanswered. No MSRP response (positive or negative) is sent to the request. The motivation is that if you SEND with Report-Failure set to no, you really don't care if it gets even to the next hop or not–you'll willing to take your chances. If Report-Failure is set to "partial," success (200-class) responses are squelched, but failure responses are returned in addition to failure reports.

The is-composing indicator

A popular feature of most messaging systems is knowing when the person you are communicating with is working on a message to send you. SIMPLE defines a special body type[25] with this information that can be sent either in a page mode message or during an MSRP session. The body has a MIME type of "application/im-iscomposing+xml," and consists of an XML document that lets the recipient know when the sender has started composing, and when the sender has gone "idle" (started composing, but stopped contributing for some time), along with how long it has been since the sender last contributed to the composition. The message can indicate what kind of content is being composed, be it plain text, an audio clip, or a web page. The message can also tell the recipient when to expect an update refreshing this information (if that time passes without an update, the recipient can throw the current information away as stale).

---

[25] RFC 3994: "Indication of Message Composition for Instant Messaging," by H. Shulzrinne. IETF, January 2005.

A typical indication might appear as follows:

```
<isComposing xmlns="urn:ietf:params:xml:ns:im-iscomposing">
  <state>active</state>
  <contenttype>text/plain</contenttype>
  <refresh>90</refresh>
 </isComposing>
```

An endpoint receiving these messages can display the information however makes sense. For traditional IM, there will be something along the lines of an "is typing" message displayed along with the conversation history whenever the is-composing messages indicate the peer is actively contributing to the message being composed.

Chapter 6

SIP-based Collaboration and Conferencing

Introduction

Audio and video conferences are common events in corporate life. Text conferencing, i.e. chat rooms, are common in entertainment. Increasingly, the term collaboration is being used instead of conferencing. It evokes a higher level of interaction and productivity between people in various organizations that may or not be actually achieved. In this section, we will discuss typical conferencing and collaboration scenarios, additional functionality that SIP-based collaboration provides, and some other Internet conferencing and conference control protocols. Finally, application scenarios and call flows will be presented.

Problem Statement

Conferencing is a multi-billion dollar business in the US today and a familiar part of a professional's working life. Audio conferencing over the Public Switched Telephone Network (PSTN) is most common, although video conferencing and web conferencing are gaining popularity.

PSTN Audio Conferencing

Audio conferences can be "dial in" or "dial out." In the dial in mode, a phone number and a "passcode" is distributed to participants, perhaps using email. The conference server or bridge plays a greeting then prompts the participant for the passcode. The passcode is used as both a conference identifier (multiple conferences can use the same dial in phone number) and as an authentication token. In some cases, each participant has a unique passcode which can be used to pull up their personal profile. Often the participant is prompted to record their name, which is sometimes announced by an automated attendant when the participant joins or leaves the conference. In the dial out mode, the conference bridge places telephone calls and plays a prompt to whoever answers the call, perhaps prompting them for a passcode before joining them in the conference.

Once in the conference, the conference bridge performs the media mixing. A typical mixing algorithm is called "mix minus." In this mode, each participant's received audio stream contains the audio from the set of active speakers (perhaps the three loudest speakers at any given instant) but never their own sent audio.

Audio mixing can be performed locally or centrally. Some high end telephone sets have conferencing capabilities. In addition, some PBXes provide mixing functionality that a telephone set can invoke. A common endpoint-invoked audio conferencing service is also known as "3 way calling" in which a telephone requests that a telephone switch place multiple calls and bridge the resulting audio calls.

Conferences can also be scheduled in advance, or created in an *ad hoc* manner. Conferences can be cascaded, with mixing being performed at multiple locations.

In general, PSTN audio conferencing does not provide the most pleasant experience. Often, a single participant with a noisy line or with music on hold (the participant had by mistake accepted an incoming call on another line and has put the conference line on hold) can degrade the experience of all participants. One participant generating echo (or noise from a broken echo canceller) can also ruin the experience. Tracking down and disconnecting the noisy line can be difficult with IVR interfaces. Also, knowing who is participating in a call is difficult.

Video Conferencing

Video conferencing has developed in the PSTN using ISDN standards. Room-based systems that link conference rooms and show participants sitting around a table are common. These systems can include camera controls.

Other corporate systems use a single camera per participant, and centrally "mix" the images into a tiled (or "Hollywood Squares") view of the conference with an N-by-N matrix of squares.

The H.323 protocol was developed specifically for video conferencing over IP networks. It defines interworking with the set of ISDN video conferencing standards. As a result, there are some deployed H.323 video systems.

Mixing latency is a critical issue in both audio and video conferencing. Audio mixing typically does not introduce large amounts of latency. However, video mixing can require significant processor resources depending on the codecs. In addition, a change in video layout can require a "fast update" command to be sent from the mixing bridge to the endpoint.

H.323 video conferencing has not really taken off on the Internet due the difficulty in setting up, scheduling, and running video conferences. Also, low bandwidth connections can make the quality poor and the experience poor.

Web Conferencing

Web conferencing is a relatively new service offered using a web browser over the Internet. In addition to a telephone number and a passcode for the audio, web conferences offer a HTTP URL which provides a web page with information about the conference.

Application sharing is the main feature. Typically a presenter stepping through a set of presentation slides is given the ability to skip having to say "Now turn to slide 3." In addition, membership information about the conference and active speaker indications can be provided. Text messaging with the presenter or with other participants is sometimes offered. A mechanism to provide feedback to the presenter is also sometimes provided.

In most web conferencing systems, a web browser plug-in or Java applet must be enabled or installed or the service does not work. This causes bad user experiences and delays in using systems for the first time. Also, web conferencing does not work well for devices with small screens such as PDAs and cell phones.

Technology Potential

A goal of SIP conferencing is to go beyond PSTN and ISDN audio, video, and simple web conferencing as the following sections will detail. Many of the limitations discussed in the previous sections will be addressed.

The Promise of SIP Conferencing

SIP conferencing offers the promise of more advanced and usable functionality. Some of the key points are:

- Indicating in the SIP protocol itself that the UA is in a conference. This allows the UA to inform the user and invoke special call control operations.
- The ability to discover if a URI is related to a conference *without having to call the URI.*
- The ability to add and invite participants to a conference without having to manually say or type a telephone number and passcode.
- The ability to display basic conference information such as the participant list on any SIP device with a screen without requiring a browser with a plug-in.
- The ability to provide synchronized current speaker indication for identification, to detect noisy lines, music on hold, etc.
- The ability to integrate conferencing with applications such as calendars and scheduling applications.
- The ability to build distributed conferencing systems using building blocks and open standards approach instead of a closed vertical stack.

- The ability of a participant to control their view of the conference, adjust controls, volumes, levels, etc., rendered by a user interface chosen locally by the device or by the user.
- The ability to support multiple mixing modes from centralized mixing to fully distributed mixing (full mesh), to tandem selection.
- The ability to distribute a conference across a number of conferencing platforms but still be able to get a complete picture of conference state such as the membership.

The full set of requirements on which the SIP conferencing work was developed is detailed in the SIP conferencing requirements document.[1] The mechanisms and protocols to implement these are described in the next sections.

Basics of SIP Conferencing

SIP conferencing can take on many forms, from a conventional centrally-mixed conference to a multicast broadcast session as will be shown in the following sections.

The simplest conferencing model is to use the SIP UA of one participant as the central conference point, both for signaling and for media mixing. Figure 6.1 shows an example of a UA that will host up to seven conference participants as the processing power of the PC and the network bandwidth will allow.

SIP endpoint-based conferencing using the UA as the central signaling and media server has two interesting properties:

- Quite a significant number of conferences can be held without any central server. This is another case where bandwidth and processing power in the endpoints compete with centrally provided services.
- Peer-to-peer SIP described in Chapter 14 can make good use of this model.

[1] Levin, O. and R. Even, "High Level Requirements for Tightly Coupled SIP Conferencing." draft-ietf-sipping-conferencing-requirements-01 (work in progress), September 2004.

Figure 6.1 – Endpoint-based conferencing
(Courtesy of Xten Networks)

Various models of SIP conferencing are described in the informational conference framework document.[2]

Centralized Conferencing

In the following section, the discussion will be restricted to the case where there exists a single centralized point of signaling, authentication, and authorization. Without this assumption, the problem of discovering conference state and performing deterministic operations on that state are extremely difficult, and have been the subject of much academic research. This assumption underlies the work of the IETF Centralized Conferencing working group.[3]

Focus—The Centralized Point of Control

The assumption of this centralized point, known as a "focus," allows many useful and interesting conferencing scenarios to take place. Note that this does not require centralized mixing—the resulting media sessions established by a focus can be full mesh or a mixed mode. In addition, it is

---

[2] Rosenberg, J., "A Framework for Conferencing with the Session Initiation Protocol." draft-ietf-sipping-conferencing-framework-02 (work in progress), June 2004.

[3] http://www.ietf.org/html.charters/xcon-charter.html

possible to connect multiple foci to form a cascaded conference. A single focus may also control a number of mixers which may be, for example, geographically distributed.

Each participant establishes a separate dialog with the focus in a peer-wise manner—each dialog is completely separate, but is coupled through the focus. In this manner, a focus acts as a Back-to-Back User Agent (B2BUA).

The focus is formally defined in SIP in the call control document for conferencing.[4]

Conference URI—The Conference Identifier

A conference in SIP is defined by the Conference URI, a SIP or SIPS URI which resolves to a unique focus. Establishing a dialog with this focus (by sending an INVITE) brings a participant into the conference. The Conference URI can be passed to other participants who can use it to join the same conference instance. Note that a Conference URI is not the same as a PSTN Conference bridge access number—often an access number is shared across multiple conferences, and a participant must input a PIN or passcode to identify which conference to join. A Conference URI by itself must have all the information necessary to identify and join a conference. (Note that it is possible to include PIN or passcode within the conference URI itself.) Authentication is typically performed using standard SIP mechanisms such as a shared secret (SIP Digest) or SIP identity or certificate.

"isfocus" Feature Tag

SIP has defined mechanisms by which a UA can provide information about the capabilities and characteristics of the device. The fact that a SIP UA is a focus is indicated by the "isfocus" feature tag which is carried as a parameter in the Contact header field in requests and responses generated by the focus. The "isfocus" feature tag is defined in the Callee Capabilities document[5] while the usage is defined in the SIP call control for conferencing document.[4]

Since feature tags are returned in responses to OPTIONS capability queries, it is possible for a UA to tell *in advance* of actually joining a conference that the resulting session will be part of a conference. That is, prior to

[4] Johnston, A. and Levin, O., "Session Initiation Protocol Call Control—Conferencing for User Agents." IETF Internet Draft, November 2004.

[5] RFC 3480: "Indicating User Agent Capabilities in the Session Initiation Protocol (SIP)," by J. Rosenberg, H. Schulrzinne, and P. Kizivat. IETF, August 2004.

sending an INVITE to the URI, the UA can send an OPTIONS request and learn from the presence of the "isfocus" tag that the URI is actually a Conference URI and present this information to the user. For example, the UA might be able to find out the conference roster or media types supported by the conference. This information can be presented to the user who can utilize this for decisions about which device to use or whether to join the conference.

Conference Aware or Unaware UA

A UA which recognizes the "isfocus" and as a result can initiate conference specific services and features to the user is known as a Conference Aware UA. A UA which does not recognize the "isfocus" tag is known as a Conference Unaware UA. A user behind a Conference Unaware UA will have a similar conference experience as a PSTN conference participant. However, a Conference Aware UA can enable many of the advanced SIP conference capabilities to be used.

Conference Creation

Any number of non-SIP means may be used to create a SIP conference. The creation of a conference involves the creation of a unique identifier in the form of a Conference URI. The creation of this conference URI also results in the creation of a focus. To join a conference, a participant establishes a SIP dialog with the focus. This will typically also result in the establishment of media sessions, such as audio, video, and text sessions.

Admission and control is performed by the focus by accepting or denying dialog establishment. While a participant can control its own media sourced and received, it cannot change the media sent or received by other participants. To do this, it needs to request the focus to take action.

Conference Factory URI

A SIP mechanism has been defined for the creation of a SIP conference in an *ad hoc* manner. A SIP INVITE request is sent to an entity known as a Conference Factory.[6] The Conference Factory is a User Agent that creates and allocates a Conference URI and a corresponding focus. The Conference URI is returned to conference creator using SIP. Typically, this is performed by redirecting (a 3xx SIP response) with the Contact URI containing the

[6] Johnston, A. and Levin, O., "Session Initiation Protocol Call Control—Conferencing for User Agents." IETF Internet Draft, November 2004.

Conference URI and the "isfocus" parameter. The conference creator can then send an INVITE to the Conference URI and establish a dialog with the focus and bring the conference into existence. Alternatively, the Conference Factory can create the conference and automatically add the participant into it. The Conference URI would be returned in a Contact header field in the 200 OK response or in a re-INVITE.

Note that a Conference Factory is not the same as an application server which can create a conference after human interaction, such as operation of an IVR or a web page form. The Conference Factory is fully automated, and requires no human or other interaction to create a conference. The conference policy is set at the start to a default, but it may be manipulated. However, as the largest user of the Conference Factory will be *ad hoc* conferencing users, this does not seem likely.

Once a conference has been created by a Conference Factory, a conference aware User Agent will learn that it is in a conference and be able to invoke a set of conference control features, such as those described in the next section. Note that it is also possible for a conference unaware UA to utilize a conference factory and create a conference. However, the UA will not be aware of this and non-SIP means will be necessary to invite others to the conference.

An example of conference establishment using a Conference Factory URI follows:

```
INVITE sip:conf-factory@example.com SIP/2.0
Via: SIP/2.0/UDP client.chicago.example.com
  ;branch=z9hG4bKhjhs8ass83
Max-Forwards: 70
To: <sip:conf-factory@example.com>
From: Carol <sip:carol@chicago.example.com>;tag=32331
Call-ID: d432fa84b4c76e66710
CSeq: 45 INVITE
Contact: <sip:carol@client.chicago.example.com>
Allow: INVITE, ACK, CANCEL, OPTIONS, BYE, REFER, SUBSCRIBE,
  NOTIFY
Allow-Events: dialog
Accept: application/sdp, message/sipfrag
Supported: replaces
Content-Type: application/sdp
Content-Length: 274
(SDP not shown)
```

```
SIP/2.0 200 OK
Via: SIP/2.0/UDP client.chicago.example.com
  ;branch=z9hG4bKhjhs8ass83;received=192.0.2.4
To: <sip:conf-factory@example.com>;tag=733413
From: Carol <sip:carol@chicago.example.com>;tag=32331
Call-ID: d432fa84b4c76e66710
CSeq: 45 INVITE
Contact: <sip:3402934234@example.com>;isfocus
Allow: INVITE, ACK, CANCEL, OPTIONS, BYE, REFER, SUBSCRIBE,
  NOTIFY
Allow-Events: dialog, conference
Accept: application/sdp, application/conference-info+xml,
message/sipfrag
Supported: replaces, join, gruu
Content-Type: application/sdp
Content-Length: 274

v=0
o=focus431 2890844526 2890842807 IN IP4 ms5.conf.example.com
s=-
i=Example Conference Hosted by Example.com
u=http://conf.example.com/3402934234
e=3402934234@conf-help.example.com
p=+1-888-2934234
c=IN IP4 ms5.conf.example.com
t=0 0
m=audio 49170 RTP/AVP 0
m=video 51372 RTP/AVP 31
```

Ad Hoc Conferencing with Resource Lists

In another scenario, a conference creator may provide a URI list to the Conference Factory.[7] This will result in the creation of the conference and also result in the participants in the URI list be invited ("dialed out") to join the conference.

An example is given on the next page:

---

[7] Camarillo, G, and Johnston, A., "Conference Establishment Using Request-Contained Lists in the Session Initiation Protocol (SIP)." IETF Internet-Drafts, November 2004.

```
INVITE sip:conf-factory@example.com SIP/2.0
Via: SIP/2.0/TCP client.chicago.example.com
 ;branch=z9hG4bKhjhs8ass83
Max-Forwards: 70
To: Conf Factory <sip:conf-factory@example.com>
From: Carol <sip:carol@chicago.example.com>;tag=32331
Call-ID: d432fa84b4c76e66710
CSeq: 1 INVITE
Contact: <sip:carol@client.chicago.example.com>
Allow: INVITE, ACK, CANCEL, OPTIONS, BYE, REFER, SUBSCRIBE, NOTIFY
Allow-Events: dialog
Accept: application/sdp, message/sipfrag
Content-Type: multipart/mixed;boundary="unique-boundary"
Content-Length: 690

--unique-boundary
Content-Type: application/sdp

v=0
o=carol 2890844526 2890842807 IN IP4 chicago.example.com
s=-
c=IN IP4 192.0.2.1
t=0 0
m=audio 20000 RTP/AVP 0
a=rtpmap:0 PCMU/8000
m=video 20002 RTP/AVP 31
a=rtpmap:31 H261/90000

--unique-boundary
Content-Type: application/resource-lists+xml
Content-Disposition: recipient-list

<?xml version="1.0" encoding="UTF-8"?>
<resource-lists xmlns="urn:ietf:params:xml:ns:resource-lists"
   xmlns:xsi="http://www.w3.org/2001/XMLSchema-instance">
 <list>
 <entry uri="sip:bill@example.com" />
 <entry uri="sip:joe@example.org" />
 <entry uri="sip:ted@example.net" />
 </list>
</resource-lists>
--unique-boundary--
```

Conference Control

Conference control is the ability of a participant to manipulate the state of the conference. Note that SIP call control mechanisms can be used by a participant to control its own individual leg (participant ⇔ focus). Conference control is the ability of a participant to manipulate the state of the conference.

SIP Conference Control using INVITE

A participant joins a conference using an INVITE—either the participant sends the INVITE to the focus ("dial-in") or the focus sends the participant the INVITE ("dial-out"). During the conference, a participant or focus can change the nature of the media session between them using a re-INVITE. For example, if an audio conference adds video, the focus can re-INVITE each participant adding a video media stream. If a participant supports video, it can accept; otherwise, it may decline and continue to participate with audio only. Either the focus or the participant may put the media streams on hold, and take them off of hold.

SIP Conference Control using REFER

A participant can control their own view of the conference using a re-INVITE as described in the previous section. However, in order to affect or control another participant's view, a third party mechanism must be used. This can be implemented in SIP using the REFER method.[8, 9]

The SIP call control operations for conferencing are described in the SIP Call Control for Conferencing document.[10] Examples of REFER requests sent by a participant to the focus are shown in Table 6.1.

Non-SIP Conference State Control

Besides these SIP controls on a conference, a new protocol is being developed in the IETF Centralized Conferencing (XCON) Working Group. This non-SIP protocol will allow most aspects of the conference state to be manipulated directly.

---

[8] RFC 3515: "The Session Initiation Protocol (SIP) Refer Method," by R. Sparks. IETF, April 2003.

[9] RFC 3892: "The Session Initiation Protocol (SIP) Referred-By Mechanism," by R. Sparks. September 2004.

[10] Johnston, A. and Levin, O., "Session Initiation Protocol Call Control—Conferencing for User Agents." IETF Internet Draft, November 2004.

Table 6.1 – Conference call control using REFER requests

SIP Request	Result
REFER Refer-To:sip:A@example.com	Requests focus send an INVITE to sip:A@example.com to add them into the conference
REFER Refer- To:sip:B@example.com ?method=REFER	Requests focus send a REFER to sip:B@example.com to request that B send an INVITE to join the conference.
REFER Refer-To:sip:C@example.com ?method=BYE	Requests focus to send a BYE to participant to remove them from the conference.

This protocol will be useful for performing more advanced conference control than the use of REFER allows, or for endpoints which are not SIP-enabled. For example, an application could provide a user interface to control a conference, and use this protocol to interact with the focus.

In addition to being able to add and delete participants, the protocol will allow display names to be set, multiple devices to be grouped under the same user and sidebars or sub-conferences to be created.

Conference State Information

There are three aspects of SIP conferencing—the actual SIP call control which is used by a participant to join the conference and establish the necessary media session. The conference state is primarily about identity—it is the roster of who is participating and with what means.

SIP Conference Event Package

Since the state of the conference changes dynamically as each participant joins, leaves, or changes their level of participation in a conference, it is useful for participants to receive updates in real time. The SIP Events (RFC 3265) framework provides an ideal mechanism for such updates. A focus hosting a conference indicates support for the SIP conference package[11] by including an Allow-Events: conference header field. A participant recognizes the presence of the isfocus feature tag in the Contact URI and subscribes to the conference package. As a result, the participant receives notifications about the conference state.

[11] Rosenberg, J. H. Schulzrinne, and O. Levin, "A Session Initiation Protocol (SIP) Event Package for Conference State." IETF Internet-Draft (work in progress), February 2004.

These conference state event notifications can contain similar information as that available in a web conference. The key difference is the data is presented in a structured way that allows the UA to render this to the user in the most efficient form. For example, a PC SIP client may display a page full of information similar to a web conference. However, a SIP phone or mobile phone with a small screen would likely only display the most critical information, such as the roster. The authors believe that in the future, any SIP UA with a screen that is Conference Aware may be able to support the SIP conference events package.

XML Conference-Info Data Schema

The conference package is an XML object that has the following organization. The basic parts of the conference-info element are the conference-description, host-info, conference-state, users, sidebars-by-ref (reference), and sidebars-by-value. The conference description contains information about the nature of the conference. This element also contains the conference URIs and information about service URIs—URIs such as web pages. Other information includes such as the maximum participant count and the available media types.

The host-info element contains details about the conference host. The conference-state element contains information about the current user count, media actually in service, etc. The users element contains a list of user elements which contain information about each participant in the conference. The sidebars-by-ref and sidebars-by-value contain information about sub-conferences known as sidebars. The sidebars-by-ref element contains URI pointers to sub conference information that can be obtained by subscribing to that URI. The sidebars-by-value element contains a list of characteristics and a roster list for the sidebars.

The user element contains some of the most useful information about conference participants. The information includes the media streams which are grouped by endpoint (since a single user may participate in a conference using a number of devices), and also the joining mode and status.

The conference package is a place where the focus can put together information from various sources. For example, the SSRC and media stream mapping information can be included.

In the example XML document below, media sent by user Bob would have his CSRC number 583398 in the actual RTP media packets sent by the mixer. Other users would have a different CSRC number. As a result, if Bob's PC is injecting noise into the conference, for example, other participants could determine that the noise came from his device and use SIP call control means to remove him from the conference or mute his session.

```
<?xml version="1.0" encoding="utf-8" ?>
<conference-info version="0" state="full"
entity="sip:conf233@example.com">

 <conference-description>

  <conf-uris>
   <entry>
    <uri>tel:+18005671234</uri>
   </entry>
   <entry>
    <uri>h323:conf545@example.com</uri>
   </entry>
  </conf-uris>
 </conference-description>

 <users>
  <user entity="bob@example.com" state="full">
   <display-text>Bob Jones"</display-text>

   <endpoint entity="sip:bob@pc33@example.com">
   <status>connected</status>
   <joining-method>dialed-in</joining-method>
    <media id="1">
     <type>audio</type>
     <src-id>583398</src-id>
   </media>
  </user>

  <user entity="sip:barbara@example.com" state="partial">
   <status>sendonly</status>
  </user>

 </users>
</conference-info>
```


Note that a single user may be using multiple devices (endpoints). The grouping of several endpoints under a single user is possible if they have authenticated the same, or perhaps they have been identified and manually grouped (see the section on Conference Control).

Conference package notifications can be full state or partial state. For large conferences, partial state notifications are preferred to reduce the traffic volume.

Another example of a conference package notification is shown below:

```
<conference-info version="0" state="full"
    entity="sip:3402934234@conf.example.com">
<conference-description>
  <conf-uris>
  <entry>
   <uri>tel:+18882934234</uri>
  </entry>
  </conf-uris>
</conference-description>
<users>
  <user entity="sip:carol@chicago.example.com" state="full">
  <display-text>Carol</display-text>
  <endpoint entity="sip:carol@client.chicago.example.com">
    <state>connected</state>
    <joining-method>dialed-in</joining-method>
    <media id="1" state="full">
    <display-text>Main Audio</display-text>
    <proto>audio</proto>
    <src-id>583398</src-id>
    <state>sendrecv</state>
    </media>
    <media id="2" state="full">
    <proto>video</proto>
    <src-id>345212</src-id>
    <state>sendrecv</state>
    </media>
  </endpoint>
  </user>
</users>
</conference-info>
```

Conference Policy

Conference policies are the rules that govern the operation of a conference. The policies can be set up in advance or as the conference is created. The policies can be fixed or they can be dynamically changed during a conference.

Note the difference between conference policy and state. While the conference policy can indicate who is authorized to join a conference, the state indicates who has actually joined the conference. It is possible for a change in conference policy to change the conference state. For example, the stop time of a conference could be changed during the conference which could cause the participants to be removed during the conference. On the other hand, a change in state will only occur if the resulting state is authorized by the conference policy.

Floor Control

In some conferences, there is a shared resource that needs to be exclusively controlled or accessed by a single or small set of conference participants. For example, a whiteboard pen can only be controlled by one participant at a time. Or, during question time during a presentation, a chair may grant one participant at a time the ability to ask a question of the presenter or the panelists.

In these cases, the shared resource is called the "floor" and the protocol used to request and access the resource is called "floor control." The basic set of semantics is defined in the Binary Floor Control Protocol (BFCP)[12] which stores attributes in TLV (Tag-Length-Value) format. (A schematic of the functionality of provided BFCP is illustrated in Figure 6.2. A description of conference floor control messages can be found in Table 6.2.)

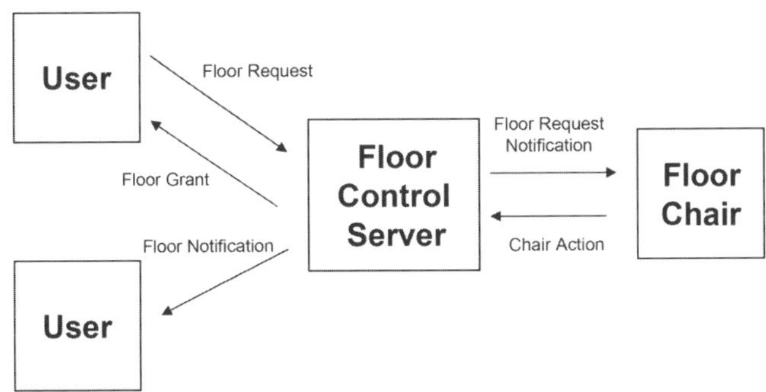

Figure 6.2 – Functionality provided by BFCP

[12] Camarillo, G., J. Ott, and K. Drage, "The Binary Floor Control Protocol (BFCP)." draft-ietf-xcon-bfcp-01 (work in progress), August 2004.

Media Mixing and Topologies

SIP conferencing can use any of the base MIME types as media: audio, video, text, and application.

The centralized SIP conferencing scenarios described in this chapter support a number of different media modes, described in the following sections.

Table 6.2 – Conference floor control messages

Request Type	Description
Floor Request	A participant requests a specific floor.
Floor Release	The floor holder releases (gives up) the specific floor
Floor Request Info	A participant or chair requests the status of a particular floor request.
Floor Request Status	A response to a Floor Request or Floor Release sent by the server to a participant.
Floor Info	A participant requests information about the floor.
Floor Status	A response to a Floor Info sent by the server to a participant.
Chair Action	A chair approves or declines a floor request.
Chair Action Acknowledge	A server acknowledges a Chair Action request.
Ping	A keep alive message sent to a server.
Ping Acknowledgement	An acknowledgement sent to a Ping request.
Error	Response to an erroneous request.

Centrally Mixed

As well as centralized signaling, a conference may have centralized mixing. In this mode, each participant sends one or more media streams to the mixer controlled by the focus, and receives back one or more mixed media streams. This mixing mode fully supports Conference Unaware UAs, and the resulting media session is indistinguishable from a normal point-to-point SIP session.

This mode also has the advantage of requiring the least amount of processing in the UA and also the minimum amount of bandwidth. In terms of security, the focus must know all media encryption keys or else it can not mix the media.

Disadvantages include extra media latency, as all media takes two hops with processing in between.

Fully Distributed (Full Mesh)

In the fully distributed or full mesh mode, a participant establishes a direct media session with each participant in the conference. As a result, the focus actually does not perform any mixing at all, but acts as a 3rd party call controller to cause the mesh of media sessions to be created. This is supported in SIP by the use of multiple media lines and multiple connection addresses in the SDP message body. Each time a participant joins the conference, the focus will re-INVITE the other participants adding a new media stream with the new participants' media information.

This mode results in the simplest focus, as it does not have to control any media mixing resources. In addition, the media latency is minimized for highest quality. However, each participant must support N-way media mixing and also have enough bandwidth for N media sessions. In terms of security, the focus does not need to know the media encryption keys, allowing participants to have the highest level of confidentiality assuming some kind of PKI infrastructure to distribute keys.

Tandem

So called tandem switching is a mixing mode that is a hybrid of centralized and distributed. Each participant sends a media stream to the focus. Instead of mixing, the focus media server merely performs the selection function on the streams. For example, if an audio conference mixes the three loudest talkers, a tandem switch would select the three loudest media streams from the complete set of participants, and send all three media streams back to each participant to mix together locally.

Since selection typically requires less processing and introduces less delay than actual mixing, the quality of this mode is likely to be higher than the centrally mixed mode. However, additional bandwidth and some local mixing capabilities in the UA are required.

Cascaded Conferences

A cascaded conference is a single logical conference that involves multiple foci working together. This is commonly done in the PSTN today where a site may have a local bridge mixing all local participants so a single media stream can be sent to a remote conference bridge.

In SIP conferencing, a focus has the ability to detect if cascading is happening, due to the "isfocus" parameter. The focus can then fetch the membership and other information from the other focus and present the complete conference state and roster to its local participants.

It is even possible for cascaded conferences to perform cooperative mixing, but this requires a conference aware application above the set of foci to coordinate this.

Applications Scenarios

We will now illustrate the various conference scenarios with high level SIP call flows that explain the success scenario for setting up the conference.

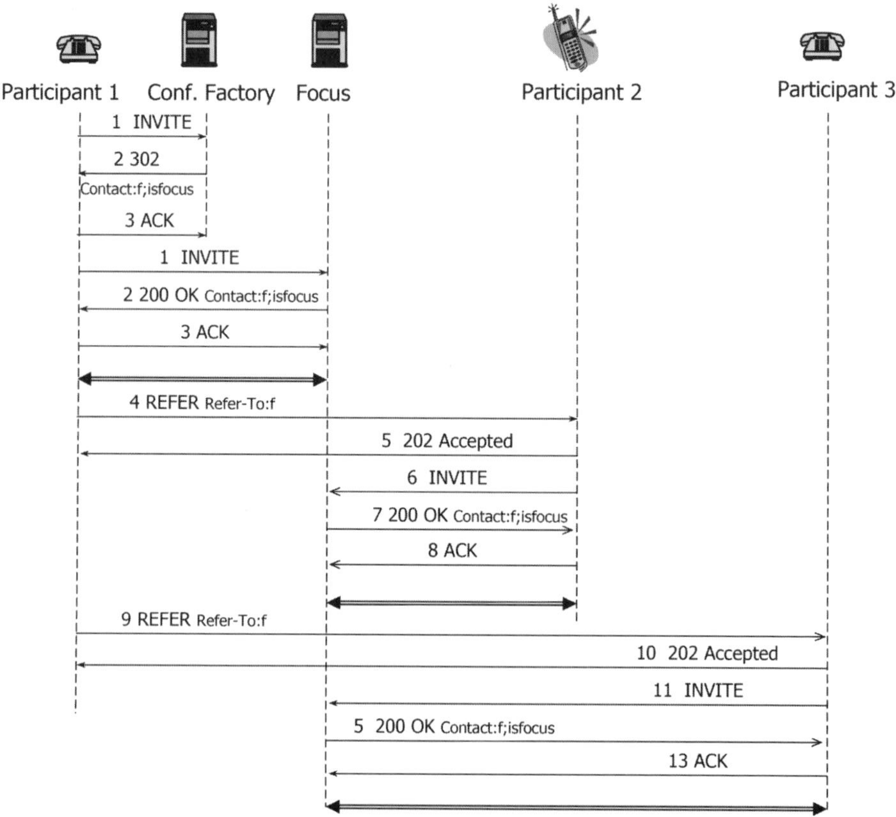

Figure 6.3 – Ad hoc conferencing scenario

Ad Hoc Conference Creation

In this scenario as illustrated in Figure 6.3, a SIP User Agent creates a conference by sending an INVITE to a Conference Factory. The Conference Factory responds by creating a focus and redirecting the UA to this focus. The UA then sends an INVITE to the focus and establishes a session. Then the UA sends invites two other participants to the conference by sending REFER messages. As a result, each UA establishes a media session with the focus which mixes them together.

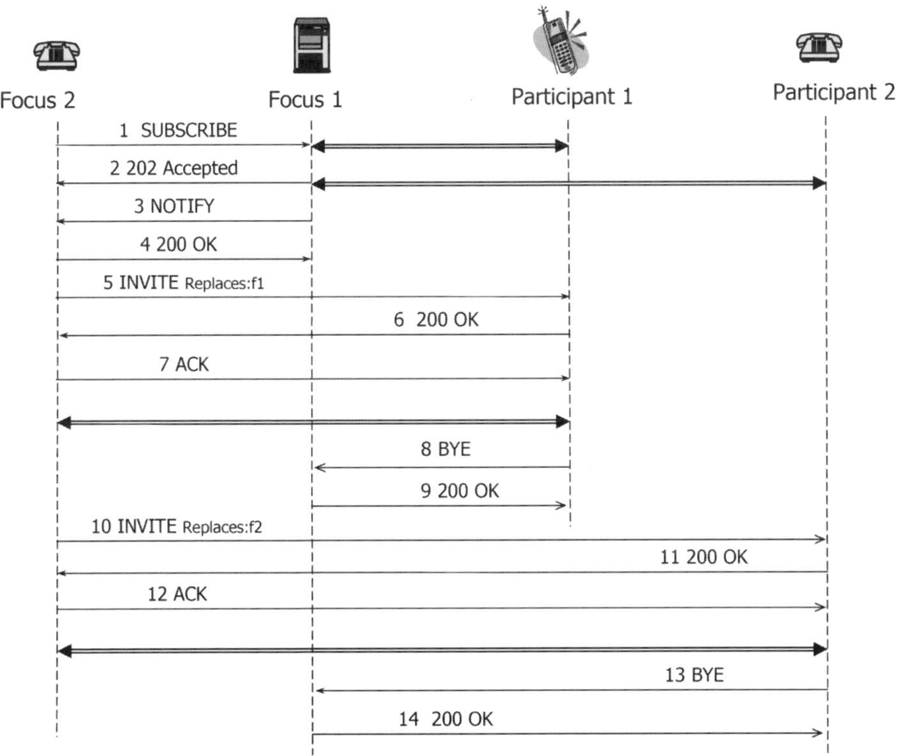

Figure 6.4 – Focus transition scenario

Transition of a conference from one focus to another

In this scenario as illustrated in Figure 6.4, a focus transitions a conference from another focus. First, the new focus subscribes to the conference package of the old focus. Using this information, the focus has the complete dialog information for each participant. The focus sends INVITE requests with Replaces header fields to each of the participants. This causes a new media session to be established with the new focus and the old media session with the old focus to be torn down.

Cascaded Conference

In this scenario as illustrated in Figure 6.5, a conference is hosted with two separate foci. One focus dials out to one set of participants, which establishes media sessions between each participant and the focus. Then, the focus dials out to the other focus, establishing a media session between the two foci. The second focus then dials out to another participant list. The resulting conferencing session is established between the complete set of participants.

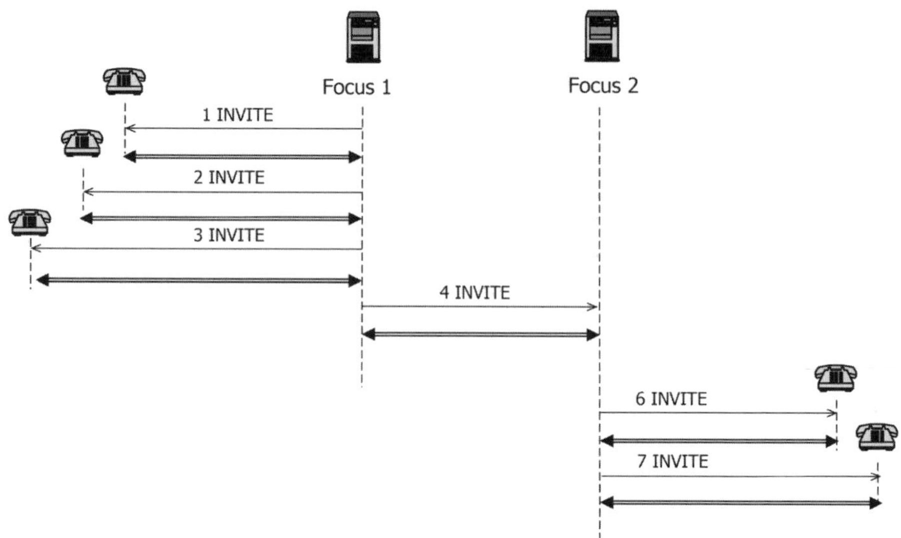

Figure 6.5 – Cascaded conference scenario

Conclusion

SIP conferencing is a good example of the capabilities of SIP beyond VoIP. The combination of SIP and other conference control protocols will result in much higher levels of interactivity and collaboration in conferences in the future.

Chapter 7

DNS and ENUM

Introduction

Interconnecting IP communication islands such as VoIP, IM, conferencing and games across the Internet requires the rendezvous with other parties and their various communication devices. This is accomplished by a two-stage process using the Domain Name System (DNS) and SIP, as illustrated in Figure 7.1:

- In the 1st step the DNS has public records that are used to identify the SIP remote proxy (having an attached location server) where the called party can be found.
- In the 2nd step the incoming SIP proxy will hold the private information about all the contact addresses, presence and personal preferences of the called party.

Since most telephony users are still on the PSTN or are using phone numbers, even for VoIP, ENUM (t**E**lephone **NU**mber **M**apping) will support finding the called party on the Internet when only a telephone number is known of the called party. ENUM is thus a valuable discovery mechanism in the long transition period from telephone numbers to native Internet addressing mechanisms.

Internet addressing is based on URLs. Internet users may prefer to use presence rather than hunt in the address book for the right phone number or URL, depending on the devices of the called party. Presence completely hides the addressing details from the caller. The discovery mechanisms shown here are applicable to presence as well.

ENUM for VoIP

ENUM is the technology that together with SIP enables all VoIP islands to interconnect. While the more detailed technology description is given further down, we show here only what ENUM is bringing to the table, and not how it works. Figure 7.1 illustrates several ENUM scenarios for telephony.

Call origination options

- An IP enabled PBX (upper left) can have the Internet as the first choice trunk group and will attempt to route the call over the Internet. The outgoing SIP proxy (SIP-1) will make an ENUM query to find the remote incoming SIP proxy and route the call to SIP-2 (the IP enabled PBX can also make an ENUM query directly if it has an ENUM resolver client built in).

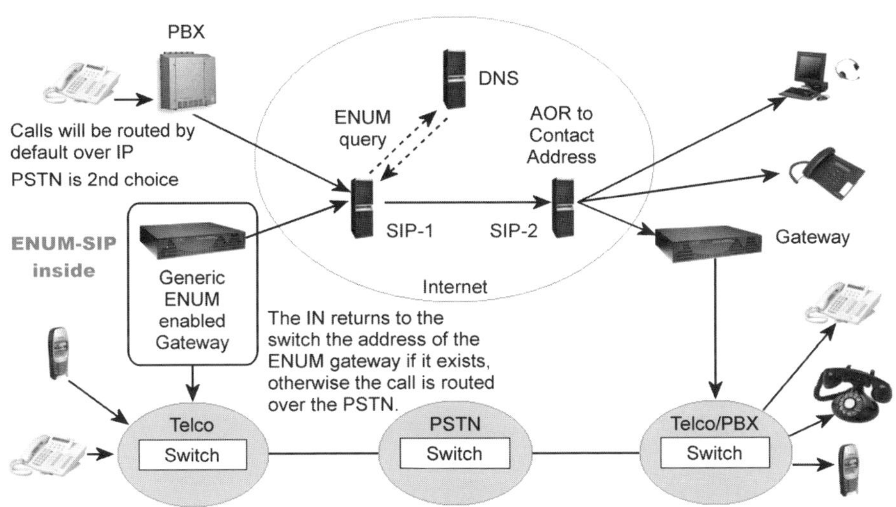

Figure 7.1 – Using ENUM and SIP for lowest cost voice call routing

The ENUM entries in the DNS for the remote SIP proxies are public records accessible to anyone on the Internet.

The incoming SIP proxy SIP-2 will check all contact addresses associated with the called party and forward the call to a selected IP telephony device according to the preferences of the called party. If the called part has only PSTN telephone service, the incoming call with be routed to the local telephone company switch and/or PBX to a traditional phone. In case no ENUM entry can be found for SIP-2 and the respective phone number, the IP choice is reported as failed to the PBX and the call will be routed over the PSTN shown at the bottom.

The contact addresses used by the incoming SIP-2 proxy server are confidential information that is not accessible from the Internet, thus preserving the privacy for the called party information.

Note the principle for least cost routing using ENUM: "*Enter the Internet as early as possible and leave it as late as possible*" when routing a call, so as to minimize the path through the PSTN or to avoid the PSTN altogether.

- A user on the PSTN or on a 2G mobile network that is ENUM enabled, will have the first call routing attempt made to a so-called

"Generic ENUM Enabled Gateway"[1] and from there call routing is analogous to the PBX example above.

Call termination options

As mentioned, the incoming call can be routed by SIP-2 as illustrated in Figure 7.2 either to

- Any IP telephony device, or
- Any PSTN, PBX phone or mobile phone, or
- Any combination thereof if SIP forking is used.

The called user preferences stored by SIP-2 determine where the incoming call is routed. This may depend, for example, on time of day, who is calling and where the called party may be at that time.

DNS for Internet Communications

ENUM is based on the Internet Domain Name System (DNS) and the DNS can be used to route IP calls without using telephone numbers as in ENUM, but using instead URIs that look like email addresses. Figure 7.2 shows the scenario where both endpoints are on the Internet and the PSTN is only a legacy endpoint of last resort.

Note that contrary to voice call routing using telephone numbers, IP connected endpoints can benefit from rich Internet communications that include, for example, Presence indication, instant messaging (IM) and multimedia. Also as a last resort, an IM call from a PC could also be routed to a legacy PSTN phone so as to make a voice call using the IM UA voice option. This is illustrated here for the MCI VoIP service using the dialer in the Microsoft Windows Messenger.

In summary, the DNS and ENUM can be used to route VoIP calls using telephone numbers and URIs for rich Internet communications. This is one of the multiple benefits of using the Internet to connect all VoIP and other IP communication islands and is much more powerful than using the PSTN for global connectivity, while at same time dramatically reducing the cost of communications.

---

[1] "ENUM in Austria," by R. Stastny. *APRICOT 2005 Conference*, Kyoto, Japan. http://www.2005.apricot.net/slides/C1-1_3.pdf

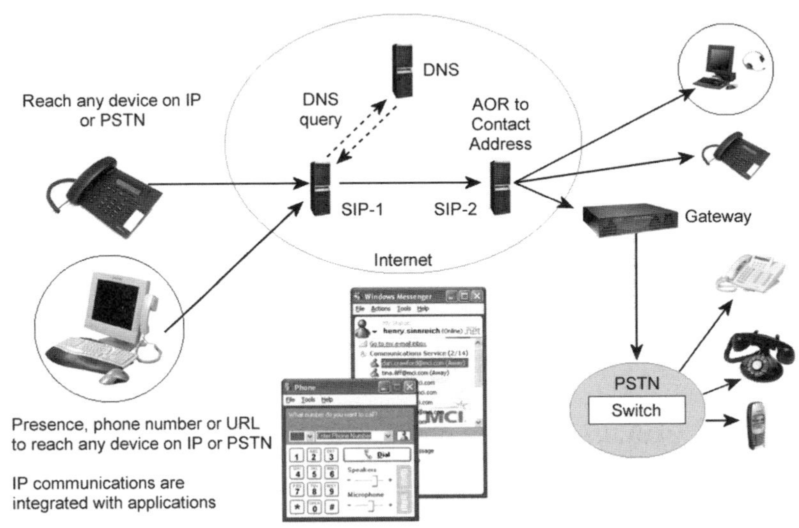

Figure 7.2 – Call routing for IP communications using DNS

What is real VoIP?

Having seen the various telephony models, arbitrage, PSTN gateway service, VoIP islands and IP endpoints using ENUM, we can now make the distinction if a service advertises as VoIP is really VoIP or just an emulation of the circuit switched voice service of the PSTN. The criteria is really amazingly simple:

- Does the VoIP service allow the user to print on the business card
  - One single phone number (using ENUM), and/or
  - The URI, such as sip: alice@example.com.

If the answer is yes, then the service is VoIP.

If, however, the user can only connect to other PSTN users by dialing phone numbers, the service is PSTN emulation, though VoIP may be part of the internal plumbing in the network.

Telephony devices for true VoIP services will also support the "dialing" of SIP URIs such as sip:alice@example.com.

Figure 7.3 shows the graphic user interface (GUI) of Microsoft Windows Messenger that allows a URI input for initiating a voice session. The Windows Messenger has two choices for the selection of the service.

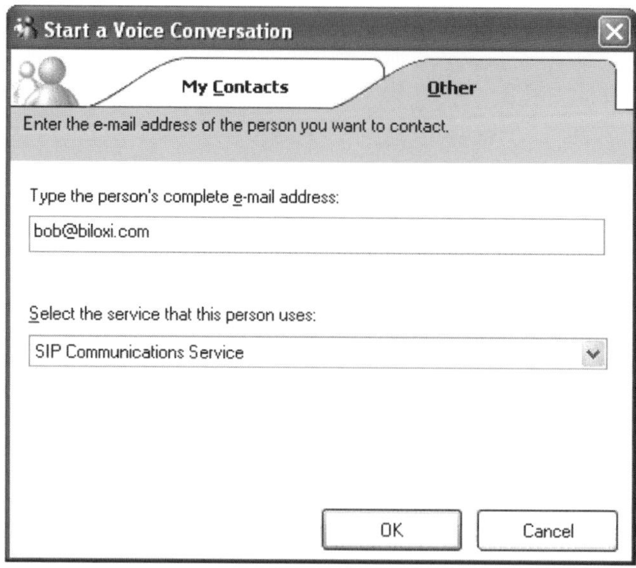

Figure 7.3 – True VoIP URI address input using the Microsoft Windows Messenger

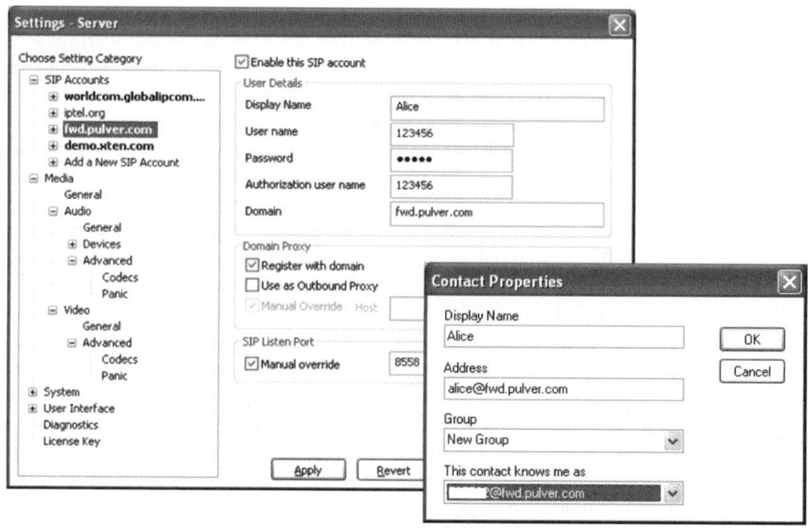

Figure 7.4 – Registration with several SIP services and choosing how to be reached using the Xten eyeBeam

Figure 7.4 shows an example for the Xten eyeBeam settings screen that allows the input of a large number of SIP registrar proxies from various service providers. This is very similar to pointing the web browser to any web site chosen by the user.

All true SIP telephony devices and soft phones allow (1) the selection of the service provider and (2) typing in the URL of the destination. Typing of the URL is accomplished on the PC and entering the value in an address book.

The Problem Space of Global Dynamic Discovery

Very large numbers: Connecting all VoIP islands and allowing all VoIP devices to discover each other is quite a challenge for the hundreds of millions of voice-enabled computers on the Internet and in private IP networks. Several trillion phones and mobile phones could be added to this number where the local phone networks, PBXs and mobile networks may be connected to the Internet via gateways.

Private addresses: Many or most users may prefer to have "unlisted numbers;" that is, fixed telephone numbers may be sometimes unlisted, mobile phone numbers are unlisted as a rule and contact URLs are unlisted for plain reasons of Internet security. A finer touch to sensitive private addresses is displayed by commercial enterprises. One may, for example, have the public URL for a company such as—

sip:support@company.com

though the location of the agent answering the call is unknown and confidential. The agent may be in a contact center anywhere in the world.

Dynamic network address: IP devices may acquire IP addresses that change when the device is connected to the network. This is especially true for mobile IP devices. The presence of a user can change rather quickly.

We will show in the following sections how these challenges are addressed by a combination of Domain Name Services (DNS) and application level protocol services such SIP and SIMPLE.

Short Glossary on Addressing

There are many types of addressing used on the Internet and in telephony networks. Addressing is a vast topic that can fill a book all by itself. We will, however, use here a very small glossary (note the addresses of record and contract addresses in Table 7.1).

Table 7.1 – Address of record and contact addresses

<table>
<tr><td colspan="2">Address of Record</td><td>One single address for the identity of the user
Long term validity
Is not associated with a device
Is public information available on the DNS
such as
sip:alice@example.com, or
+1-972-555-1234 (ENUM address)</td></tr>
<tr><td colspan="2">Contact Address</td><td>Several contact addresses for the user
May change short term
May be associated with a device
Is private and protected information
such as:
home phone
office phone
mobile phone
home fax
office fax
pager
PDA
laptop
game box
Contact addresses are application specific.</td></tr>
<tr><td rowspan="4">Application Address</td><td>Mail</td><td>mailto:alice@example.com</td></tr>
<tr><td>SIP</td><td>sip: conference-22363@example.com</td></tr>
<tr><td>Presence</td><td>pres:alice@example.com</td></tr>
<tr><td>ENUM</td><td>+1-972-555-1234</td></tr>
</table>

We will illustrate how ENUM works with the example shown in Figure 7.5. The following assumptions have been made for the example:

- Alice has the benefit of being registered with an ENUM service provided most likely by her Internet service provider. As a result, Alice needs to provide only one single phone number on her business card. Callers using the public telephone network or a PBX can use this number to reach Alice on any of the contact addresses (see Glossary) on which Alice may be reachable on a specific point in time and place and also depending on the preferences for Alice to take the call (or not to take the call and send it to voicemail).

- The caller (on left) has the benefit of using a telephony service that has a VoIP gateway. The VoIP PSTN-SIP gateway has a so-called ENUM resolver that will be explained further below.
- The ENUM database has entries for all phone numbers registered for ENUM service. This number can grow quite big if everyone would use ENUM. In the US, for example, there may be a total of 500 million phone numbers for fixed residential, enterprise and mobile phones. Because of number portability, the telephone numbers are not allocated any more in blocks for various phone companies and as a consequence, the database has to be queried (a "dip" is made) for every single call to check for an ENUM entry.

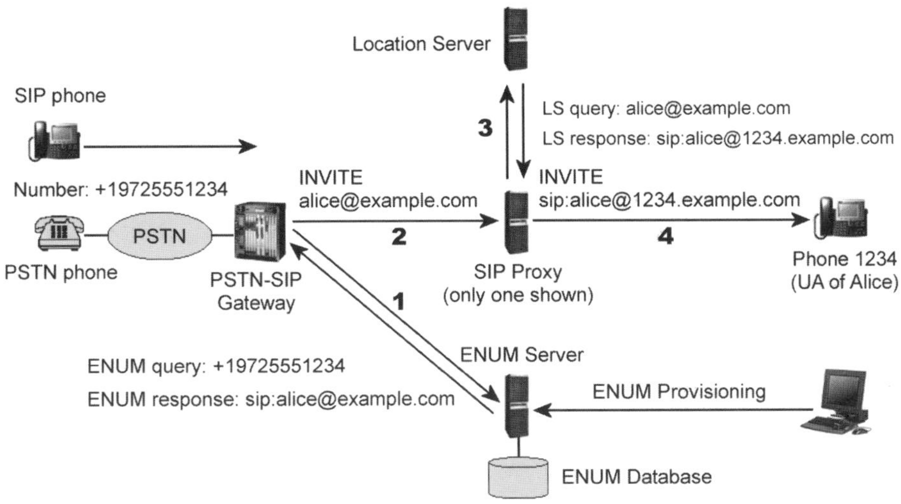

Figure 7.5 – ENUM call flow example. The ENUM resolver is in the calling UA.

In the example, the caller may be anywhere in the world—in Japan, for example. The caller looks at the business card of Alice and sees the single phone number and dials +19725551234.

1. The VoIP enabled service provider will try and route the call to the PSTN-SIP gateway. The gateway has an ENUM resolver that will check for an entry for +19725551234 in the ENUM server. The ENUM server returns a SIP URL in the form of sip:alice@example.com. If the caller has a SIP phone with an ENUM resolver in the phone, the ENUM query can be performed directly by the SIP phone as indicated in the upper left side of the diagram.

2. The gateway will send an INVITE with sip:alice@example.com in the request URI to the outgoing SIP proxy (not shown here) and the SIP INVITE will eventually be routed to the incoming SIP proxy at example.com.
3. The incoming SIP proxy (in the middle in Figure 7.5) will query the location server to determine all of the contact addresses for Alice.
4. The incoming SIP proxy checks also for the preference of Alice to take her calls. Suppose Alice happens to be in the office and takes incoming calls on her desktop SIP phone. As a result, the INVITE is forwarded to 1234@sip.example.com which happens to be the SIP desktop phone of Alice. Alice may have more than one device registered while in the office, and the incoming call may also be forked to her laptop and mobile phone. However, for simplicity, this is not shown here.

The correct usage of ENUM for SIP is discussed elsewhere.[2]

Data in the DNS which includes ENUM is characterized by the following:

- The DNS contains public available data and is not suitable for privacy.
- Changes propagate slowly (minutes). The DNS is not suitable for fast changing data.
- The DNS is not suitable for large data files, such as XML documents.

The use of SIP proxies in combination with the DNS ENUM servers is optimal, since SIP data is characterized by:

- The SIP data is private.
- SIP registration and presence can change fast.
- Presence is expressed in large XML documents.

Example of Using the ENUM Application

Figure 7.6 shows an ENUM[3] service example.

---

[2] RFC 3824: "Using E.164 numbers with the Session Initiation Protocol (SIP)," by J. Peterson, H. Liu, J. Yu and B. Campbell. IETF, June 2004.

[3] RFC 3761: "The E.164 to Uniform Resource Identifiers (URI) Dynamic Delegation Discovery System (DDDS) Application (ENUM)," by P. Falstrom and M. Mealing. IETF, April 2005.

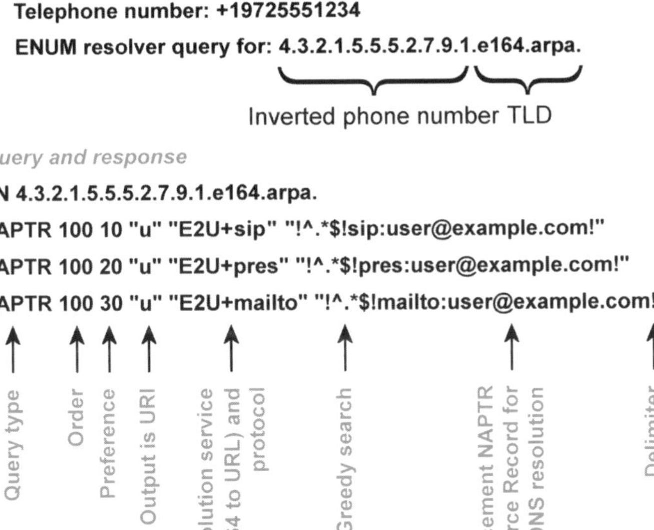

Figure 7.6 – ENUM service example

The user has a telephony number that may look in the address book like this: +1 (972)-555-1234. Let's assume the SIP phone can be linked directly to the address book and also that the SIP phone contains an application called an ENUM Resolver.

1. The ENUM resolver removes all characters except the numeric digits. The result is: 19725551234.
2. Dots are inserted between all digits: 1.9.7.2.5.5.5.1.2.3.4
3. The order of the digits are reversed: 4.3.2.1.5.5.5.2.7.9.1
4. The top level domain (TLD) e164.arpa is added to the right: 4.3.2.1.5.5.5.2.7.9.1. e164.arpa

The result from step 4 is in a form that can be understood by the DNS and is called the Application Unique String in the technology underlying ENUM: The technology is called the Dynamic Delegation Discovery System[4] (DDDS). The DDDS uses the DNS as a distributed database of rules. We

---

[4] RFC 3403: "Dynamic Delegation Discovery System (DDDS) Part Three: The Domain Name System (DNS) Database," by M. Mealing. IETF, October 2002.

refer interested readers to the DDDS specifications in RFC 3401, 3402 and 3403.

The output of the ENUM resolver in step 4 is sent to the DNS to find all the Network Address Pointer (NAPTR)[5] resource records associated with this "key." The ENUM-populated DNS will return the results as shown in Figure 7.6. The query for 4.3.2.1.5.5.5.2.7.9.1.e164.arpa will produce the following items:

- Query class: IN (Internet).
- Query type: NAPTR.
- Order: Specifies the order in which the NAPTR records must be processed to correct ordering of the rules. The order is irrelevant to our example here.
- Preference: DNS entries may express user preferences, such as showing the SIP URL first as in this example. Preference may also be used for other purposes, such as for load balancing or for directing clients to more capable servers.
- The Flag U: Specifies the output will be a URL.
- The service field specifies the services associated with this key. The service field for ENUM is E2U (E.164 address to URL) and the + sign followed by the application protocol service, such as SIP, Presence, mail, etc. Various services are listed in Table 7.2 for ENUM services.
- The delimiter between the fields is an exclamation mark: ! The responses to the ENUM query are here three fields separated by exclamation marks.
- The middle field is a "greedy regular expression (regexp)" '^.*$' that matches any starting string and indicates that further analysis of the starting string on the client side is not necessary.[6]
- The final field is an application service URL. The example shows URLs for SIP, presence and mail (the respective application services). The application service URL is used for another DNS query to find the SIP proxy servers or the presence servers or the mail servers. The next query will be a DNS service query (SRV) as will be shown.

---

[5] RFC 2915: "The Naming Authority Pointer (NAPTR) DNS Resource Record," by M. Mealling. IETF, September 2000.

[6] RFC 3725: "Using E.164 numbers with the Session Initiation Protocol (SIP)," by J. Peterson, et al. IETF, June 2004.

The Usage of Regular Expressions

Usage of the regular expressions in DNS queries as illustrated in Figure 7.6 is based on the following rules:

.*	matches any character any number of times
^	shows where to start the match
$	shows where to end the match

The rules can be applied as in these examples:

^123.*	would match any number starting with **123**
***1234$**	would match anything ending with **1234**
^123(.*)567$	would match all numbers that start with **123** and end with **567**
123123	can be used with **^** and **$**

The use of regular expressions enables very flexible filtering of phone numbers, such as for example selecting blocks of numbers allocated to an enterprise PBX.

Telephone Number or Any URL: It is extremely important to notice that instead of the URL in the form of an inverted phone number in the e164.arpa TLD as shown, any other URL could be used for the DNS NAPTR query to find all other registered services. The query could just as well start with a SIP URL or mail URL, for example.

DNS SRV Address Resolution

The next step in finding the IP addresses of the servers located by the ENUM query consists in using the DNS resolver again, this time to make an SRV[7] type of query.

For this, the DNS resolver would look up the name servers for example.com and find the following:

NS ns1.example.com
NS ns2.example.com

---

[7] RFC 2782: "A DNS RR for specifying the location of services (DNS SRV)," by A. Gulbrandsen, et al. IETF, February 2000.

```
NS   ns3.example.com
NS   ns4.example.com
```

for which the A type DNS records are as follows:

```
A    166.201.43.1
A    166.201.43.2
A    166.201.43.3
A    166.201.43.4
```

The name servers in turn can now provide the IP addresses for the SIP protocol, using either UDP, TCP or TLS as the transport level protocol.

DNS SRV Query	DNS SRV Response
_sip._udp.example.com	166.201.43.101 166.201.43.102 166.201.43.103 166.201.43.104
_sip._tcp.example.com	166.201.43.101 166.201.43.102 166.201.43.103 166.201.43.104
_sip._tls.example.com	166.201.43.101 166.201.43.102 166.201.43.103 166.201.43.104

In this example, all four SIP servers can support UDP, TCP and TLS.

Locating SIP servers has been standardized in RFC 3263[8] and the use of the NAPTR DNS resource record is standardized in RFCs 3401-3404.[9] For every new query the DNS may return the IP addresses of the SIP servers in a round robin order and the application using DNS SRV can try the first IP address for load balancing between servers.

---

[8] RFC 3263: "Session Initiation Protocol (SIP): Locating SIP Servers," by J. Rosenberg and H. Schulzrinne. IETF, June 2002.

[9] RFC 3401, 3402, 3403, 3404: "The Dynamic Delegation Discovery System (DDS)," by M. Mealing. IETF, October 2002.

DNS records are often used to select servers by using DNS SRV records with priorities and weights. This model ensures scalability, redundancy and load balancing. The load is distributed between all servers at a given priority level using their weight value. If some of them are not responding, then the other servers at the same priority will take their traffic share, redistributing the load balancing between them according to their own priorities.

Here is an example given for the SER Media Proxy by AG projects* that uses a proprietary SRV (not registered with IANA) record type "mediaproxy":

```
_mediaproxy._tcp.ag-projects.com. IN SRV 10 6 25010 nat7.dns-hosting.info
_mediaproxy._tcp.ag-projects.com. IN SRV 10 4 25010 nat8.dns-hosting.info
_mediaproxy._tcp.ag-projects.com. IN SRV 20 0 25010 nat9.dns-hosting.info
```

In this example, the load is shared by allocating 60% to server nat7 and 40% to nat8. The server nat9 is used for redundancy when neither server with priority 10 is available.

* http://ag-projects.com/SER_Media_Proxy.html

An ENUM resolution process can actually generate several successive queries as shown in Figure 7.7. The initial SIP INVITE is left in Trying state until the successive queries produce the URL for the destination SIP proxy 2 that the outgoing SIP proxy 1 can use to forward the INVITE to.

For this reason it is recommended to avoid too many intermediaries between endpoints that may generate repeated ENUM queries. Too many ENUM queries may strain the DNS system and will also significantly add to the call setup delay.

Readers can get a better feeling by using the DNS SRV resolver application that can be invoked from their PC, for example from the Command Prompt using the "nslookup.exe" utility in Windows XP or 2000. An example for the MCI SIP-based services is given in Figure 7.8.

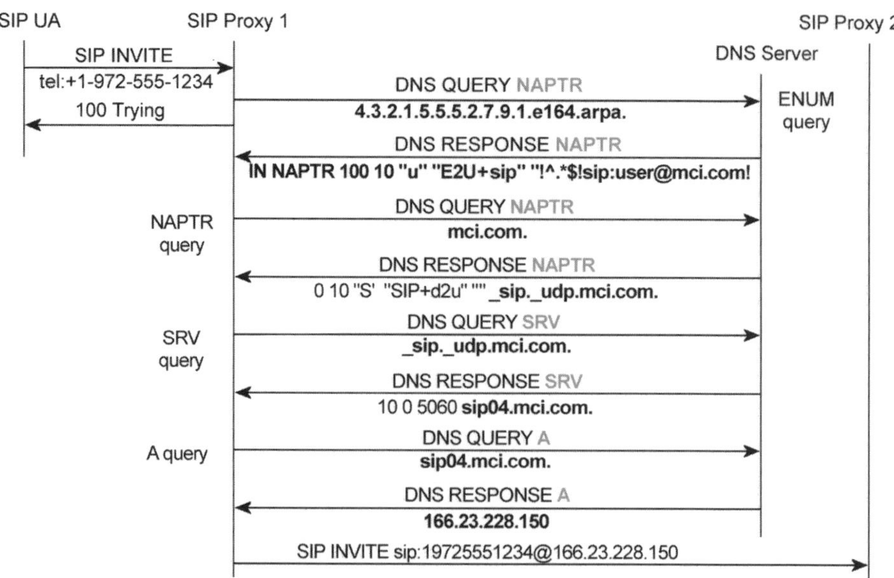

Figure 7.7 – DNS ENUM queries to find the remote incoming SIP proxy server *(Courtesy AG-Projects)*

```
Command Prompt
C:\>nslookup -querytype=SRV _sip._udp.mci.com
Server:  scmdns.mcilink.com
Address:  166.33.187.21

Non-authoritative answer:
_sip._udp.mci.com       SRV service location:
          priority       = 1
          weight         = 1
          port           = 5060
          svr hostname   = atcns01.wcomnet.com
_sip._udp.mci.com       SRV service location:
          priority       = 1
          weight         = 1
          port           = 5060
          svr hostname   = csuns01.wcomnet.com
_sip._udp.mci.com       SRV service location:
          priority       = 1
          weight         = 1
          port           = 5060
          svr hostname   = dnjns01.wcomnet.com

mci.com nameserver = DNS3.mci.com
mci.com nameserver = DNS1.mci.com
mci.com nameserver = DNJDNS2.mcilink.com
atcns01.wcomnet.com     internet address = 166.38.245.20
csuns01.wcomnet.com     internet address = 166.34.210.180
dnjns01.wcomnet.com     internet address = 166.33.198.156
DNS3.mci.com     internet address = 199.249.19.2
DNS1.mci.com     internet address = 199.249.19.1
DNJDNS2.mcilink.com     internet address = 166.33.198.196

C:\>
```

Figure 7.8 – Example of an SRV query and response using the PC

ENUM Services

The IETF ENUM working group has developed several service names, so that starting from a legacy E.164 telephone number, various other Internet communication services can be reached.[10, 11]

Table 7.2 – Registered ENUM services

ENUM Service Name	Service Type	URI schema
E2U+SIP	SIP	sip:, sips:
E2U+pres	presence	pres:
E2U+mailto	email	mailto:
E2U+fax	fax	tel:
E2U+sms	sms	tel:, mailto:
E2U+ems	ems	tel:, mailto:
E2U+mms	mms	tel:, mailto:
E2U+H323	H.323	H323:
conf-web	web conference	http, https,
conf-uri	Conference service	sip:, sips:, h323:

Near term, while telephone numbers are still the dominant directory entry, ENUM resolution makes a lot of sense. However, as the telephone system will be deprecated over time in favor of Internet communications, any other URL can serve as key for the DNS search, similar to the telephone number in ENUM to find all the other services as shown.

An ENUM-Based Directory Application

The registered types of services in Table 7.2 can support various applications, such as a simple web-based directory that returns all the various communication addresses by which someone may be found just using that person's telephone number. The SIP service alone could return various other fixed

[10] R. Brandner, et al., "IANA Registration for Enumservices email, fax, mms, ems and sms." Internet Draft, IETF, February 2005. Work in progress.

[11] A. Johnston, "IANA Registration for ENUMservices conf-web and conf-uri." Internet Draft, IETF, February 2005. Work in progress.

and mobile telephone numbers using the contact addresses for SIP. With ENUM it is possible to discover directly telephone numbers for fax, various mobile telephone messaging service addresses (SMS, EMS, MMS).

Such a directory application provides public access to data that most users may want to keep private to avoid telemarketing and spam. Businesses may, however, have an interest for some of their staff to be reachable and various means could be applied to filter out unwanted messages or to minimize their impact.

ENUM Hierarchy, Delegation and Registrars

The global DNS has proven to be extremely scalable since it is fully distributed and it uses the Dynamic Delegation and Discovery System (DDDS) described in RFC 3401, 3402, 3403, 3404 and 3405. The so-called ENUM "golden tree" has several levels that are also called Tiers, as shown in Figure 7.9. The description "golden" for the tree refers to its coherent structure that avoids any data inconsistency at all Tiers[12] down along the global tree.

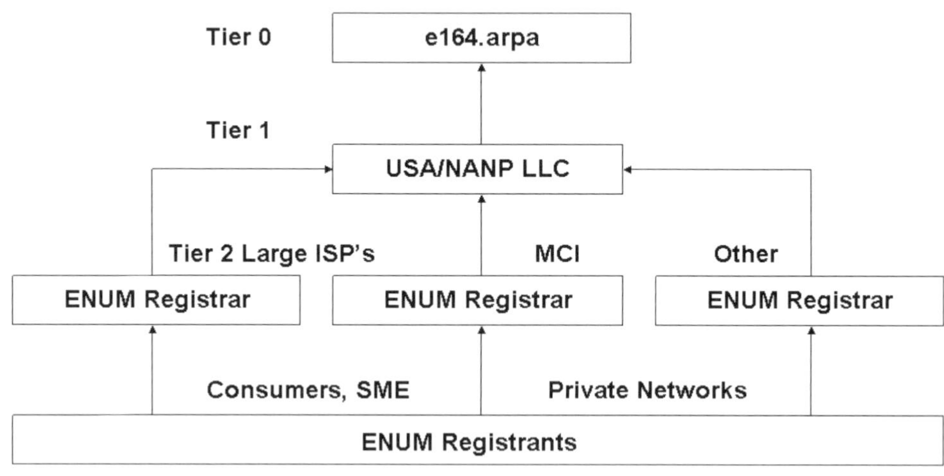

Figure 7.9 – The ENUM golden tree

[12] DNS technology can also be used in private networks and by service providers that act as registrars for various so-called "private ENUM." However, the "private ENUM" systems are not to be confused with the Internet standard "golden tree."

The various Tiers, as applicable to the market in the USA is shown in Table 7.3. The specifics for Tier 1 down to Tier 3 and below depend on the country,[13] since various countries may have slightly different registration schemas.

Table 7.3 – The ENUM Tiers

Tier	Description
Tier 0	Top Level Domain: e164.arpa
Tier 1	Country delegation (ENUM LLC[14] in North America)
Tier 2	Actual DNS name servers containing NAPTR records

In the golden tree schema, each Tier will register the name servers that are one level below.

ENUM Provisioning

Figure 7.5 shows in the bottom right a workstation for provisioning of ENUM data. Actually, for accurate provisioning, the ENUM extensions for the Extensible Provisioning Protocol (EPP) have been specified by Hollenbeck.[15]

The extensions to the EPP for ENUM consist of XML data for the E.164 domain names and for the NAPTR fields:

- Order
- Preference
- Flags
- Service
- Regular expression
- Replacement

The EPP query and transform commands support the retrieval, creation, deletion and renewal of the XML data elements for the NAPTR records.

---

[13] "ESP-SOAP Connector." White Paper for the ENUM-Trial project of T-Systems. September 2003, Berlin, Germany. http://www.enum-trial.de/

[14] The ENUM Limited Liability Corporation (LLC) has been formed at the time of this writing. Similar organizations are being formed in Europe and in Asia Pacific countries.

[15] "E.164 Number Mapping for the Extensible Provisioning Protocol," by S. Hollenbeck. Internet Draft, IETF, August 2004.

ENUM Security

The DNS has a similar role for Internet communications as the Service Control Points (SCP) have for the PSTN for call routing. While the SCPs run in highly protected telephone signaling networks, the DNS runs on the public Internet and is therefore much more exposed to attacks.[16] Only a small number of authorized companies can access and modify data in the SCP, but a very large number of users can access the DNS and a reasonably large number of users can modify provision and modify data in the DNS.

The security and privacy of the ENUM and SIP services is enhanced by policy driven control of the incoming calls in the incoming SIP proxy.

The provisioning of the data in ENUM has the benefit of the high security mechanisms available in the EPP.

Once provisioned, the security of the DNS is well understood and can be taken care of.

As mentioned, ENUM DNS servers do not support and privacy at all, but SIP does. The judicious combination of ENUM and SIP can however support privacy adequately.

ENUM lookups determine actions by the resources of the users. Arbitrary provisions of ENUM data may produce devastating results. Other actions may be less harmful, but could disclose information about resources that may facilitate attacks on those resources[1].

The ENUM provisioning has to be restricted to the sponsoring client only to make the transform operations in the EPP[8].

Recent work on DNS security is aimed at radically enhancing the security of this critical resource for the Internet. See RFC 2535 and its updates.[17]

Conclusions

VoIP, instant messaging and various other IP communication services are at present more or less isolated communication islands, in spite of being connected to the Internet. The most common bridge between VoIP islands is still the legacy telephone network.

---

[16] "Privacy and Security Considerations in ENUM," by R. Shockey, et al. Internet Draft, July 2003. work in progress.

[17] RFC 2535: "Domain Name Security Extensions," by D. Eastlake. IETF, March 1999. This RFC has been updated by RFC2931, RFC3007, RFC3008, RFC3090, RFC3226, RFC3445, RFC3597, RFC3655, RFC3658, RFC3755, RFC3757 and RFC3845.

The DNS and ENUM are technologies that will support global connectivity across the Internet between PSTN, VoIP and IM enabled networks. A wide range of ENUM services has been defined, such as for SIP, presence, email, various mobile phone messaging systems, and other.

ENUM and SIP are the optimum combination for public records and sensitive data on private location and device information. ENUM and SIP are also well suited to use stable, long term DNS data entries in combination with fast changing SIP registrations and presence.

The ENUM hierarchy based on the golden tree assures consistent data on a global scale for registered domains and phone numbers.

The ENUM address resolution is based on the successive use of NAPTR resource records, SRV resource records and finally on host address A type records.

The security and provisioning aspects of ENUM are quite complex given the fact the DNS servers live on the public Internet, contrary to equivalent servers for the telephone networks that function in well isolated environments.

Chapter 8

XCAP, the Extensible Configuration Access Protocol

Introduction

Managing application and device configuration data is an important and, all to often, difficult task for users of communication systems. Configuring a single endpoint with the various settings it needs to use a service can be complex enough. Manually keeping data like buddy lists in sync across multiple devices can be overwhelming.

SIMPLE provides a standard mechanism that gives service providers and users the ability to maintain such configuration as a network hosted service. This data store is leveraged to assist with automatic configuration and synchronization of data between endpoints using SIP events.

XCAP, the Extensible Markup Language Configuration Access Protocol,[1] is a standardized way to use HTTP to store, retrieve, and manipulate configuration and application data. XCAP defines the basic structure of the data store, and a framework for adding new configuration or application data types to this store.

Where XCAP fits into a communication service

One of the strengths of SIP and its related protocols is flexibility. A wide range of service architectures can be realized. While there is no single globally-correct architecture, many deployments will have structures similar to that in Figure 8.1.

A user connecting to a service from a new endpoint will use XCAP to retrieve his or her current settings. This contains data like buddy lists and can also be how the user's endpoint discovers basic configuration data such as the name of the SIP proxy to use to access the service. This channel will also be used to tell the service items like who is allowed to subscribe. Inside the service, a presence server can use XCAP to obtain the permissions the user provided and a copy of the user's current buddy list to use when serving eventlist subscriptions.[2]

The user can then use SIP events to subscribe to changes in any of the configuration data. If the user adds a buddy to his buddy list using a web interface, or another endpoint, this endpoint will get notified of the change.

---

[1] "The Extensible Markup Language (XML) Configuration Access Protocol (XCAP)," by J. Rosenberg. Internet Draft, IETF, November 2004.

[2] "A Session Initiation Protocol (SIP) Event Notification Extension for Resource Lists," by A.B. Roach, B.Campbell, J. Rosenberg. Internet Draft, IETF, December 2004.

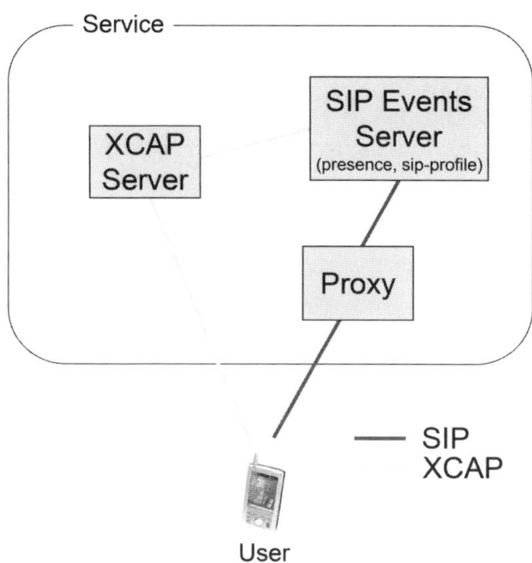

Figure 8.1 – XCAP in the service architecture

Application Usages

XCAP is a framework that can be used to store any kind of configuration data. New types of data are added to the framework by defining XCAP "application usages" for them. All XCAP data is represented in XML. A usage defines the structure of the data it contains (using XML schema) and the initial authorization policies for documents within that usage.

The first application usages defined for XCAP are used to manipulate presence rules and resource lists.

Presence Rules

Alice has to grant permission to Bob before he can see her presence data. When Bob tries to subscribe, Alice's presence server looks for this permission. If it can't find anything it gives Bob a "pending" subscription while it asks Alice what she wants it to do.

XCAP's pres-rules application usage[3] gives Alice a standard way to provide that permission to the presence server. This usage holds a set of rules, each

---

[3] "Extensible Markup Language (XML) Formats for Representing Resource Lists," by J. Rosenberg. Internet Draft, IETF, October 2004.

expressed in XML as a set of conditions, actions, and transformations. The conditions determine to whom each rule applies. The actions tell the presence server whether to allow the subscription. The transformations control what parts of a presence document this particular subscriber gets to see. Alice might provide a rule granting Bob permission to subscribe as follows:

```
<?xml version="1.0" encoding="UTF-8"?>
<cr:ruleset xmlns:cr="urn:ietf:params:xml:ns:common-policy"
        xmlns:pr="urn:ietf:params:xml:ns:pres-rules">
 <cr:rule id="fjieiownx93">
  <cr:conditions>
   <cr:identity>
    <cr:id>bob@example.com</cr:id>
   </cr:identity>
  </cr:conditions>
  <cr:actions>
   <pr:sub-handling>allow</pr:sub-handling>
  </cr:actions>
  <cr:transformations>
   <pr:provide-person>true</pr:provide-person>
   <pr;provide-services><pr:all-services/></pr:provide-services>
   <pr:provide-devices><pr:all-devices/></pr:provide-devices>
  </cr:transformations>
 </cr:rule>
</cr:ruleset>
```

For more details on how presence rules work, see Chapter 5 on "Context Aware Communications."

Resource Lists

Users frequently keep lists of URIs. These may be buddy lists in a presence application, or bookmarks in a web browser. A presence service can offer eventlist subscriptions, allowing users to subscribe to a single resource in order to receive presence for everyone on their buddy list.

The XCAP resource-list application usage Rosenberg[4] provides a standard way for users to maintain these lists on a centralized service and for services

---

[4] "Presence Authorization Rules," by J. Rosenberg. Internet Draft, IETF, October 2004.

to access them. This usage defines an XML document format for representing lists of resources, where a resource is represented by any URI. These lists can contain sub-lists, nested arbitrarily deep. Alice's buddy list and bookmarks on an XCAP server could look like this:

```
<resource-lists xmlns="urn:ietf:params:xml:ns:resource-lists">
  <list name="presence-list">
     <display-name>My Buddies</display-name>
     <list name="Co-workers">
        <entry uri="sip:carol@example.com">
           <display-name>Carol</display-name>
        </entry>
     </list>
     <list name="Friends">
        <entry uri="sip:bob@example.com">
           <display-name>Bob</display-name>
        </entry>
     </list>
  </list>
  <list name="Bookmarks">
     <entry uri="http://www.example.com"/>
     <entry uri="http://www.example.com/hr/2005/holidays">
        <display-name>Holiday Schedule</display-name>
     </entry>
  </list>
</resource-lists>
```

Figure 8.2 – A resource list document

For more detailed information on representing and using resource lists, see our chapter on "Context Aware Communications."

Structure of the configuration data store

XCAP simply defines a way to use HTTP. The protocol consists only of agreements of how to use HTTP to manipulate XCAP resources and what those resources look like. Thus, XCAP resources are identified by HTTP URIs. A web server providing access to XCAP resources will keep them all under a common place in its document tree called the "XCAP root," for example:

https://xcap.example.com/xcap-root

All XCAP data is kept below this root (see Figure 8.3). The next segment in the HTTP path below this root names a particular XCAP application usage (https://xcap.example.com/xcap-root/pres-rules). There are always two trees below the application usage, a global tree, and one for per-user data.

The global tree contains information that applies to all users for that application usage. Typically, only the administrator for a service can make changes to documents in the global tree. This is where a service provider might provide configuration information like which SIP proxy to use in a future application usage.

The users tree contains information specific to each user. The user's XCAP identifier (XUI) is the next segment of the path below users. For instance, in the example given in Figure 8.3, Alice's resource lists would be kept at https://xcap.example.com/xcap-root/resource-lists/users/alice. It is likely that a service will reuse a user's SIP username as an XUI, but it is possible to use different names.

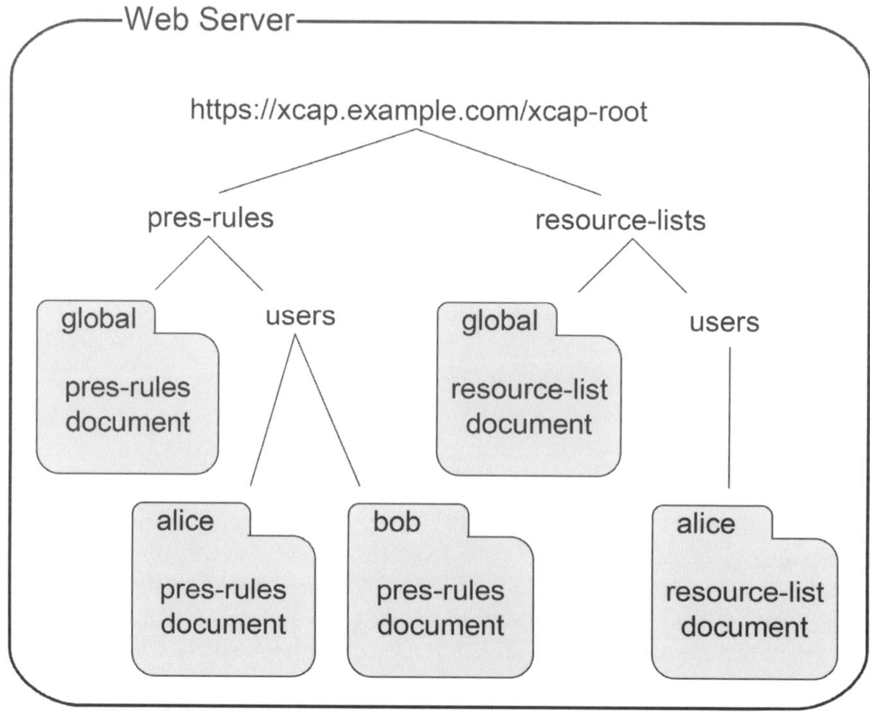

Figure 8.3 – Example of XCAP resources (global and user trees) under XCAP root

Referring to configuration data

XCAP uses HTTP URIs to refer both to documents and the XML structured data inside those documents. All references to XCAP resources will have a document selector followed optionally by a node selector. The document selector is the regular collection of path segments separated by "/" characters familiar from typing paths into web browsers. The node selector is an XPATH[5] expression (though only a subset of XPATH is valid as an XCAP node selector). The document and node selectors are separated by two tildes (~~).

Document Selector Node Selector

https://xcap.example.com/xcap-root/resource-lists/users/alice/~~/resource-lists/list[@name="presence-list"]/list[@name="Friends"]

Figure 8.4 – A URI for use with XCAP

The URI in Figure 8.4 selects Alice's resource list document, and then selects the node containing her list of friends. Assuming the document from Figure 8.2, an HTTP GET using this URI would return:

```
<list name="Friends">
   <entry uri="sip:bob@example.com">
      <display-name>Bob</display-name>
   </entry>
</list>
```

Node selectors are formed using a subset of the XPATH language. Each segment of the node selector must uniquely identify an element immediately below what the previous part of the expression selects. That's why it is necessary in the example URI in Figure 8.4 to qualify each list element it selects by specifying a value for its name attribute.

In addition to qualifying elements by attribute values, a node selector can choose an element by position. A node selector of /resource-lists/list[2] applied to the document in Figure 8.2 would select Alice's bookmarks. These tools can be combined, and a wildcard character, "*", can be used to match any element below the current selection, allowing very complex node selectors

---

5 "XML Path Language (XPath) Version 1.0," by Clark, J. and S. DeRose. W3C REC REC-xpath-19991116, November 1999.

to be constructed. The XCAP specification has several good examples of constructing non-trivial node selectors.

A node selector can also point directly to an attribute of an element. A GET against the resource containing the document in Figure 8.2 using a node selector of /resource-lists/list[1]/@name would return simply "presence-list."

Basic XCAP operations

XCAP uses HTTP's methods for manipulating the data that it stores. GET retrieves data, PUT stores or modifies data, DELETE removes data. POST is not used. Any attempt to POST to a URI indicating an XCAP resource will result in an error. The data being manipulated can be a whole document, or only a piece of a document identified by a node selector.

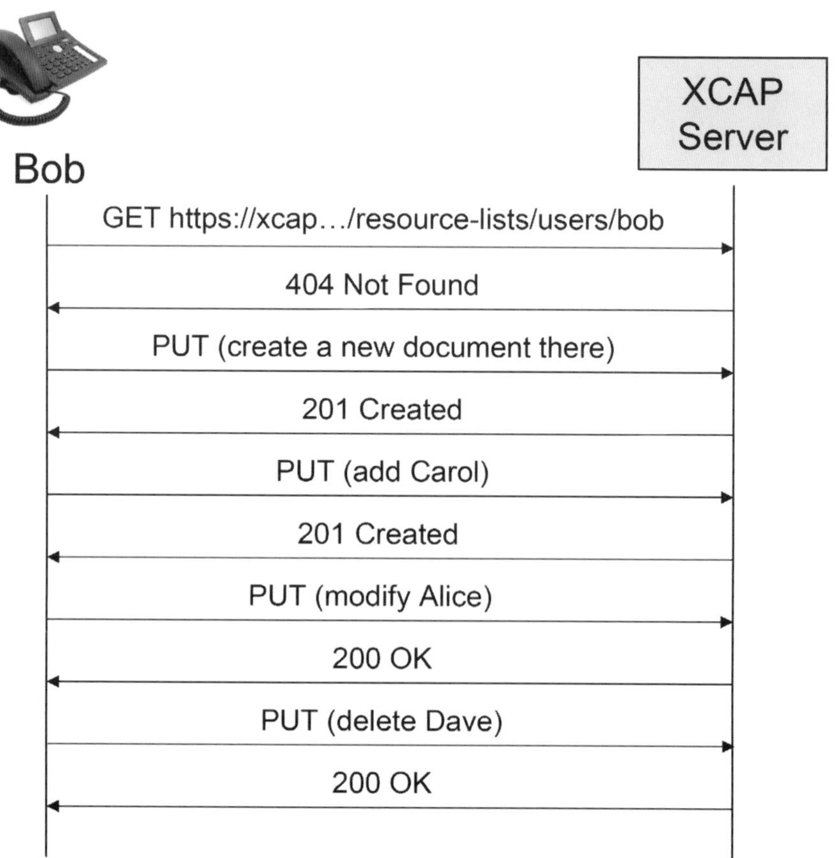

Figure 8.5 – Bob is changing his presence document

To see these methods in action, we'll follow Bob as he creates and edits a new presence list, as shown in Figure 8.5. Bob creates a list that initially contains only Alice and Dave. He then adds Carol, updates his description of Alice, and deletes Dave.

Bob's initial GET returns a 404 since he has no resource-list resource at this XCAP server yet. His first PUT provides an initial document containing Alice and Dave. Only select header fields from the actual HTTP request are shown here.

```
PUT https://xcap.example.com/xcap-root/resource-lists/users/bob HTTP/1.1
Content-Type: application/resource-lists+xml

<?xml version="1.0" encoding="UTF-8"?>
<resource-lists xmlns="urn:ietf:params:xml:ns:resource-lists">
  <list name="buddies">
    <entry uri="sip:alice@example.com"/>
    <entry uri="sip:dave@example.com"/>
  </list>
</resource-lists>
```

The XCAP server responds with a 201 Created response containing the Etag (entity tag) for the resource it just created. Bob then adds Carol to the list just after Alice. The URI in the message below is folded only for readability here.

```
PUT https://xcap.example.com/xcap-root/resource-lists/users/bob/
        ~~/resource-lists/list[1]/entry[2][@uri="sip:carol@example.com"]
HTTP/1.1
Content-Type: application/xcap-el+xml

<entry uri="sip:carol@example.com">
```

This node selector doesn't match any existing node in the document (before this PUT, a GET with that URI would return a 404). The XCAP server notices this and checks to see if the node selector *would* match the provided element if it were inserted as the second entry in the selected list. In this case, that's true, so the server makes the insertion and returns a 201. If it hadn't matched, the server would return a 409 Conflict response.

This matching principle is important. Any XCAP PUT operation must maintain the property GET(PUT(X))=X. In other words, if you PUT some content X using a URI, and immediately GET using that same URI, the server has to return X. This property ensures that the PUTs that modify only a portion of a document are unambiguous. Without it, a client couldn't issue a series of PUTs modifying a document without a GET between every one to make sure the server did what it intended. Any attempt to PUT content where GET(PUT(X)) doesn't equal X will be rejected with a 409 Conflict response.

Notice the difference in the Content-Type between Bob's first two PUTs. The initial request created a whole document, and had a MIME type reflecting the document. The second modified a piece of that document and used the special application/xcap-el+xml MIME type to signal "this is just an element that is meant to be a piece of some xcap document." XCAP also defines the application/xcap-att+xml MIME type for use when manipulating only an attribute of an element.

Next, Bob replaces his current entry for Alice with something that is more descriptive.

```
PUT https://xcap.example.com/xcap-root/resource-lists/users/bob/
      ~~/resource-lists/list[1]/entry[@uri="sip:alice@example.com"]
  HTTP/1.1
Content-Type: application/xcap-el+xml

<entry uri="sip:alice@example.com">
  <display-name>My good friend Alice</display-name>
</entry>
```

The node selector in this URI matches the existing <entry> element for Alice, so the XCAP server replaces the existing element with the new content.

Finally, Bob deletes the entry he has for Dave:

```
DELETE https://xcap.example.com/xcap-root/resource-lists/users/bob/
      ~~/resource-lists/list[1]/entry[@uri="sip:dave@example.com"]
  HTTP/1.1
```

DELETE requests can only be accepted if the URI matches nothing after the delete. Attempting to use a positional selector such as /resource-lists/list[1]/entry[1] will always fail if there was more than one entry in the first list.

Bob's resulting resource-lists document is as follows:

```
<?xml version="1.0" encoding="UTF-8"?>
<resource-lists xmlns="urn:ietf:params:xml:ns:resource-lists">
  <list name="buddies">
    <entry uri="sip:alice@example.com">
      <display-name>My good friend Alice</display-name>
    <entry>
    <entry uri="sip:carol@example.com"/>
  </list>
</resource-lists>
```

Conditional XCAP operations

Like any HTTP server, an XCAP server maintains an entity tag (Etag) for each resource it holds. This tag acts like a version identifier. Whenever a resource gets changed, its Etag changes. Each of the 200-class responses in our earlier example contained an Etag: header field containing the new tag value for Bob's resource list document. In XCAP, the Etag value is associated with the resource identified by the document selector part of a URI. Change any part of a document using a node-selector and the tag for the entire document changes. If you retrieve any part of an XCAP document, the HTTP response carrying the fragment will say it has the same Etag as the entire document.

XCAP clients use Etags to discover when the local version of a document and the version on the XCAP server are out of sync. It lets them discover when someone else has modified a document since they last touched it.

HTTP (hence XCAP) requests can use If-Match and If-None-Match header fields containing Etag values to make the request conditional. A PUT with an If-Match value will only succeed if the tag value of the document currently stored at the server is the same as the value in the header. Similarly, operations with an If-None-Match header will only succeed if the listed Etag value no longer matches what's on the server.

If-Match is used to say "Don't make this change if someone else has modified the document since I last worked with it." If a request containing an If-Match has a value that doesn't match the current document, the server will return a 412 Precondition Failed response.

If-None-Match can be used to make sure a PUT creates a new document, or inserts a new element into a document instead of replacing something that's already there. By including an If-None-Match header with the wildcard value "*", the request will fail if the URI (document and node selector) matches anything on the server. If-None-Match can also be used to check if a document has been modified without retrieving it. A GET with an If-None-Match tag value that actually matches the existing document stimulates a 304 Not Modified response.

Suppose Carol heads off to a trade show. On her way out the door, she asks her administrative assistant to go through her buddy list and make sure the full names that get displayed are spelled correctly. At the event, Carol makes some good business contacts and adds them to her buddy list. By chance, Carol and her assistant start modifying the list at the same time, as depicted in Figure 8.6 below.

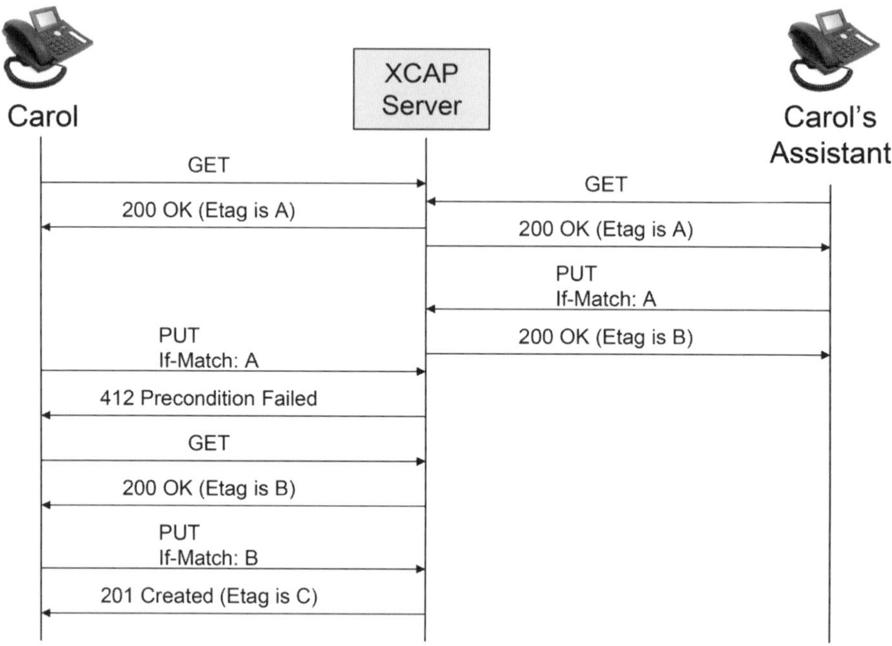

Figure 8.6 – Illustration of two users attempting to simultaneously modify a buddy list

Carol and here assistant both start out by getting the current document. Carol's assistant then modifies the spelling on one of the existing entries, causing the Etag value of the document to change. When Carol tries to insert a new contact, she learns that the Etag she currently holds is no longer valid. She fetches the changed document and retries her request, this time successfully creating a new entry in her presence list.

Subscribing to changes in configuration data

Carol would prefer that the changes her assistant makes show up on her computer's copy of her buddy list immediately. Similarly, when Carol adds new entries to her list while at the show, they should already be reflected on her desk computer when she gets back to the office. SIMPLE leverages SIP Events and the SIP configuration framework to make this possible.

The SIP configuration framework[6] defines the "sip-profile" event, along with four profile types: application, user, device, and local. The application type is used to access application configuration data, such as that stored on an XCAP server. Carol can subscribe to her resource list document with a SUBSCRIBE containing the following information:

```
SUBSCRIBE sip:carol@example.com SIP/2.0
Event: sip-profile;profile-type=application;app-id=resource-lists
```

With this subscription in place, she'll see any changes other UAs make to her document immediately, as can be seen in Figure 8.7.

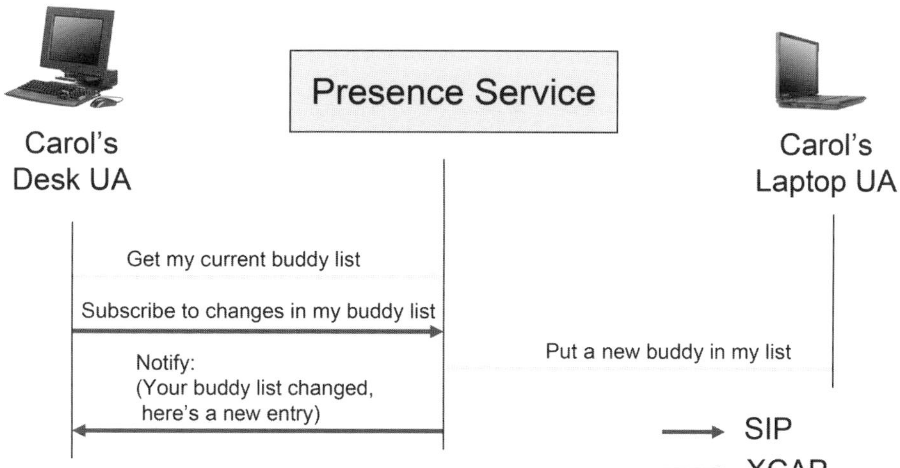

Figure 8.7 – Example of how a user's subscription to a resource list document allows for immediate notification of the user if another User Agent makes changes to the document

6 "A Framework for Session Initiation Protocol User Agent Profile Delivery," by D. Petrie. Internet Draft, IETF, October 2004.

Summary

The Extensible Configuration Access Protocol allows users to keep their application configuration data, like buddy lists, on a service hosted by a provider in a standard way. It uses standard HTTP between clients and the server, and keeps the configuration data in XML documents with standard structures for each kind of application. XCAP is a framework, allowing new types of application data to be managed at any time.

A SIP Events server combined with an XCAP server provides a complete solution for keeping application data in sync across multiple devices.

Chapter 9

Mobile Communications Using SIP

Introduction

Wireless Internet Access Options

Taking a cue from the fact that the number of mobile phones worldwide is already exceeding that of wired phones, it is also likely that the number of personal wireless IP devices will soon exceed the number of wired PCs. Since true mobility implies the use of both wireless and wired networks, the six networks that a user may be connected to are at present:

1. Wired LAN: 802.3.
2. Wireless LAN (WLAN): 802.11 a, b, and g.
3. 3G mobile networks, such as 3GPP and 3GPP2.
4. 4G broadband wireless metropolitan area network: 802.16.
5. So-called 2.5G networks with Internet access.
6. Dial-up Internet access: 56 kb/s and ISDN (just for the sake of completeness).

2G mobile networks such as GSM and CDMA are not counted here since they do not provide transparent Internet access, though some "Internet-like" functionality is accomplished for messaging and using web browsing gateways. For simplicity we will also not discuss here the so-called 2.5G and 3.5G transition networks between 2G, 3G and 4G, respectively.

Multi-Modal Wireless Devices

Most PCs and laptops have interface modules to at least three of the above network types and it is expected 4G mobile (802.16) network interfaces will be added in the near future. New types of dual mode mobile phones can work in both 2G/3G and WLAN mode. Some phones can also connect using Bluetooth wireless and wired LAN on the desktop. Many 2.5G networks provide laptop cards for connectivity. A short summary of communication devices includes the following:

1. Desktop SIP phone.
2. PC.
3. Laptop.
4. PDA.
5. 2.5G-3G mobile phone.
6. 2G mobile phone.
7. SIP adapter for analog phones.

New Mobility Requirements

Under these circumstances, mobility has to include the notion of moving from one type of network to another, from one device to another, while maintaining not only the capability for rich communications, but also maintaining the session, for example a phone call or a multimedia collaboration session.

By contrast, traditional mobility implies moving between wireless cells or wireless LAN segments, thus changing the point of attachment to the same type of network and using the same device. In the case of mobile phone networks, mobility is defined even more narrowly, since it also implies keeping the same service provider. The 2G and 3G mobile phones are thus locked to traditional mobile service providers as well.

We will show in the following sections that SIP-based application layer mobility can support the establishment and maintaining of communications when moving between different network types, between different points of attachment to the network and changing devices. Naturally, as with all SIP-based communications, accounts with various service providers can be used on different "lines" on the same device and on the same access network to the Internet.

Mobility Network Access Protocols

Each of the various Internet access networks that a mobile user may encounter has its own set of protocols required for authentication, authorization and accounting (AAA).

From a business perspective, any financially sustainable mobile service has to put the main focus on payments. A scenario for multimode mobile communication devices is shown in Figure 9.1 to illustrate how the variety of network protocols can nevertheless lead to a uniform view on payments to get network access. The common platform here for payments is the RADIUS AAA server chain. We will show further below how the SIP and SIMPLE protocols can act for the common delivery of these services.

Individual users and enterprise customers depend on a central payment service (shown on the right) that acts as the ultimate AAA node for all fixed and mobile networks where mobile users may roam.

- Mobile 2G-2.5G networks have a back-end infrastructure based on the Home Location Register (HLR) and SS7 signaling that use a MAP proxy to connect to the RADIUS server that belongs to the payments service. The secure front end AAA protocols associated with the SIM card in the mobile phone are not shown for simplicity.

- WLAN 802.11x networks use the port-based network access protocol (IEEE P802.1X draft) and the IETF Extended Access Protocol (EAP) for network access to provide RADIUS-based AAA for network access. The WLAN RADIUS server will outsource its AAA functions also to the RADIUS server belonging to the payment service.
- Wired Ethernet LANs may also use EAP or some other, simpler network access mechanisms. In some hotels Ethernet access to the Internet is part of the room charge ('free').

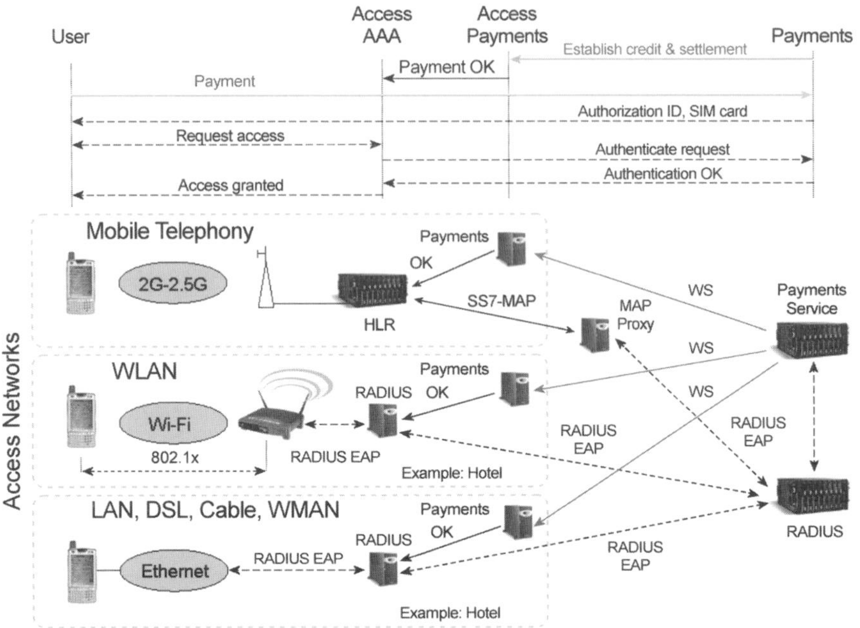

Figure 9.1 – Examples of mobile access to the Internet

The main point made here is that network access for the mobile device includes specific AAA protocols, some of them, like RADIUS having extensions for SIP and HTTP authentication.[1] Wireless IP access networks can also use the RADIUS attributes for IEEE 802.1x and DHCP, so that the

[1] "RADIUS Extension for Digest Authentication," by B. Sterman, et al. Internet Draft, IETF, June 2004.

DHCP server may send appropriate configuration parameters to the mobile device.[2]

Mobility Management at Various Layers

We will explore briefly how the mobility management function can be accomplished at several layers of the IP protocol stack:

- Radio: L2 link layer mobility,
- Network: L3 IP layer Mobile IP,
- Application: L4 SIP mobility,
- Combinations of the above, such as L2-L3 and L3-L4.

L2 Mobility Example: 802.11

Mobility for wireless LANs, such as roaming in hotels between the areas covered by wireless access points (WAP) or in cities with continuous hot spot coverage can be accomplished using L2 mobility as shown in Figure 9.2.

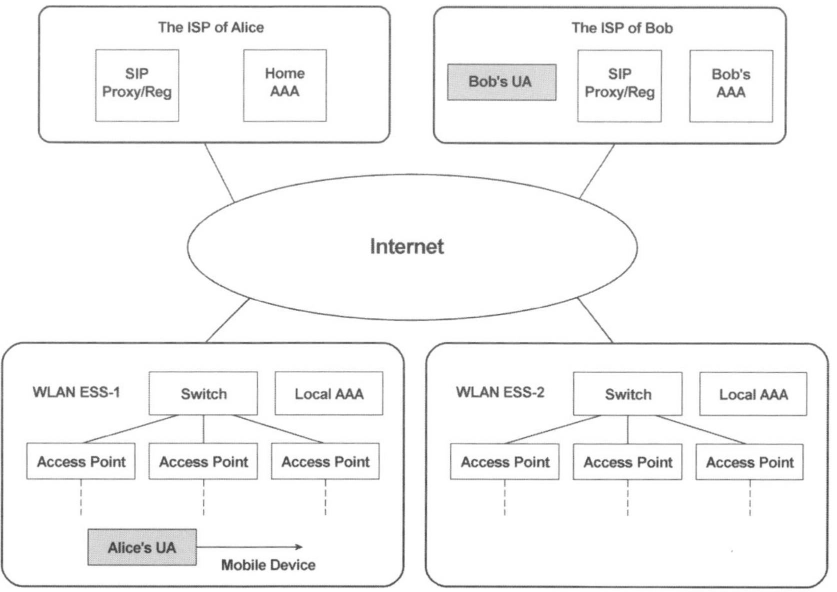

Figure 9.2 – Mobility in wireless LANs

[2] "RADIUS Attributes Sub-option for the DHCP Relay Agent Information Option," by R. Droms, et al. Internet Draft, IETF, April 2004. Work in progress.

The scenario shown in Figure 9.2 shows Alice roaming between various access points within one wireless LAN as well as moving between different LANs. The visited networks (wireless LANs) can be shared by multiple ISPs using proper AAA mechanisms and the Internet for connectivity. The example here shows Bob's ISP also to be reachable by Alice from the visited WLANs. Such service models have been explored in detail[3] and the handover performance studied.[4] The handover performance in 802.11 WLANs and the AAA chain composed of RADIUS servers using EAP over TLS is in the range of 80ms to 200ms, without adding any propagation delay over the Internet. This handover performance is probably satisfactory for voice.

It is also possible to combine L2 handover with L3 Mobile IP (see the next section) and obtain consistent small handover times[5] of about 100ms for propagation delays between the UAs in the range of 10 to 100ms over the Internet.[6]

Mobility for 802.16 Mobile Wireless MAN

Broadband wireless metropolitan networks (MAN) based on the 802.16 family of standards have the potential for true broadband wireless access to the Internet and the transparency that may not be available on "walled garden" type of other of mobile services. The 802.16e standard is being developed to add link layer mobility to 802.16 wireless MAN, but this is still work in progress.

L3 Mobile IP

As mentioned, mobility management can also be accomplished at the network layer L3 using Mobile IP.[7] Mobile IP (for IPv4) has found wide deployment in CDMA 2000 3G mobile networks. There is also a significant

---

[3] "A Roaming Architecture for IP-Based Mobile Telephony in WLAN Environments," by J. Vatn. Stockholm Mobility Roundtable, 22-23 May 2003, Stockholm, Sweden. http://web.hhs.se/cic/roundtable2003/papers/S13-Vatn.pdf

[4] "An Experimental Study of IEEE 802.11b Handover Performance and its Effect on Voice Traffic," by J. Vatn. Royal Institute of Technology, Stockholm, Sweden, July 2003. http://www.it.kth.se/~vatn/research/handover-perf.pdf

[5] "Link Layer Assisted Mobile IP Fast Handover Method over Wireless LAN Networks," by H. Yokota, et al. Paper presented at the MOBICOM 2002 conference. http://portal.acm.org/citation.cfm?id=570661

[6] "Performance Evaluation of Two Layered Mobility Management Using Mobile IP and Session Initiation Protocol," by Jin-Woo Jung, et al. Globecom Conference 2003. http://w3.antd.nist.gov/pubs/sip-mip-jwjung-globecom2003.pdf

[7] RFC 3344: "IP Mobility Support for IPv4," by C. Perkins. IETF, August 2002.

momentum to implement Mobile IPv6 in state of the art mobile network for a number of reasons, mostly however due to the expectation of the large number of mobile devices, each requiring its own IP address.

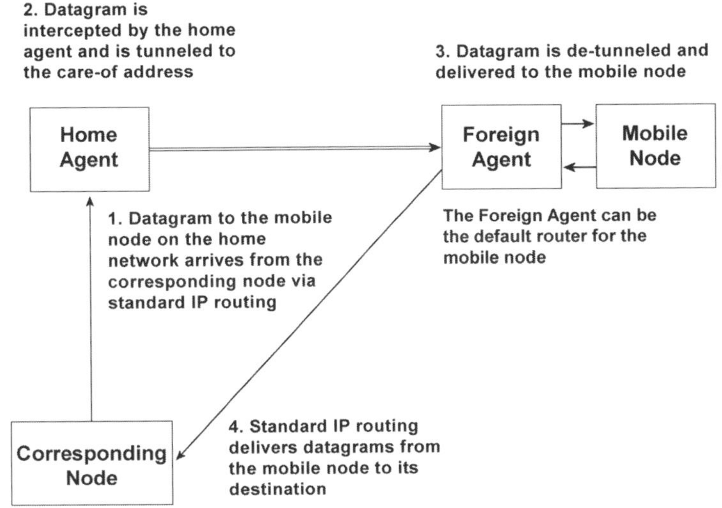
2. Datagram is intercepted by the home agent and is tunneled to the care-of address
3. Datagram is de-tunneled and delivered to the mobile node
Home Agent
Foreign Agent
Mobile Node
1. Datagram to the mobile node on the home network arrives from the corresponding node via standard IP routing
The Foreign Agent can be the default router for the mobile node
Corresponding Node
4. Standard IP routing delivers datagrams from the mobile node to its destination

Figure 9.3 – Operation of Mobile IPv4

A short overview of Mobile IPv4 can be given with the aid of Figure 9.3. Mobile IPv4 has the following key elements, shown here:

Mobile Node (MN)	Changes its point of attachment from one network or subnet to another, without changing its IP address as seen by the application layer L4.
Home Agent (HA)	A router in the home network of the mobile node. The HA tunnels IP datagrams for delivery to the mobile node when it is away from the home network and maintains the current location information for the MN.
Foreign Agent (FA)	A router in the visited network which provides service to the MN while it is registered there. The FA de-tunnels the datagrams arriving from the HA for the MN and delivers them to the MN. The FA serves as the default router for the outgoing IP packets from the MN.
Correspondent Node (CN)	A peer that communicates with the MN. A CN may be either fixed or mobile as well.

Note that all packets from the CN to the MN have to be routed via the home network. This is called triangular routing.

Mobile IPv6[8] for IPv6 uses similar principles as MIPv4, but is integrated into IPv6 and has several improvements based on the experience with MIPv4. Mobile IPv6 will be an attractive implementation option once IPv6 becomes more widely deployed across the Internet.

Note the opposite models used by Mobile IP and SIP (as will be shown) to support mobility:

- L3 Mobile IP does not change the IP address, as seen from the application layer.
- L4 SIP mobility copes with changes of the IP address.

Issues with Mobile IPv4

The Mobile IPv4 standard based on RFC 3344 has been developed over several years in the IETF and has also been adopted by other standards organizations. It has also found wider deployment in 3G CDMA 2000 networks, as mentioned. Still, MIPv4 has also some drawbacks:

- Mobile IPv4 is not widely deployed on the Internet, so it is unlikely that users will (1) find a home ISP that deploys the home agent for Mobile IPv4 and (2) it is even less likely to find support for the Mobile IPv4 foreign agent when away from the home network. It is not trivial for ISPs to support the HA function when giving users a dynamic IP address using DHCP.
- The triangle IP routing in one direction shown in Figure 9.3 adds additional delay for the media. For example, two MNs having their home network in Texas but visiting a network in Tokyo must have their packets routed all the way to the home network and back. The extra propagation delay from the home network adds to the handover delay between two FAs in a linear fashion, as can be seen in Figure 9.4.
- Handover increases in a linear fashion with the distance of the MN from the HN, even when moving between adjacent network points of attachments. This problem is being addressed by recent work on low latency handoffs,[9] but it will take time for the standard to be

[8] RFC 3775: "Mobility Support in IPv6," by D. Johnson, et al. IETF, June 2004.

[9] "Low Latency Handoffs in Mobile IPv4," by K. El Malki. Internet Draft, IETF, June 2004. work in progress.

developed and widely deployed. Low latency handover in Mobile IPv4 is based on combining triggers from L2 wireless access points to initiate early registration with the new FA (pre-registration), or still use the old FA while already having registered with a new FA (post-registration).

- IP tunneling from the HN to the FA ads significant IP overhead (8, 12 or 20 bytes) to voice packets that may be as short as 10 to 20 bytes.[12]

It is not trivial for Mobile IP to be deployed at present in Virtual Private Networks (VPNs), protected by firewalls and NAT. Though mobility inside the private network presents no problem, mobility between the outside and inside of the protected network is still work in progress.[10, 11]

L4 Application Layer Mobility Using SIP

SIP can provide mobility at the application layer and SIP extends the notions for mobility as shown here (courtesy Henning Schulzrinne):

Terminal Mobility	The mobile device can move between points of attachment of the same network, for example between Wi-Fi access points. This is similar to the mobility in 2G/3G mobile telephone networks.
Session Mobility	SIP mobility allows the user to change the device and/or the network and still remain in the established session. For example a user logged into a conference call with a mobile phone, can when entering the office move to the PC without having to leave and re-join the conference.
Personal Mobility	Users can be reached on any device they may have, on any network. When in the office, a user can be reached for example on more than one device at the same time.
Service Mobility	Users can change the location, the device and the access network and can still keep all their services and preferences, such as the personalized GUI, directory and telephony dial plan. An example is a user on travel without the personal laptop, in an Internet cafe.

---

[10] "Problem Statement: Mobile IPv4 Traversal of VPN Gateways," by F. Adrangi, et al. IETF, October 2004. Work in progress.

[11] "Mobile IPv4 Traversal across VPN or/and VPN Gateways," by F. Adrangi. IETF, February 2002 (archive).

Application layer mobility using SIP was first described by Schulzrinne and Wedlund[12] and it has the following properties:

- Independence of the underlying layers: Changes in the IP network layer and the various L2 link layers. The change of IP address is well-supported.
- SIP level mobility is not dependent on Mobile IP. Users are thus not dependent on their home network and the visiting networks to support Mobile IP. The media delay of Mobile IP is also avoided.
- User who are not moving during a session and are not dependent on smooth handover performance will need no other network support for mobility.
- Handover for SIP mobility when moving between points of attachment to the network require (1) DHCP IP address allocation and (2) SIP re-registration. The DHCP address allocation can take up to 2 seconds and are thus the biggest delay in the handover process.
- The handover time can be significantly reduced by:
  - Combining SIP mobility with Mobile IP, and/or
  - Combining Mobile IP with WLAN mobility.

Figure 9.4 shows the effect on handover performance of combining local SIP registration and mobile IPv4 in the home network.[13] The use of Mobile IP eliminates the delay due to DHCP. It can be seen that handover performance is excellent when the MN is close to both the home network and the SIP registrar/proxy. In the 10 to 30 ms delay interval, the increase in handover time is linear with the propagation delay.

The conclusion from reported work in the field[13] and illustrated in Figure 9.4, is that SIP combined with Mobile IPv4 will support very short handoff times that can be considered smooth enough for good quality of service. However, as will be seen, in many instances, where smooth handoff is either not required or is not critical, SIP application level mobility can be used very effectively without Mobile IP.

---

[12] "Application Layer Mobility Using SIP," by H. Schulzrinne and E. Wedlund. *Mobile Computing and Communications Review*, Volume 1, Number2. March 2003. http://www1.cs.columbia.edu/~hgs/papers/Schu0007_Application.pdf

[13] "Performance Evaluation of Two Layered Mobility Management using Mobile IP and the Session Initiation Protocol," by Jin-Woo Jung, et al. Presentation at the Globecom 2003 Conference.

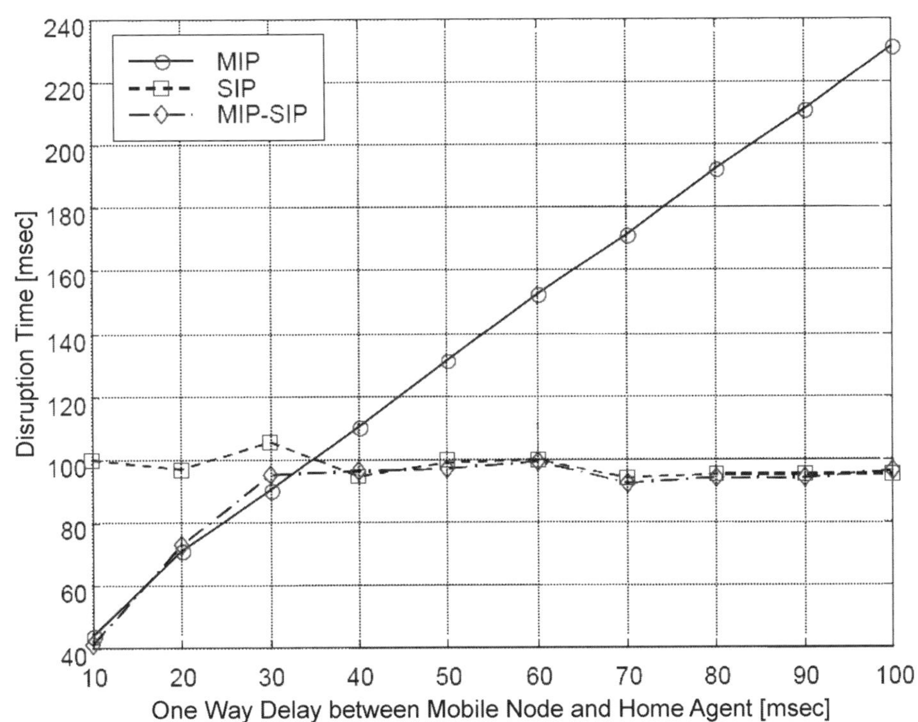

Figure 9.4 – Using SIP with Mobile IP for optimum handover performance[13]

Mobility in P2P Overlay Networks

Recent research in peer-to-peer (P2P) overlay networks for mobility have shown the following:

- The mobility agent can reside in the P2P node[14] and IP network-based mobile is no longer required.
- The handover performance is improved in P2P mobility hand-over.[15]

---

[14] "IPv4 Mobility through Peer Signaling," by S. Goswami. Internet Draft, IETF, February 2005. http://www.ietf.org/internet-drafts/draft-goswami-mip4-peer-signaling-00.txt

[15] "Rapid Mobilty via Type Indirection," by B. Zhao, et al. Computer Sciences Division, UC Berkeley. IPTPS, February 2004. http://www.cs.berkeley.edu/~ravenben/tapestry/

Mobility in overlay peer-to-peer networks may have in our opinion a profound impact on mobile communications, possibly making obsolete many existing mobile network infrastructures.

SIP Terminal Mobility

Terminal mobility refers to the ability of the user to connect the mobile device to any type of network that provides Internet access. Terminal mobility is a "built-in" SIP feature, since the terminal will (1) first acquire a network address using DHCP and then (2) register with the SIP registrar. After these steps, the mobile device can both initiate and receive calls.

The complexity of the Internet access services poses two challenges to this simple concept of terminal mobility:

- Getting Internet access from a L2 network, such as a WLAN hot-spot.
- NAT and firewall traversal.

Figure 9.5 shows the high level message flows required for terminal mobility. In the following we will use the terms Mobile Node (MN) and Mobile Station (MS) interchangeably. The term MN is used in the SIP mobility literature.

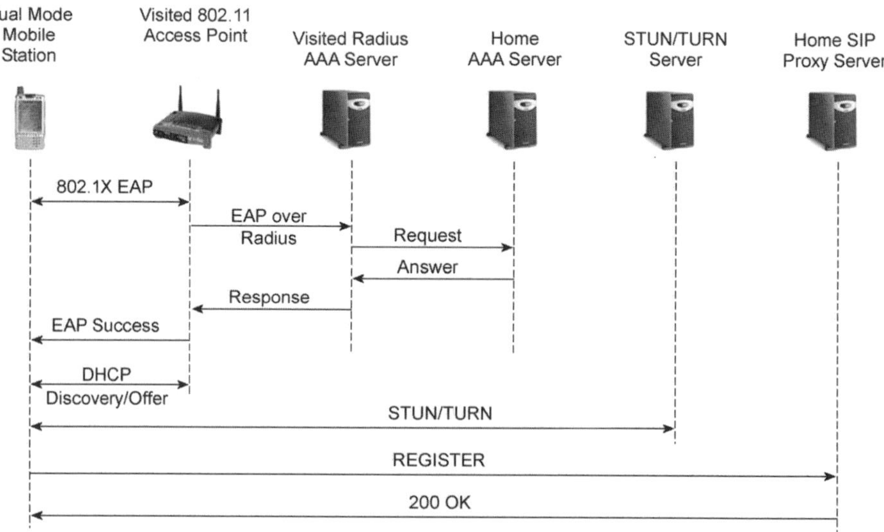

Figure 9.5 – Terminal mobility with message flows for network access and NAT/FW traversal

The following generic steps are required to establish a SIP registration for a mobile station (MS) on a wireless LAN:

1. The MS requests port-based access to the WLAN using the Extended Authentication Protocol (EAP).
2. The wireless access point forwards the EAP request to its local authentication, authorization and accounting (AAA) RADIUS server.
3. The local RADIUS server forwards the AAA request to the home AAA RADIUS server.
4. After a successful authentication (EAP Success) the MS gets a local IP address from the DHCP server and is ready for Internet access. Still, there are the challenges to real-time communications posed by eventual NAT and firewall that may protect the visited network.
5. The MS runs the STUN and if necessary, also the TURN protocols, so as to reach the home SIP proxy.
6. The MS registers with the home SIP proxy and is ready for SIP-based communications.

Pre-Call Terminal Mobility

The high level call flow for SIP pre-call mobility is shown in Figure 9.6 for the scenario where a corresponding station on the Internet is trying to reach the mobile station in its home network. The home network will reply to the first INVITE with "302 moved temporarily" that includes the latest known address of the mobile node. The corresponding host can now initiate a 2nd INVITE and establish the session with the mobile station.

Pre-call mobility for SIP is a very simple scenario, since once the UA has acquired an IP address and registered with the home proxy, it can originate and receive calls.

The home proxy registrar has to have the most recently acquired IP address of the UA, in case the network point of attachment has changed. For this reason, mobile UAs must send register updates every few seconds or send notifications of IP address change to the home SIP proxy.

Note that for pre-call mobility there is no need for mobile IP. Users moved to new locations just use SIP as usual and discover that everything works as usual. This is a familiar scenario for people moving their SIP phones around in an enterprise network or travelers carrying with them a SIP phone or SIP adapter that they connect in any hotel room in the world that has broadband Internet access (provided their home network assures some service such as STUN for NAT traversal, see Chapter 13).

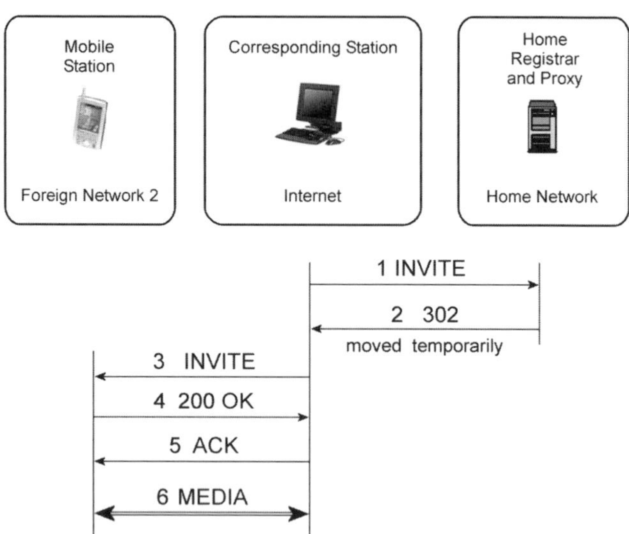

Figure 9.6 – SIP pre-call mobility call flow

Mid-Call Terminal Mobility

Mid-call mobility for SIP can be accomplished using a re-INVITE message to the corresponding UA, without requiring the intervention of the home SIP proxy. This is shown in Figure 9.7.

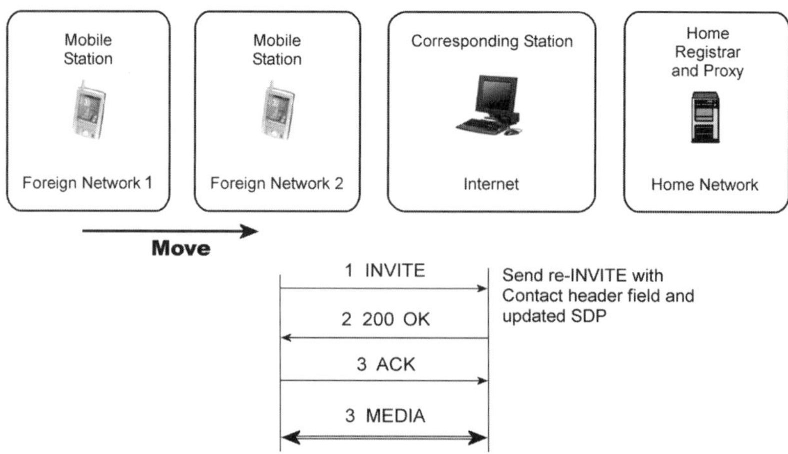

Figure 9.7 – SIP mid-call terminal mobility call flow

The SIP re-INVITE message shown in Figure 9.7 can be sent as soon at the UA has sensed the new IP address. The new IP address requires a DHCP message exchange that may take 1-2 seconds, during which the media stream is interrupted.

In addition to the perceivable time for the acquisition of the new IP address, the handoff from the old network address to the new network address will also require additional time for the processing of the SIP re-INVITE. The time required for the re-INVITE exchange between the mobile station and the corresponding station is quite small, such as in the 100 ms range or less, plus the propagation time that depends on the distance.

If several seconds handover between networks can be tolerated, the mid call terminal mobility does not pose any special technical challenges. The actual message flows for mid-call mobility will be however more complex than shown in Figure 9.7 if SIP digest authentication between the UAs is required. The interested reader may want to review Chapter 12 on SIP authentication to fully understand all processes required for a secure re-INVITE.

Smooth handover for the IP address change is not a trivial task, but can be accomplished by combining SIP mobility with Mobile IP. As shown in Figure 9.4, by combining SIP mobility with Mobile IP, the delay due to DHCP reacquisition can be avoided and very small handover times can be obtained, especially in high speed WLAN networks.

SIP Session Mobility

Users can change for example between the mobile phone while driving to work to a large screen multimedia fixed device (UA) in the office and still maintain the session using SIP session mobility. An example is shown in Figure 9.8 where the user of a mobile phone A or PDA is already in a voice session with a corresponding station C. On entering the office, the user can transfer the existing session from the mobile device to a multimedia PC with audio, video and data collaboration (as well as having the benefit of IM on the large PC screen).

The transfer of the session from one device to another using SIP REFER is a local peer-to-peer action and does not require any interaction with the SIP servers that have initially established the session.

SIP Personal Mobility

Users can be located at different devices at the same time and can be reached using a single Address of Record (AOR) as detailed in Chapter 7 on ENUM, where the single AOR is a phone number or a URL. This is shown in Figure 9.9. Separate private and work accounts can be maintained on one single SIP service, or separate SIP services can be used as

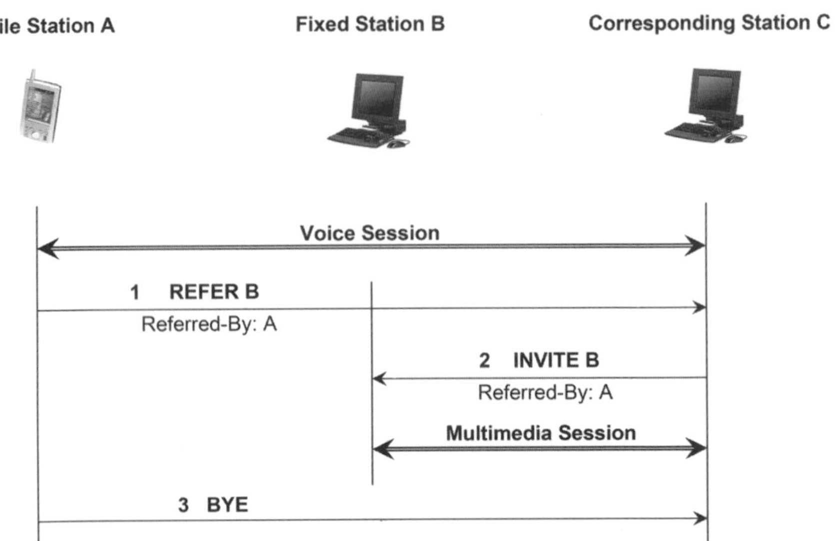

Figure 9.8 – SIP session mobility: Moving from voice session to a multimedia session

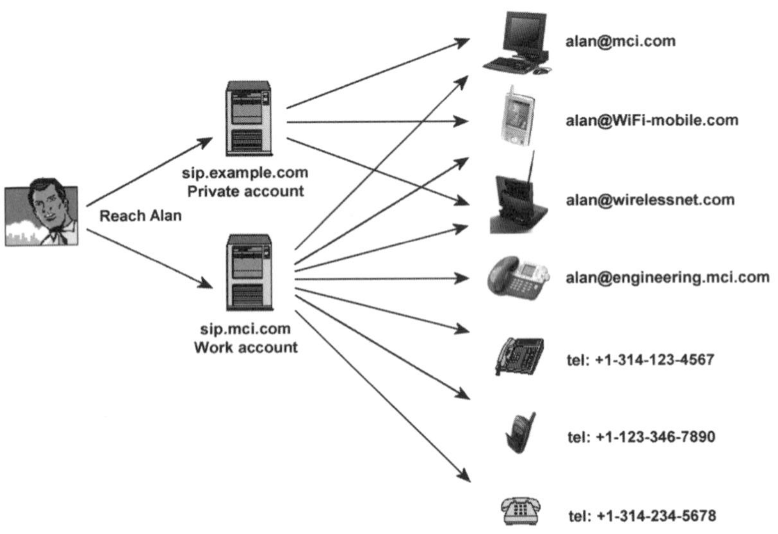

Figure 9.9 – SIP personal mobility—reachable on any device at work and in private life

shown in Figure 9.9. The SIP forking proxies can ring several or all of the contact addresses (CA) stored for the user, according to the called user preferences that constitute the users policy for forking. These preferences will usually include the day and time and also the domain and URL of the caller.

SIP Service Mobility

Users can move between networks and change devices and still maintain their communication services and applications, such as buddy lists and presence filtering, incoming call handling, voicemail, address book, media preferences, conference rooms and other. An example is a user on vacation without taking the usual laptop computer or SIP VoIP adapter along on the trip. The user can however log in for example at an Internet cafe, use a PC SIP softphone and/or IM application and log on the home SIP registrar and get the use of all services that are hosted by the service provider, such as language, the buddy list, IM filtering and policy, VoIP directory and short calling list, user preferences, etc.

It is envisioned by some researchers (see footnote 12 on page 218) that traveling users may be identified by physical tokens or biometrics to log in to the home SIP registrar.

Summary

Application level mobility for SIP can support a wide spectrum of new services that are not possible or just not practical on existing mobile networks:

- Terminal mobility
  - Pre-call
  - Mid-call
- Session mobility
- Personal mobility
- Service mobility

No other mobility management protocols are required neither at the L2 link layer nor at the L3 IP layer (Mobile IP) if smooth handoff is not critical or not required for roaming users. However, L2 link layer mobility and L3 Mobile IP can contribute to smooth handover.

SIP mobility combined with Mobile IPv4 can provide smooth handover performance that is independent of the link layer and is therefore useful when moving from one type of network, for example wireless 802.11x LANs to another network type, such as 802.3 wired Ethernet.

Chapter 10

Accessibility to Communications for Disabled People

Introduction

Deaf, hard of hearing, speech-impaired or blind people are often unable to use the phone or even the computer without special facilities and require special devices for communications. Current communication devices for users with disabilities are traditionally geared to the use of the telephone network, have limited functionality and are also expensive. Lack of widely implemented standards makes it even harder for disabled users. For example, many text phone models in different countries are unable to communicate with each other. Additionally, many of these users would rather use sign language in a conversation, because it is so much more fluent than typing in a real-time conversation. For that purpose, sign language relay services are needed to translate between sign language and voice. Automatic selection and invocation of such services would ease the communication situation for the users.

SIP-based Internet multimedia communications are ideally suited to provide deaf, hard of hearing, speech impaired and blind individuals access to worldwide communications using any combination of text, voice and video that is suitable to their needs.

In the following section we will use the shorter term "accessibility" when referring to accessibility for disabled person to communications.

The concept of accessibility using multimedia has been promoted also under the name of Total Conversation.[1] The proponents of Total Conversation make the valid argument that capability such as Text over IP (ToIP)[2] is valuable not only for disabled individuals, but also for all Internet users.

While the use of SIP for voice and video are fairly well understood and treated elsewhere extensively, ToIP is a relative new concept and will be discussed subsequently in more detail.

Scenarios for Accessibility

Some of the usage scenarios are shown here to serve as a guide for service requirements and design.

---

[1] Presentation made by Gunnar Hellstrom to the SIPPING WG at the 59th IETF meeting. See also other presentations of this concept at http://www.totalconversation.org/

[2] "Framework of requirements for real-time text conversation using SIP," by A. van Wijk , G. Hellstrom and R.R. Roy. IETF, February 2004, work in progress.

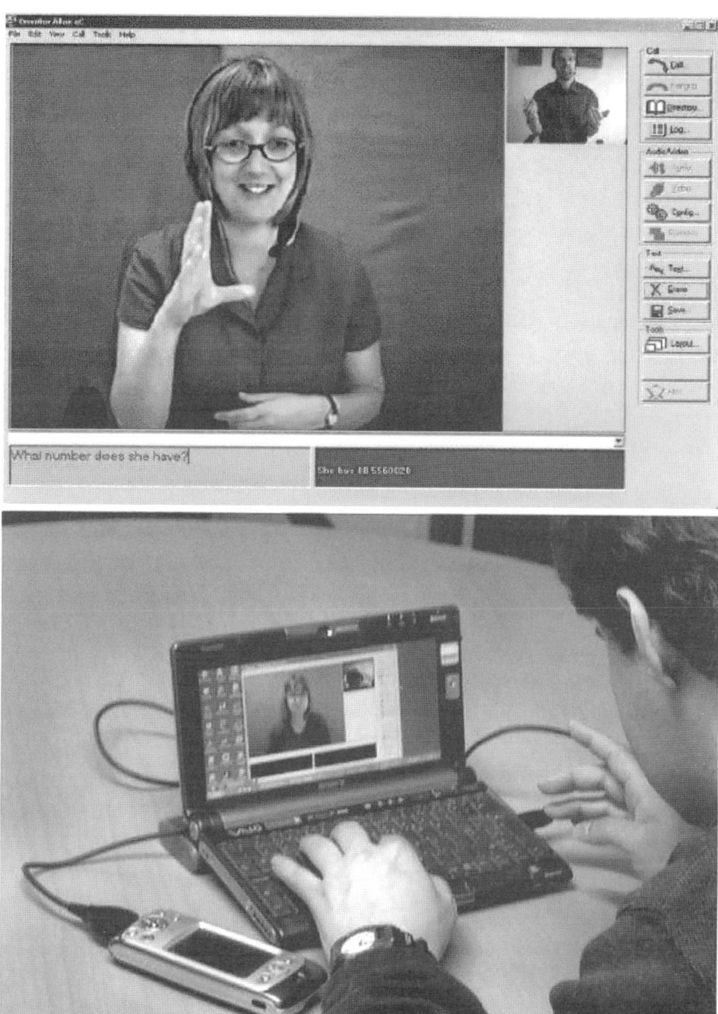

Figure 10.1 – Using text, voice and video with sign language
(Courtesy Omnitor AB, http://www.omnitor.se/)

1. Transcoding Service

A hearing user calls the household of a deaf person and a hearing person answers the call. During the conversation, the caller asks to talk to the deaf person while keeping the voice channel open so that the voice communication can continue if required.

A relay service is invited into the conversation so that the voice of the caller can be translated and the text displayed to the deaf person. The deaf person can type text for the reply and the text is translated by the relay service to voice for the caller to hear.

The hearing caller can ask by voice to speak again to the hearing person in the called household. The relay service withdraws from the call.

2. Media Content Provider

A deaf person would like to follow important foreign news on the radio through a text stream transcoded from the program's radio stream (voice to text could be transcoded locally on the PC as well). The UA of the deaf person queries the UA of the radio station and not finding a text capability will invoke a relay service to provide the audio to text conversion and the text stream.

An alternative is for radio stations to provide text streams as well, a practice that should be encouraged, we believe.

3. Sign Language Interface

A deaf person may have the capability to set up the UA to receive the voice stream, use an application to convert the audio to XML data, so as to operate an Avatar to display sign language. The voice to sign language conversion could also be performed by a relay service.

For outgoing communication, the deaf person could type text that is converted by a local application into voice, or by using a relay service.

4. Synthetic Lip-speaking Support for Voice Calls

This is an application similar to sign language, except that lip speaking images instead of sign language is displayed to the hearing impaired user.

A hard of hearing person may use a lip-speaking avatar software on a PC to receive voice calls. The lip-speaking software processes voice (audio) stream data and displays the synthetic animated face, so that a hard of hearing person may be able to lip-read. During the conversation, the hard of hearing person uses the lip-speaking software as support for understanding the audio stream.

5. Voice-Activated Menu Systems

This application may be useful when contacting merchants that still have no web site for order taking or for customer support, but have only legacy PSTN-style interactive voice response (IVR) systems in place. The hearing impaired person will interact with the IVR using DTMF, a relay service or a local voice-text application.

6. Conference Call

Multi-party conferences can be accomplished with participants that are not impaired at all and with participants that have various types of impairments:

- Not impaired: Can listen and speak.
- Hearing OK, but no speech: Listens and types text.
- Deaf or hearing impaired: Speaks and reads text.
- Sign language user: Can read sign language and text, answers with signs.

7. Emergency Call

A disabled person makes an emergency call using a relay service or a local application for transcoding to match the specific impairments of the user. This is similar to the other application scenarios mentioned before, except the added requirements for emergency calls will apply, as described in Chapter 5.

Relay Services vs. Local Applications

In all applications scenarios, either a relay service or a local application could be used to perform the required transcoding. Though local applications on PCs are becoming ever more powerful, relay services are still preferred at present. Relay services with human interpreters are still simply superior to machine transcoding applications, thus justifying their higher cost.

Requirements for Accessibility

The power of SIP-based Internet communications for the disabled has been recognized quite early and has undergone intense work in the IETF. One of the first RFCs to address this area is not surprisingly about the requirements for SIP to support impaired individuals.[3] We will provide here a short overview of such requirements.

[3] RFC 3351: "User Requirements for the Session Initiation Protocol (SIP) in Support of the Deaf, Hard of Hearing and Speech impaired Individuals," by N. Charlton, et al. IETF, August 2002.

The usage scenarios in the preceding section can be translated into SIP call flows and system design in straight forward manner and detail design examples are beyond the scope of this book. There are however generic requirements for accessibility that have to be considered when designing for accessibility that we will briefly mention here.

Media Types: SIP UAs for the disabled and SIP proxies in the network must support user preferences with regard to media types and the insertion of a suitable relay service on a call by call basis.

Confidentiality: The SIP-based service must also support confidentiality, without revealing for example that a deaf person is calling.

Deaf, hard of hearing and speech-impaired people can keep their preferences and abilities confidential from others, to avoid possible discrimination or prejudice, while still being able to establish a SIP session.

All third-party or intermediaries (transcoding services) employed in a session for deaf, hard of hearing and speech-impaired people must offer a confidentiality policy. All information exchanged in this type of session should be secure and confidential and the information exchange erased after use.

Accessibility and mobility using any network: SIP/IP to PSTN gateways must support the conversion of protocols that enable the use of text telephones on the PSTN side and ToIP on the Internet side. The same is true for gateways between the Internet and mobile phone networks, such as 2G (CDMA and GSM), 2.5G and 3G networks.

A complete disability service should actually work properly when the disabled person is using either the Internet, or a mobile phone or a legacy PSTN device for the hearing or seeing disabled individuals.

Seen from this perspective, it is becoming obvious that enabling accessibility from any network is best accomplished by placing the service on the Internet and considering PSTN devices and mobile phones as SIP endpoints seen though the respective gateways to the Internet. SIP application level mobility is directly applicable for this requirement, see Chapter 9.

Text Conversation and Text over IP (ToIP)

When using text for a real-time text conversation, as a counterpart to a voice call, the most direct feeling of contact is achieved when transmitting each character at the moment it is typed.

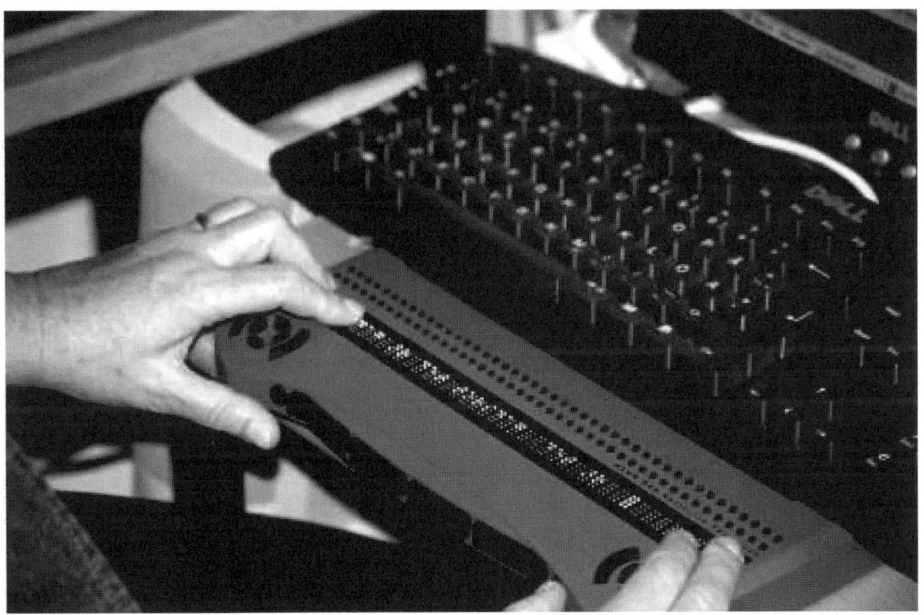

Figure 10.2 – Braille display for a blind person
(Courtesy Omnitor AB, http://www.omnitor.se/)

Text conversation should not be confused with either the Short Messaging Service (SMS) on mobile networks or with instant messaging (IM) on the Internet.

Replies or interruptions using text conversation from the remote part are possible, even before the whole message is sent. Text conversation is therefore highly interactive, since the transmission is mostly character by character, though pasted in words or blocks of characters can also be transmitted. SMS and IM by contrast transmit whole (though usually short) messages after using a send command. Users of IM are familiar with waiting for the other side, while the "is typing" information is displayed.

Presence is a useful feature that can be used in relation to real-time calls as well as to messaging exchange.

ToIP requires very simple software in SIP user agents and is therefore proposed to be included in all SIP telephony devices.[4]

---

[4] "SIP Telephony Device Requirements and Configuration," by H. Sinnreich. Internet Draft, IETF January 2005, work in progress.

The RTP Payload for Text Conversation

ToIP can be used alone or with other media such as video and voice, to support multimedia conversation services. Text in multimedia conversation sessions is sent character by character as soon as it is available, or with a small delay for buffering.

The text is intended to be entered by human users from a keyboard, handwriting recognition, voice recognition or any other input method. The speed of character entry is usually of a few characters per second or less. Only one or a few new characters are expected to be transmitted with each packet. Small blocks of text may be prepared by the user and pasted into the user interface for transmission during the conversation, occasionally causing packets to carry a slightly bigger payload.

The RTP payload for text conversation was first standardized in RFC 2793 and is under revision in the I-D RFC 2793 bis.[5] It is based in part on other standards for defining characters such as ISO 10646-1[6] code and UTF-8[7] and also in the T.140 text conversation protocol[8] standard.

ToIP is defined as an RTP payload designed to support the arrival of single encoded UTF-8 characters in correct order, without duplication and with detection and indication of loss.

The RTP payload format for ToIP is:

text/t140

An example of SDP describing RTP text transport on port 11000 appears as follows:

```
m=text 11000 RTP/AVP 98
a=rtpmap:98 t140/1000
```

Protection against loss of data is mainly based on using the sequence numbers of the RTP packets. Missing sequence numbers are used to detect lost packets at the reception point. Various redundancy techniques can be used to protect against data loss. One main method for protection from

---

5 "RTP Payload for Text Conversation (RFC 2793bis)," by G. Hellstrom and P. Jones. IETF, August 2004, waiting for publication.

6 ISO/IEC 10646-1: (1993), Universal Multiple Octet Coded Character Set.

7 Yergeau, F., "UTF-8, a transformation format of ISO 10646," RFC 3629, December 2003.

8 ITU-T Recommendation T.140 (1998)—Text Conversation Protocol for multimedia application, with Amendment 1, (2000).

loss is to use redundancy according to RFC 2198. This is the default, specified in rfc2793bis on RTP payload for text conversation.

Based on the information in the received packets, the receiver can:

- Reorder text received out of order.
- Mark where text is missing because of packet loss.
- Compensate for lost packets by using redundant data.

Experience has shown that an average character transmission rate during a complete session is around 2 characters per second. The data rate can, however, be quite variable, for example if redundancy is used and the typing speed is 10 characters per second, the data rate can be around 3000 bit/s.[5]

The software required to implement ToIP is very minimal in size and complexity. For this reason it is recommended as best practice for SIP telephony devices to support ToIP.[4]

Transcoding Services

Hearing or speech disabled individuals or deaf-blind people using a Braille-style display may find it impossible to establish a communication session due to their own disability or due to incompatible media capabilities in the user agents. Transcoding services, also called relay services can solve this problem by inserting an intermediary that does the necessary transcoding so as to enable communications between the parties.

Discovery of the capabilities of the remote party is also an important capability when using transcoding services. For example, before establishing a session between a deaf party A and another party B, party A may for example use the SIP options method and find out that party B has a SIP telephony device that can support ToIP as well and thus communicate directly with each other. Should this not be the case, an intermediary can be invoked to act as a transcoding service. The text box on the next page discloses some general issues concerning intermediaries.

Invoking a transcoding service (labeled T for further use here) between two parties A and B involves establishing two media sessions:

Media between A and T

Media between T and B

Note on Intermediaries

Intermediaries are a contentious subject on the Internet: Intermediaries can perform many useful services in the network, but may at the same time produce even more damage to security, can block new services, may deteriorate performance and could hurt various applications. For these reasons, intermediaries, if they cannot be avoided, have to meet the requirements for Open Pluggable End Services (OPES) articulated in RFC 3238.

For transcoding services at least the following recommendation applies:

One-party consent: *The use of any OPES service be explicitly authorized by one of the application-layer end-hosts (that is, either the content provider or the client).*

There are two possible models for invoking a transcoding intermediary T: Use a central conference bridge model or use the 3rd party call control (3pcc) model.[9] We show one example for each model. In the examples the following terminology is used:

SDP A: A session description generated by A. It contains the media description and transport address, (IP address and port number) where A wants to receive media for each particular stream.

SDP B: A session description generated by B. It contains the media description and the transport address where B wants to receive media for each particular stream.

SDP A+B: A session description that contains the media description and the transport address where A wants to receive media and the transport address(es) where B wants to receive media. Note: While we refer here to one single transport address, multiple transport addresses can also be used.

SDP TA: A session description generated by T and intended for A. It contains the media description and the transport address where T wants to receive media from A.

---

[9] "Transcoding Services Invocation in the Session Initiation Protocol." by G. Camarillo, et al. Internet Draft, IETF, Feb. 2003, work in progress.

SDP TB: A session description generated by T and intended for B. It contains the media description and the transport address where T wants to receive media from B.

SDP TA and TB: A description of where T wants to receive media given (originally) to A.

Conference Bridge Model for Transcoding

In this model the transcoding service acts like a centralized conference bridge and we can think that for a two-way communication the bridge provides a conferencing service between two participants. Two different scenarios are possible:

Transcoding invoked by the calling party
Transcoding invoked by the called party (callee)

The example in Figure 10.3 shows the high level call flows for the scenario where the calling party A invokes the transcoding service T.

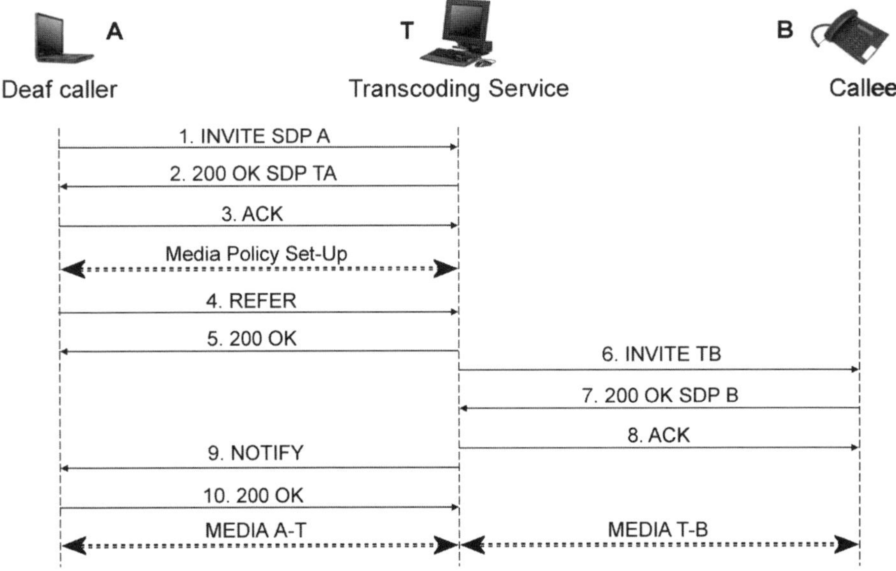

Figure 10.3 – Caller A invokes a transcoding service T (conference bridge model)

In this model, the transcoding service is set up the same way as a conference,[10] see also Chapter 6. The media policy for the session is set up similar to the conference policy. A media policy could specify for example outgoing voice and incoming text for the deaf party A and voice in both directions between T and called party B.

The message sequence in Figure 10.3 is as follows:

- The caller A dials into the conference bridge T (messages 1 to 3)
- The caller A sets up the media policy with T
- Caller A refers T to the called party B (messages 4-5)
- The conference bridge T 'dials out' to party B (messages 6-8)
- T notifies party A that B has accepted the call (messages 9-10)
- Media flows between A-T and T-B to support the transcoded service.

3rd Party Call Control Model for Transcoding

In this scenario the calling party A uses 3rd party call control (3pcc) for the transcoding intermediary T and also for the called party B. The advantage of this approach is that only the user agent A of the deaf person needs to support 3pcc capabilities and does not need to assume any special SIP capabilities for either T or B. As is common with 3pcc, there are some security concerns for T and B that may however be addressed if the network provides the calling party ID.

It is also possible for the called party to use 3pcc to invoke the transcoding service T if it knows that the incoming call is from a disabled user or if the caller speaks a language that the called party does not understand and desires a translation service to continue the call. In Figure 10.4 we show however only the scenario where the caller invokes the translation service T.

In this example, the deaf user A wants to determine what media will be used in both sessions between A-T and T-B, so the call control is slightly different than what can be found in examples given by others.[11]

---

[10] "A framework for conferencing with the Session Initiation Protocol" by J. Rosenberg. Internet Draft, Internet Engineering Task Force, Nov. 2002, work in progress.

[11] RFC 3725: "Best current practices for third party call control in the Session Initiation Protocol," by J. Rosenberg, et al. IETF, April 2004.

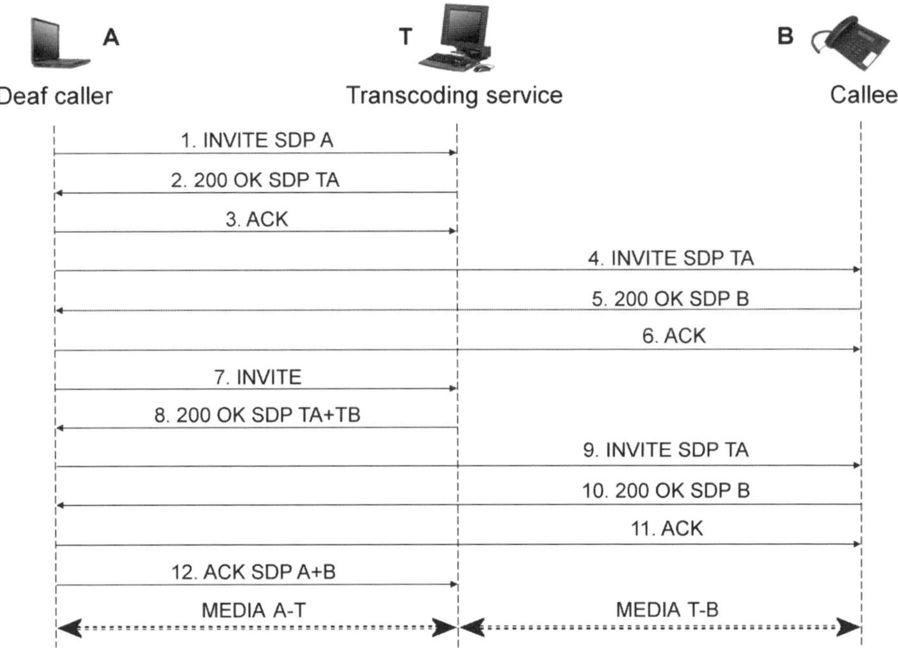

Figure 10.4 – Caller A uses 3rd party call control to invoke a transcoding service T

Here the UA A specifies its session description in SDP in the first INVITE, in contrast to the media-less SDP in the original 3pcc examples of Rosenberg.[11]

The message sequence in Figure 10.4 is as follows:

- A invites T (message 1) and communicates its media in SDP A , for example ToIP outgoing and voice using the iLBC codec for the incoming media. It also stores the media capabilities received from T in message 2, for example, the audio codec that T can support.
- A invites B and communicates the media capabilities of T. It stores the media capabilities and other SDP data from B (messages 4-6).
- As is characteristic for 3pcc, A re-invites T using the SDP media capabilities from B in its SDP data. T confirms it can support the media for the A-T leg and the T-B leg.
- A re-invites B and sends to B the media description from T.
- A sends the ACK (message 12) to T with the SDP data for media and the transport addresses for A and B.
- Finally, both T and B believe they talk to A, but T talks not only to A (the 3pcc controller), but also to B.

Transcoding Services in Parallel

Transcoding services in parallel are useful in some scenarios, such as:

- An automated transcoding service, where a machine in one direction performs text to speech conversion and another machine performs voice recognition (speech to text) in the other direction.
- Two different human relays are used for the different directions, so as to avoid one single person to have access to both directions of a sensitive private conversation.

Figure 10.5 shows the media sessions when using two different transcoders T1 and T2 for the different directions in one conversation.

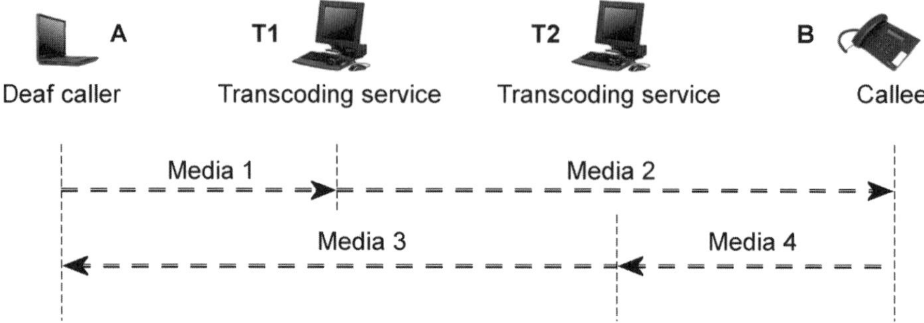

Figure 10.5 – Transcoding services in parallel

For decisions on invoking transcoding services, it is also feasible to issue media preferences at registration time, and let this preference influence service invocation.

Readers interested in more detailed examples and call flows for transcoding services should consult the T.140 ITU-T Recommendation.[9]

Conclusions on Accessibility to Communications Using SIP

We have seen that accessibility to communications for users with disabilities can include various scenarios such as transcoding services, media content providers, emergency calls and conference calls.

Accessibility requirements can be quite complex and include the need for various media types as well as the normal need for confidentiality.

Communication modes and tools include Text over IP (ToIP), sign language interface, synthetic lip speaking, voice activated menus and other. ToIP is a specific new media type on the Internet used for accessibility. Interactive text conversation is a specific communication mode that should not be confused with instant messaging.

Transcoding services for people with disabilities can be invoked using SIP in various call control models, such as by using either the conference model or the 3rd party call control model. The examples illustrate how SIP-based Internet communications are ideally suited to support accessibility to communications by disabled persons.

The availability of all three media of video, text and voice provides an opportunity to communicate in any suitable mode directly in a manner that suits the communication participants. It increases accessibility to a large extent as compared to the classical single media services. Thus, SIP-based services provide a good platform for accessible communication for people with disabilities as well as for all others.

Chapter 11

Internet Customer Care – A Holistic Approach

Introduction

In consumer to business, the telephone call center is the most important link between any business and its customers. The customer experience when calling a 1-800 or free-phone number (name often used outside the US) shapes the impression and confidence of customers. Telephony call centers are therefore rightly considered the most critical telecommunications resource of a business in dealing with customers. Telephony call centers use the following building blocks:

- PBX and/or large circuit switch.
- Interactive voice response (IVR) systems.
- Voice recognition and voice browsing based on VoiceXML are IP-based.
- Automatic call distributor (ACD).
- Computer Telephony Integration[1] (CTI) to integrate communications with applications. The use of CTI in call centers dates back to the early 1980's and CTI is still the core of circuit switch call center technology.
- Distinct call management systems for internal and external communications.
- Information technology (IT) systems.

Call centers are often geographically distributed across the country or on a global scale for the following reasons:

- Call routing depends on the time convenient to the call center (time zone).
- Small call center teams or individual agents that are working from home.
- Outsourcing of call centers across the globe. This is an especially significant development, since outsourcing may reduce the cost substantially.

At present, the legacy PSTN is used almost exclusively to place calls from a customer to the call center and within call centers. VoIP is barely emerging as an option for internal telephony in the call center. Some call centers are using besides telephony email as well, and IM internally too, but telephony, IP communications and IT systems are not integrated.

---

[1] *Computer Telephony Integration*, by William Yarberry. 2nd edition, CRC Press, 2003. ISBN 0-8493-1438-0.

As we will show in this chapter, PSTN telephony network routing and legacy call centers (1) provide a very poor customer experience, (2) require costly PSTN network resources and (2) require a costly call center infrastructure. Given the huge market for consumer to business communications, we believe this is about to change and we will examine some generic aspects of moving this traffic from the PSTN to IP and to transform call centers into Internet customer care (CC).

The Customer Experience

The poor customer experience on the PSTN is probably the greatest incentive to migrate all consumers to business communications to the Internet.

Table 11.1 – Customer experience on the PSTN and on the Internet

TDM Switching Experience	Internet Experience
Voice only	Web and IP multimedia
PSTN Scenario: ▪ Look up phone number ▪ Call an 800/freephone number ▪ *Navigate a multilevel menu* ▪ *Musing on hold* ▪ *Speak to an agent* ▪ *Transfer of call, more than once* ▪ *Sometimes get a disconnect* ▪ *Call again, menu, wait, etc.* ▪ Talk to agent, take notes, etc. Make purchase	Internet Scenario: ▪ Search the web ▪ Examine web pages and ads ▪ See agent presence and queue ▪ Click to connect ▪ Secure IM, voice and web share Make purchase

The comparison in Table 11.1 between the customer experiences on the PSTN is self explanatory. The PSTN has the following drawbacks:

- Comparison shopping requires too many PSTN calls to be effective.
- The interactive voice response (IVR) menus, long touted as an advanced voice technology, when combined with music on hold and disconnects are nothing short of a punishment and disincentive for the customer.

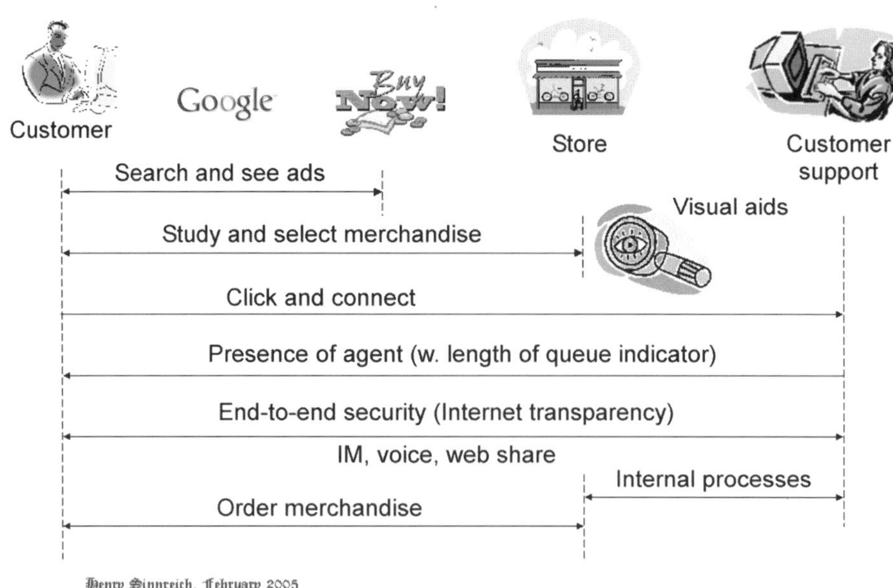

Figure 11.1 – The customer experience on Internet contact with business

By contrast, the customer experience in an all Internet environment is shown in Figure 11.1.

In the case of shoppers, the emerging technologies for visualization allow the shopper to visualize the discovered information, so as to better make sense of it.[2] Visual aids enhance the competitiveness of both the search engine deployed as well as those of the selected web sites, and is believed to be an increasingly valuable technology for Internet customer acquisition and customer care.

Note the following distinctions of the Internet model for consumer to business communications:

- Use of web searching to find the objects of interest.
- Comparison shopping requires little effort. Visual aids may help.
- Merchandise value can be examined without pressure.

---

[2] "Visualization Strategies end Tools for Enhanced Customer Relations Management" by S. Ganapathy, et al. *Communications of the ACM*, November. 2004, p. 93-99.

- Check on agent presence and length of queue before to click to connect.
- Automatic call back by the agent is an option.
- IM and voice can support clear communications and logs of transactions.
- Both the customer and the agent can multiplex their work using IM.
- IM allows an agent to communicate with several customers at the same time, thus enhancing productivity.

Broadband Internet access is preferable, but where not available this is not necessarily a show stopper. IM and low bit rate voice codecs may work acceptably even on dialup lines with only 40 kb/s data rates.

As with all other applications on the Internet, the extent of the disruption of the traditional call center industry is hard to envisage, given that many inventions have still to happen. Figure 11.1 can give however already an astonishing insight: The first action of a user who may need customer support may by to use a web search engine, such as Google.

Internet End-to-End Transparency is Strictly Required

Note also that both (1) secure end-to-end communications between the customer and agent and also (2) the application dependent detailed message flows (not shown here) require end-to-end transparency over the Internet. Customers having Internet access through intermediaries, such as Session Border Controllers may find they cannot communicate adequately with a CC application, since the intermediary may or may not understand the CC application in the UA, where special UA are deployed, its messages and state machines.

Network Aspects for PSTN and Internet CC

The network aspects of call center and CC are summarized in Table 11.2.

The comparison in Table 11.2 is self explanatory and makes one wonder how long the PSTN may still be used for consumer to business communications. We offer here some explanations:

- Internet penetration is still not 100% as compared to the PSTN.
- The loss of revenue is strongly resisted by phone companies.
- The early write off for the huge PSTN installed base for call center routing is probably also resisted by phone companies.

Table 11.2 – Call routing and call control comparison between the PSTN and the Internet

Circuit Switched Telephony	Internet Call Control
Separate Carrier and Call Center Routing Carrier call routing ▪ Intelligent Network Control ▪ 800/freephone numbers are location dependent ▪ Dedicated capacity/trunks for each CC and each application/ product ▪ Moving calls between CCs require special telephony trunk pairs. One single call requires many switch ports in the PSTN networks. ▪ Complex IT dependencies between LD and local phone networks. CC/enterprise call routing PBX and automatic call distributor (ACD).	Integrated call control using SIP on the public Internet and in the CC/enterprise ▪ SIP call control ▪ URLs have global meaning ▪ No dedicated capacity ▪ Lower bandwidth requirements ▪ Caller preferences, such as "I will not talk to an IVR!" ▪ SIP certification of identity ▪ End-to-end security.

Internet access by cable companies and 3G/4G wireless networks may however accelerate the migration to Internet CC usage.

Internet Customer Care Architecture

After examining in the previous section the public network aspects of business to consumer communications, let's also take a brief look how voice-based call centers are impacted by the Internet. We make a distinction between

- The impact of the Internet and an all-IP design, and
- The impact of IP technology that may be already used in a spotty manner inside PSTN connected call centers.

Table 11.3 – Comparison between TDM call center and Internet CC architecture

TDM technology	All-IP design
▪ PBX for circuit switching ▪ IVR for customer guidance ▪ ACD for call routing to agents ▪ CTI for telephony applications ▪ Multiple protocols: H.1xx, S.1xx, H.32x, etc. ▪ Distinct communication systems o With the PSTN outside o Internal call routing ▪ Complex external/internal call routing ▪ CTI and IP agent workstation ▪ Distinct IT systems and complex interworking.	End-to-end and multi-party SIP call control ▪ SIP events ▪ SIP presence ▪ IM, voice and document sharing ▪ Embedded conferencing ▪ IP agent workstation application ▪ Integrated IT is possible ▪ SIP and IM logs can serve for auditing and archiving.

Table 11.3 is also self explanatory, so we would only like to note the fact that SIP events and SIP presence enable context aware communications and seamless integration of communications and applications, as discussed in Chapter 5.

Conclusions

Though telephony call centers have started to deploy VoIP and even SIP, the partial deployment is far from reaching the full potential of Internet customer care. By contrast, customer acquisition and customer care on the Internet have a completely different model, where a voice call may be mostly avoided, or if unavoidable, has to be part the positive user experience when looking for an answer on the Internet.

Telephony style call centers must therefore go far beyond partial inside deployment of VoIP and migrate to the Internet service models for customer care. SIP applications beyond VoIP are part of this migration.

Chapter 12

SIP Security

Introduction

Our daily experience with file transfer, email and the Web is a good start for envisaging the advantages of open global communications over the Internet. It also points out the challenges posed by the required security when using the Internet. Real time Internet communications based on SIP have the added complexity that SIP signaling packets and RTP media packets may use different paths across the network, several transport protocols (UDP, TCP, TLS) and a large number of ports for the corresponding transport addresses (a transport address is defined as the combination of IP address and port number). This fact points to the need of more complex security technologies and also more challenges for NAT and firewall traversal than required for the familiar FTP, messaging protocols and HTTP.

The vulnerabilities for Internet communications are not yet fully explored, since this is an emerging industry. But there is no doubt that malicious people will find ways to stage various attacks, such as denial of service (DOS), stealing and misuse of URLs and VoIP phone numbers for such purposes as telemarketing, spam, impersonation, illegal intercept of communications and, last but not least, determining the private IP addresses behind NAT and firewalls of private networks connected to the Internet for other exploits.

NATs and firewalls are used to help protect private IP networks, but they pose many challenges to Internet communications. NAT and firewalls usually block both SIP signaling and RTP media packets, so that special technologies are required for NAT and firewall traversal for Internet communications.

We will show that a complete solution for security and NAT/firewall traversal require adequate support by protocol design, in the SIP endpoints (phones, IP-PSTN gateways), in the NAT itself and in dedicated network servers. The overall system design for security has also to include such services as proving the identity of the participants.

Hoping that buying a single "box" can solve the security and NAT/firewall traversal issues is very dangerous and purveyors of such solutions in a box are quite guilty in our opinion of misleading their customers. The proliferation in the market of various "solutions in a box" has been an incentive for the authors to write about the security challenges for Internet communications.

SIP Security and Identity

This section will go over the basics of SIP security and identity mechanisms. Starting with the SIP trapezoid model, simple authentication approaches such as HTTP Digest will be explained. Next the Secure SIP or sips URI scheme will be introduced and the use of TLS transport for authorization and confidentiality will be covered. A simple SIP identity approach suitable for closed trusted networks will be discussed in the Network Asserted Identity section. Finally, more robust Internet suitable identity schemes such as the SIP Authenticated Identity Body (AIB), the SIP Identity header field and the use of certificates for global interdomain communications will be discussed.

The Trapezoid Model

The trapezoid model, as introduced in Chapter 1, is the basic interdomain structure for SIP networks. As shown in Figure 1.2 of Chapter 1, each domain has a SIP server that provides services for the SIP User Agents within the domain. Incoming and outgoing requests to and from the domain are routed through these SIP servers. They provide a place where authentication can be performed and policy can be enforced, especially if these SIP servers are coupled with a firewall function which blocks unauthorized communications. Mapping from private address spaces to public address spaces can be performed here as well if required. If the use of a media relay is required (due to security or logging requirements, for example), this server can control the media relay.

It is assumed that each domain authenticates the User Agents within the domain. As such, we will see how it is natural for this SIP server to make various assertions about identity within that domain. Since the basic identity in SIP is a SIP URI, SIP identity assertions are about SIP URIs, usually Address of Record (AOR) URIs. It is possible for a SIP network to assert another identity, for example an E.164 telephone number. However, the differences between the Internet and PSTN addressing spaces makes it virtually impossible to securely validate such an assertion without requiring transitive trust between the private IP network and the PSTN.

Digest Authentication

Digest authentication is a simple authentication mechanism that SIP borrowed from HTTP and must be supported by all SIP User Agents. It allows a SIP provider to issue a shared secret to a SIP User Agent, and allows the User Agent to provide a hash of this shared secret to the provider's server upon challenge without transporting the secret in the clear. The shared secret is only provided as part of a Message Digest (MD) hash, the exact algorithm known as MD5. Upon receipt of a SIP request, a SIP Server can challenge a UA using a 407 Proxy Authentication Required or 401 Unauthorized response code. This challenge includes a nonce, which is to be used by the UA to perform the hash. The UA performs the MD5 hash across the shared secret (and important SIP header fields) using the provided nonce and returned in a Proxy-Authorization or WWW-Authentication header field. The Server calculates the MD5 hash over the same set of values, and if the hash matches that provided by the client, the authentication is successful. It is extremely difficult to reverse the direction of the hash—that is, go from the MD5 hash to the shared secret. SIP digest authentication provides strong cryptographic security.

This simple shared secret challenge/response mechanism is useful within a domain for authorizing registration, or access to resources such as PSTN gateways or conferencing bridges. However, requiring proxies to share secrets with each other is clearly not a useful authentication approach for use on the open Internet.

Digest authentication provides replay protection (through the use of nonces), and can provide integrity protection over the bodies of SIP requests. It does not provide any integrity protection of the SIP header fields. TLS or S/MIME can be used to protect that part of the message.

An example Digest response header is shown below:

```
Proxy-Authorization: DIGEST username="joe",
  realm="example.com",
  nonce="f9d26bd9c4766eacd3101d8d2dc5f38d.1087694984",
  uri="sip:913145551212@example.com",
  response="fe1545a816d698b993b83bade8428c0f"
```

In this example, realm and nonce were provided by the challenging server, which in this case is in the example.com domain. The presence of the realm domain allows a UA to be provisioned with a number of sets of credentials, and the appropriate one provided based on the realm of the challenge. The username is carried in the clear to allow the server to lookup the appropriate shared secret; the URI is the Request-URI of the request. The response contains the actual MD5 hash.

Secure SIP and TLS

The Secure SIP or sips URI scheme was introduced in SIP in RFC 3261[1] to provide message protection capabilities beyond what was available in the first SIP specification RFC 2543.[2] SIPS extends SIP in an analogous way that Secure HTTP, HTTPS extends HTTP. The use of the sips URI scheme requires that TLS[3] transport be used at each hop, although a possible exemption is given on the last hop, provided it is secured using some other mechanism.

The use of TLS transport provides two key properties to SIP. It provides confidentiality and integrity protection using hop by hop encryption. It also allows the use of certificates for authentication, as the certificates can be exchanged during the TLS connection setup. The host names and the assertions in the certificate can be compared to the identity in the SIP request for authorization.

The TLS handshake is shown in Figure 12.1. An example of a Secure SIP message is shown beginning below:

```
INVITE sips:4443333@gw1.a.example.com SIP/2.0
 Via: SIP/2.0/TLS ss1.a.example.com:5061;branch=z9hG4bK2d4790.1
 Via: SIP/2.0/TLS client.a.example.com:5061;branch=z9hG4bK74bf9
 ;received=192.0.2.101
 Max-Forwards: 69
 Record-Route: <sips:ss1.a.example.com;lr>
 From: Alice <sips:+13145551111@ss1.a.example.com;user=phone>
 ;tag=9fxced76sl
 To: Carol <sips:+19185553333@ss1.a.example.com;user=phone>
 Call-ID: 2xTb9vxSit55XU7p8@a.example.com
 CSeq: 2 INVITE
 Contact: <sips:alice@client.a.example.com>
Content-Type: application/sdp
 Content-Length: 154
```

---

[1] RFC 3261: "SIP: Session Initiation Protocol," by J. Rosenberg, H. Schulzrinne, G. Camarillo, A. Johnston, J. Peterson, R. Sparks, M. Handley, E. Schooler. IETF, June 2002.

[2] RFC 2543: "SIP: Session Initiation Protocol," by M. Handley, H. Schulzrinne, E. Schooler, J. Rosenberg. March 1999.

[3] RFC 2246: "The TLS Protocol Version 1.0," by T. Dierks and C. Allen. IETF, January 1999.

```
v=0
o=alice 2890844526 2890844526 IN IP4 client.a.example.com
s=-
c=IN IP4 client.a.example.com
t=0 0
m=audio 49172 RTP/AVP 0
a=rtpmap:0 PCMU/8000
```

In this message, note the presence of the TLS transport identifier in the Via header field, the sips URI schemes in the To, From, and Contact URIs and in the Request-URI.

Secure SIP uses the well known port of 5061, and must be supported by proxy servers. User Agents may support Secure SIP.

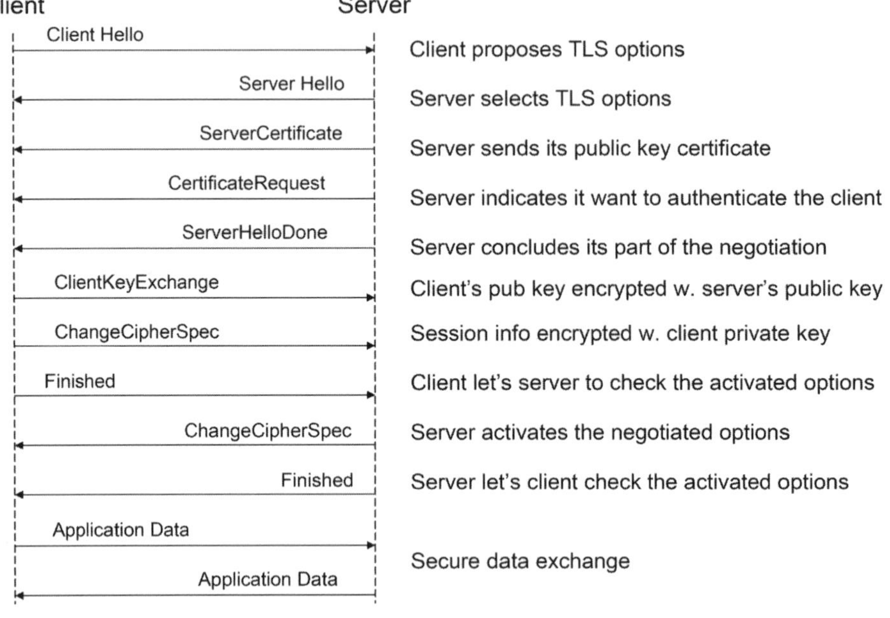

Figure 12.1 – TLS Version 1.0

Unlike https:, secure SIP using the sips: URI scheme *only* protects the message hop-by-hop, and each intermediary must be trusted to do the right thing. Any proxy in the path of a sips: protected message can see, copy, and even modify the message unless other protection mechanisms are also employed.

SIP Identity

The basic SIP specification contains identity information in the From header field. However, like email, From URIs can be arbitrarily populated in a SIP request by a UA. Identity over a single hop can be verified using TLS, but a SIP request may be forwarded by a set of intermediaries before reaching the destination. As a result, a number of enhanced identity schemes have been developed for SIP and are detailed in the following sections.

Network Asserted Identity

This section describes the use of the P-Asserted-Identity SIP header field, as defined by RFC 3325.[4] This approach, known as Network Asserted Identity, is suitable for identity only within a trust domain. An example of a trust domain is shown in Figure 12.2.

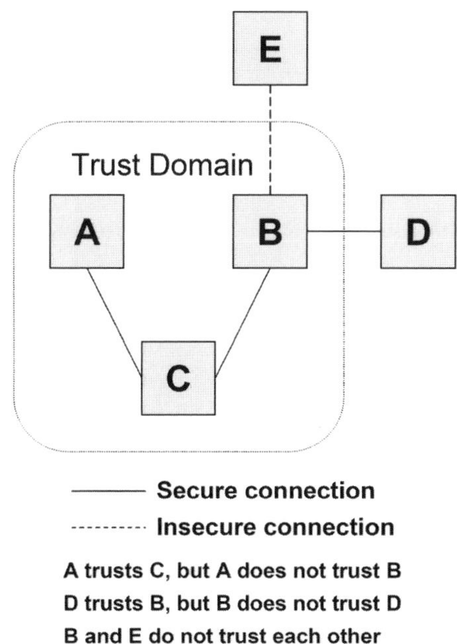

Figure 12.2 – Trust Domain Example

[4] RFC 3325: "Private Extensions to the Session Initiation Protocol (SIP) for Asserted Identity within Trusted Networks," by C. Jennings, J. Peterson, M. Watson. IETF, November 2002.

In a SIP network, a Proxy server may insert a P-Asserted-Identity header field in a request it forwards inside its trust domain indicating the identity of the requestor. A Proxy server receiving a P-Asserted-Identity header field in a request may accept the identity provided it was received from a proxy within its own trust circle.

Looking at Figure 12.2, since A and B do not trust each other, they would remove or ignore P-Asserted-Identity header fields sent by the other. However, if the request was routed through C, whom they both trust, they would accept the P-Asserted-Identity. Since E is not trusted by any of the other networks, a P-Asserted-Identity header field would never be sent or received by E.

Example P-Asserted Identity header fields are shown below:

```
P-Asserted-Identity: "Alice" <sip:alice@atlanta.example.com>
 P-Asserted-Identity: tel:+19725551212
```

Authenticated Identity Body (AIB)

The SIP Authenticated Identity Body[5] is an approach to SIP identity that utilizes the SIP trapezoid and multiparty MIME to deliver a cryptographically secure identity object with a SIP request.

Carrying identity information in a message body is problematic in two ways:

1. A simple SIP request with a message body (such as an INVITE with SDP) turns into a request with a multiparty MIME body, which not all currently deployed UAs can support.
2. Since proxies likely won't share the keying material needed to decrypt an AIB, the identity information is not always available for request routing decisions.
3. Identity information can not be inserted by a proxy since they can not add message bodies to a request. For an AIB to be inserted by a third party server, the request must first be sent to the server, which then redirects with the AIB, then the UA sends the same requests plus the AIB to the recipient.

[5] RFC 3893: "The Session Initiation Protocol (SIP) Authenticated Identity Body (AIB)," by J. Peterson. IETF, September 2004.

These problems have led to the development of a similar identity object but carried in a header field where it can be inspected and inserted by proxies as described in the next section.

Identity Header Field

A more recent approach uses a new Identity and Identity-Info header field.[6] The Identity header field contains a cryptographic signature validating the identity in the From header field and including the following header fields: Contact, Date, Call-ID, CSeq To, and From. These header fields are chosen to prevent the Identity header field from being replayed for different calls or by different UAs.

The Identity-Info header field contains a URL in which the certificate can be downloaded.

An example is shown below (although the identity signature would be all one line).

```
Identity: nAkHrH3ntmaxgr01TMxTmtjP7MASwliNRdupRI1vpkXRvZXx1ja9knB2
W+v1PDsy32MaqZiOM5WfEkXxbgTnPYW0jIoK8HMyY1VT7egt0kk4XrKFCHYWGCl
sM9CG4hq+YJZTMaSROoMUBhikVIjnQ8ykeD6UXNOyfI=
Identity-Info: https://example.com/cert
```

A typical call flow is shown in detail in Figure 12.3 which has the following steps:

1. UA A generates SIP request and responds with MD5 hash of username password when challenged by Proxy A.
2. Proxy A challenges the request using SIP digest to authenticate UA A. If successful, then it adds and signs the Identity header with Proxy's A private key and forwards the request to Proxy B.
3. UA B fetches certificate of Proxy A using URI in Identity-Info and uses it to validate caller identity URI in the Identity header.
4. UA B begins alerting user after UA A's identity is validated.

[6] Peterson, J. and Jennings, C., "Enhancements for Authenticated Identity Management in the Session Initiation Protocol (SIP)." IETF Internet-Drafts, March 2002.

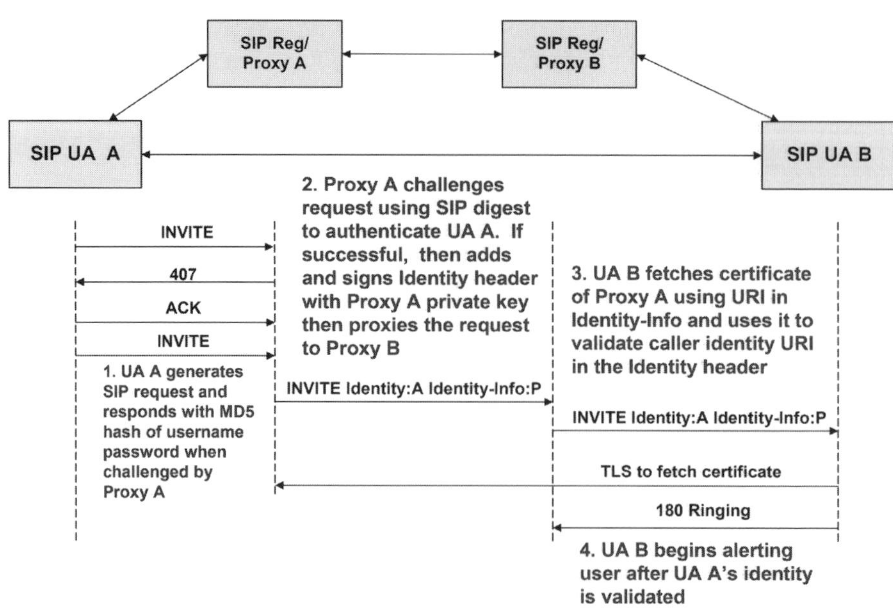

Figure 12.3 – Interdomain SIP identity

Certificate Management Service for SIP

The use of certificates by SIP servers such as proxy servers is very similar to the way certificates are used by web servers on the web today. A given domain, example.com, will get one certificate for each proxy server used to route interdomain SIP requests. This certificate will be presented during the TLS handshake with other SIP servers in other domains. Within the domain, UAs registering or being challenged can also view this certificate to ensure that they are connected to a valid server for the domain and not a server spoofing the domain.

These certificates can be identical to the standard e-commerce certificates supported today by web browsers (checking the security settings on your web browser will show you which certificate authorities the browser supports).

It is also possible that a UA could have an e-commerce certificate and use it in a similar way to a server. However, at hundreds of dollars per year, this is not a scalable approach for networks of thousands and even millions of UAs.

The alternative is for UAs to use self-signed certificates. This way, the only cost is that of creating the certificate. There are two models in which self-signed certificates are useful. One is the "leap of faith" approach used in SSH (Secure Shell) today; the other is a certificate server hosted by the domain of the UA.

The "leap of faith" approach is commonly used in SSH today. The first time a successful session is established with a UA, the user can confirm (using non-technical means, such as the sound of someone's voice, or their image) the other user's identity, the current certificate can be stored and used next time. This provides assurance that at least you are communicating with the same UA as before. This can even be useful within a single session. For example, a UA can confirm that the BYE received to terminate the session was sent by the same UA as the one that established the session by sending an INVITE.

The certificate server is a relatively new approach being developed by the SACRED Working Group in the IETF. The work has been applied to SIP[7] and results in the architecture shown in Figure 12.4. A UA generates a self-signed certificate which is uploaded to a certificate server in the same domain. Whenever the UA uses the self-signed certificate in a request, it provides a URL which points to the certificate server for that domain (that is, if the identity is sip:joe@example.com, then the URL of the certificate server must also be in the example.com domain—otherwise there is no strength in the assertion). A recipient can then fetch the certificate and use it to authenticate the other UA.

An example is shown in Figure 12.4. The steps are as follows:

UA B generates and publishes a self-signed certificate with its Certificate Server. A TLS connection is opened with the Certificate Server, and UA B validates the certificate of the Certificate Server. The Certificate Server challenges UA B using SIP Digest and validates UA B's credentials. The PUBLISH method is used to upload the certificate using the credential event package.

Other UAs under the control of B can SUBSCRIBE and receive a NOTIFY with this certificate and private key.

UA A wants to establish a secure session with UA B. A one time encryption key is exchanged using an S/MIME message body. To get the certificate of UA B, UA A sends a SUBSCRIBE with event package certificate to the Credential Server for UA B. The SUBSCRIBE is sent over a TLS connection,

---

[7] "Certificate Management Service for The Session Initiation Protocol (SIP)," by C. Jennings and J. Peterson. Internet Draft, IETF, February 2005. Work in progress.

and UA A is able to validate the certificate of the Credential Server. The certificate of UA B is sent in a NOTIFY over the TLS connection.

UA A uses the certificate to encrypt the S/MIME message body and sends the INVITE to UA B.

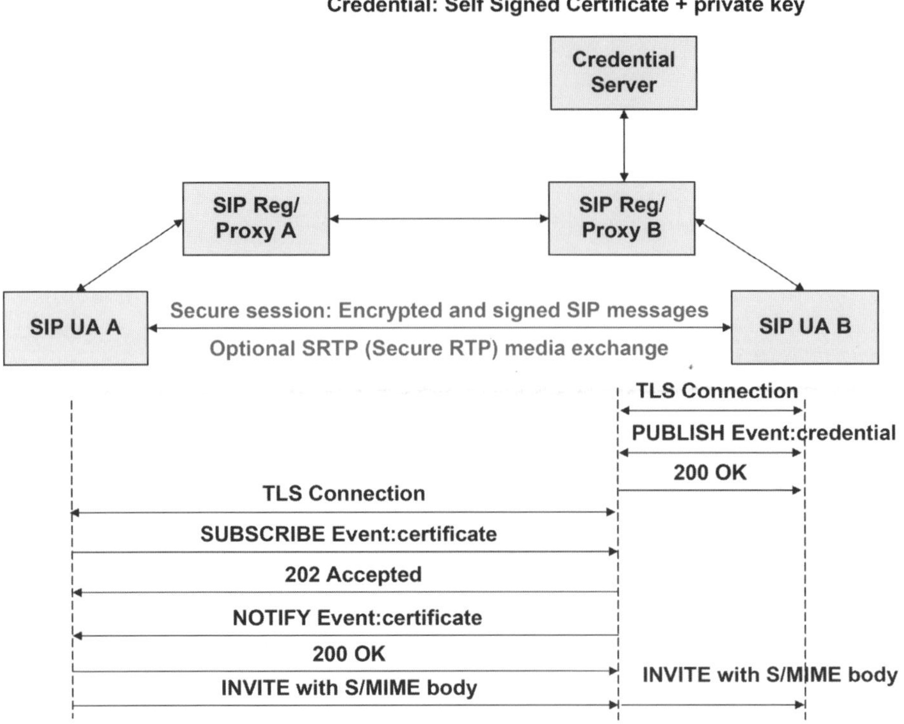

Figure 12.4 – Certificate management in SIP

Conclusion

This chapter discusses several security mechanisms for SIP. SIP provides authentication mechanisms such as Digest authentication and the use of certificates. Certifcates can be used between SIP proxies or can be provided for one-time use to the UA by the outgoing SIP proxy and verified at the destination SIP proxy or UA.

Chapter 13

NAT and Firewall Traversal

Introduction

Network Address Translators (NATs) and Firewalls are common elements in IP networks today, and a communication protocol such as SIP must be able to traverse them, and establish media streams that traverse them as well.

Early approaches to NAT and Firewall traversal used ALGs (Application Layer Gateways) that coupled the signaling and media and relayed both. While such devices are widely used today, they break the end-to-end nature of the SIP and media sessions, rendering many of the security approaches described in Chapter 12 ineffective.

This chapter describes Internet friendly end-to-end approaches to NAT and Firewall traversal using protocols such as STUN, TURN, and ICE.

NAT and Firewall Traversal

Firewalls

Firewalls are a rather complex topic that is outside the scope of this book. However, in order to explain the necessary techniques for SIP-based Internet communications to deal with firewalls, we provide here a short summary of the basics, in the form of a Q&A table (see Table 13.1). Interested readers are referred to the references for further reading.[1, 2]

Network Address Translators

The need to route packets between private IP networks and the public Internet has led to the standardization of the address allocation in private networks in RFC 1918.[3] Private IP networks have three address ranges assigned by the Internet Assigned Numbers Authority (IANA). The address ranges are:

10.0.0.0 to 10.255.255.255, 10/8 prefix, 24-bit block, one Class A address
172.16.0.0 to 172.31.255.255, 172.16/12 prefix, 20-bit block
192.168.0.0 to 192.168.255.255, 192.168/16 prefix, 16-bit block

---

[1] *Firewalls and Internet Security: Repelling the Wily Hacker*, by W. Cheswik, S. Bellovin and A. Rubin. W. Addison-Wesley Professional; 2nd edition (February 24, 2003). ISBN: 020163466X.

[2] RFC 3511: "Benchmarking Methodology for Firewall Performance," by B. Hickmann, et. al. IETF, April 2003.

[3] RFC 1918: "Address Allocation for Private Internets," by Y. Rekhter, et al. IETF, February 1996.

Table 13.1 – Questions and Answers Concerning Firewalls

What is a firewall?	Firewalls are network elements placed at the edge of private IP networks and the Internet, or between segments of private IP networks. Personal firewalls are also deployed for PCs and laptops. Firewalls implement a control policy for both permitting traffic and blocking traffic, according to well defined rules. The most basic policy is usually to permit all traffic originated from inside the private IP network to flow outside and permit only those outside packets to flow inside, if they are in response to outgoing packets from some application protocol, such as SMTP, FTP, HTTP, SIP, RTP, etc. Firewalls can act as packet filters, looking at each packet at a time for making the forwarding decision, or can perform a stateful inspection that takes into account the history for certain packet flows. A firewall that is not SIP-aware will likely block incoming SIP INVITE messages, thus blocking all incoming calls. Incoming RTP media packets will also be blocked.
Why use firewalls?	Firewalls protect, to some extent (see the limitations below), the private IP network from various attacks originating from the Internet. Firewalls are a convenient control point to enforce policies for network security. Firewall logs are also a useful tool for monitoring possible intrusion attempts. Last but not least, corporate firewalls are a convenient way to prove network security to auditors, within the limitations of the protection provided by firewall technology. Firewalls have their limitations and are just another component of a comprehensive security architecture, security policies and practices.
Can firewalls protect from against all attacks?	Firewalls cannot protect from attacks originated from inside the private IP network or from configuration mistakes that enable various attacks. Firewalls cannot protect from tunneling malicious applications over various application protocols, such as HTTP or SMTP. There is also no protection against malicious servers contacted from the inside. Firewalls cannot provide protection against viruses, spyware and other malware.

IP packets in these address ranges are not routable over the Internet, but only inside private networks. Various private networks can therefore re-use these addresses without risking any address collisions between the inside networks and the Internet outside.

The re-use of the private address ranges in countless private IP networks has provided considerable relief to the problem of exhausting the IPv4 address space[4] that was a matter of concern in the early 1990s. The router at the edge of private IP networks was then called a Network Address Translator or NAT. The IP router industry has since flooded the market with NATs to meet the rapid growth of RFC 1918 compliant private IP networks.

NATs provide some protection from attacks originating from the outside of the private network, since attackers have to know the IP addresses of their targets. NATs are placed at the edge of private IP networks and are often combined with firewalls for better protection. The combination of NAT and firewall cannot provide however protection at the application level, as described above for firewalls.

The routing experts authoring RFC 1918 have cautioned that solving the reachability and routing between private networks and the public network may give new problems for applications that rely on IP address information to work properly. Real time communications using SIP rely on the IP addresses in the SDP payload to communicate where they expect to receive RTP media packets. SIP endpoints inside a private IP network will communicate a private IP address that makes no sense on the Internet where the other SIP endpoint or SIP proxy server may be located, or in another private IP network. Other protocols affected by NATs are FTP, HTTP, IPsec and Mobile IP.

The loss of transparency for the Internet due to NATs and other intermediaries is a very serious problem for its effectiveness. This problem has been documented in RFC 2775 on Internet Transparency.[5] Various attempts have been made to solve this problem, attempts that have been *categorized*

---

[4] IPv4 has a theoretic address space of 2^{32} or 4,294,967,296 unique values, but the fact that IPv4 addresses are allocated in blocks reduces the effective address space. The rapid proliferation of IP devices such as mobile phones and appliances is also expected to deplete the IPv4 address space and was the main incentive to develop IPv6 with an address header of 128 bits, instead of the 32 bits in IPv4.

[5] RFC 2775: "Internet Transparency," by B. Carpenter. IETF, February 2000.

as short term fixes and named UNilateral Self-Address Fixing (UNSAF) in RFC 3424[6] issued by the Internet Architecture Board.

The solutions for SIP-based Internet communications that are "NOT UNSAF(e)" are described further down in this chapter. As will be seen, significant complexity is required for NAT and firewall traversal for SIP signaling/messaging and RTP media transport.

Understanding and Classifying NATs

The lack of early standardization for NAT has led to a plethora of implementations, since vendors have designed NATs as best as they could or have believed would make them competitive in the market. Only after the fact, application designers have tried to understand NAT and describe their behavior. Understanding NATs involves explaining how NAT work and classifying the behavior of NATs.

How NAT Works

The first description in the IETF of a NATs is given in RFC 1631[7] and industry experience with NAT has produced extensive vendor literature on this topic, such as the Cisco tutorial[8] listed in the references. A solid tutorial on "Traditional NAT" is given in RFC 3022.[9]

Figure 13.1 shows the basic diagram with two "stub" (private IP) networks connected over the Internet and is self explanatory to a large degree.

Both stub networks in Figure 13.1 have the same address space 10.0.0.0. Packets from host A to host B have the "inside" source address and the public destination address: S=10.33.96.5 and D=198.76.28.4, note that 198.76.28.4 is a public Internet address.

The NAT for stub A will change the inside source address to the outside source address for A, for routing across the Internet: S=198.76.29.7 and keep D=198.76.28.4

---

[6] RFC 3424: "IAB Considerations for UNilateral Self-Address Fixing (UNSAF) Across Network Address Translation," by L. Daigle. IETF, November 2002.

[7] RFC 1631: "The IP Network Translator (NAT)," by K. Egevang and P. Francis. IETF, May 1994.

[8] Cisco Document ID: 6450 "How NAT Works."
http://cisco.com/en/US/tech/tk648/tk361/technologies_tech_note09186a0080094831.shtml

[9] RFC 3022: "Traditional NAT," by P. Srisuresh and K. Egevang. IETF, January 2001.

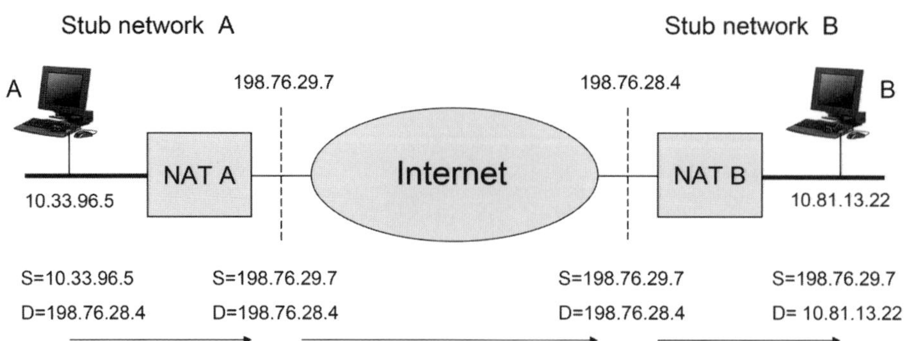

Figure 13.1 – Basic NAT Operation

The NAT for stub B will change the incoming destination address from D=198.76.28.4 to D=10.81.13.22

Packets in the reverse direction from host B to host A will be treated in a similar fashion. An excellent flash animation that illustrates packet by packet handling is available online at the time of this writing at http://www.cisco.com/warp/public/556/nat.swf

The border routers with the NAT function should never advertise the internal IP addresses to the Internet, but Internet addresses can be advertised to the inside of the stub networks for proper inside routing.

The bindings within the NAT between the inside and outside addresses have a timeout, depending on the implementation. The timeout is also dependent on the direction of the packet flow. If there is no more packet flow, the bindings will disappear. Timeout values may differ widely.

Note that,

- IP packet routing between the two stub networks requires no address changes to the hosts in the stub networks, nor any changes in the routing over the Internet.
- Since a small number of hosts in the stub network communicate at any given time with the Internet, only a small number of public Internet addresses is required on the outside of the NAT. Residential IP networks in most cases can cope with one single outside address. Also, many ISPs allocate NAT addresses to residential subscribers, so that residential hosts are often double NAT-ed and in some cases more than two levels of NAT are experienced.
- Stub networks A and B may have the same address space and hosts A and B even have the same private IP addresses without any

overlap, as long as the stubs A and B belong to different private networks.

- If stubs A and B belong to the same private IP network and share a common private IP address space, care has to be taken to have no overlap of the private IP addresses for hosts A and B. This is the case of private IP networks, such as a corporate network that is spread over several geographic locations and interconnected over the Internet. Internet partitioned stubs must be behave like a non-partitioned stub with non-overlapping private IP addresses.

Besides changing the IP addresses, the NAT has also to perform certain IP header manipulations. The NAT must also modify the IP checksum so as to forward properly formatted IP packets. RFC 1631 also specifies the NAT to be aware of basic IP applications, such as ICMP and FTP and modify the places where IP addresses may appear in the application protocol.

Given however the large number of applications and the requirement that NAT should be application unaware, the general approach is to make instead the applications to be NAT aware, as will be shown here for SIP-based communications.

Even without considering the application protocols, just at the IP level only, there are several NAT issues to be aware of, as are described in Table 13.2.

The NAT properties described here and the lack of standards for NAT can lead to widely different implementations. Worse, effects such as public address overload can make the NAT change its behavior in unpredictable ways, depending on the traffic load.

Readers may be interested in a commercial survey of commercial NAT products on the market that shows symmetric NAT to be a very seldom found legacy product on the market,[10] though there may still be an installed based out there.

NAT Behavior

The complexity of NAT, the lack of standards for NAT and the resulting ingenuity by designers have created something of a monster that many Internet researchers have tried to explain. At the time of this writing there is not even a completely agreed view in the IETF on NAT behavior,

---

[10] "NAT Classification Test Results," by C. Jennings. Internet draft, IETF, February 2005.

Table 13.2 – NAT Issues at the IP Level

Static NAT	The mapping of each inside address to an outside address, if enough outside addresses are available.
Dynamic NAT	The mapping of internal addresses to a pool of outside addresses varies in time, depending on the active communications.
Overloading and multiplexing using port and address translation (NAPT)	In case the pool of outside addresses is not big enough (there may be even one single outside address), different outside port numbers are used for the outside IP address(es). The combination of IP address and port number is called a **transport address** and will be used in the definition of application aware NAT traversal methods for SIP.
UDP port parity preservation	RFC 3550[11] prescribes the use of even-numbered ports for RTP and odd ports for RTCP.
Outside port ranges	Range 0-1023 is for "well known" ports for specific protocols Range 1024-49151 is for "registered" ports for application protocols. Range 49151-65535 is for "dynamic/private" ports.

but rather a series of studies that have been published. It is safe to assume that more recent documents provide a more accurate description of NAT behavior and solutions for NAT traversal by application protocols such as SIP and RTP.[12, 13, 14, 15] A more detailed description of the various behavior models for NAT is, however, beyond the scope of the book.

---

[11] RFC 3550: "RTP: A Transport Protocol for Real-Time Applications," by H. Schulzrinne, S. Casner, R. Frederick, and V. Jacobson. IETF, July 2003.

[12] RFC 3027: "Protocol Complications with the NAT," by M. Holdrege and P. Srisuresh. IETF, January 2001.

[13] RFC 3489: "STUN-Simple Traversal of UDP Through NAT," by J. Rosenberg, et al. IETF, March 2003.

[14] "NAT Behavioral Requirements for Unicast UDP," by F. Audet and C. Jennings. IETF, October 2004. Work in progress.

[15] "Anatomy" by Geoff Huston. *The Internet Protocol Journal*, September 2004. http://www.cisco.com/ipj

As a result of NAT complexity and NAT non-deterministic behavior, the IETF has formed the working group named "Behavior Engineering for Hindrance Avoidance (BEHAVE)" to develop requirements and best practice documents for NAT to function as deterministic as possible.[16] We recommend interested readers to follow this work that is available online at http://ietf.org/html.charters/behave-charter.html.

SIP NAT/FW Traversal

The difficulties in getting SIP and SIP-initiated media sessions through NATs can clearly be seen in a message capture of a SIP message sent from behind a NAT, shown below:

```
INVITE sip:bob@client.biloxi.example.com SIP/2.0
Via: SIP/2.0/UDP ss2.biloxi.example.com:5060;branch=z9hG4bK721e4.1
Via: SIP/2.0/UDP 10.1.1.3:5060;branch=z9hG4bK74bf9
  ;received=192.0.2.101
Max-Forwards: 69
Record-Route: <sip:ss2.biloxi.example.com;lr>
From: Alice <sip:alice@atlanta.example.com>;tag=9fxced76sl
To: Bob <sip:bob@biloxi.example.com>
Call-ID: 4Fde34wkd11wsGFDs3@atlanta.example.com
CSeq: 2 INVITE
Contact: <sip:alice@10.1.1.3>
Content-Type: application/sdp
Content-Length: 151

v=0
o=alice 2890844526 2890844526 IN IP4 10.1.1.3
s=-
c=IN IP4 10.1.1.3
t=0 0
m=audio 49172 RTP/AVP 0
a=rtpmap:0 PCMU/8000
```

The non-routable private IP address 10.1.1.3 appears in three important places in the message (in boldface): the Via header, the Contact URI, and the SDP Connection (c=) line. The Via header has been automatically fixed

---

[16] The IETF working group charter for "Behavior Engineering for Hindrance Avoidance (behave)." http://ietf.org/html.charters/behave-charter.html

with the received= parameter, but the Contact URI will not be routable for SIP messages, and the SDP Connection IP address will not be routable for the RTP media.

If the above SIP request had been routed through a NAT with an Application Layer Gateway (ALG), the ALG would have rewritten the private IP addresses with the public IP address (192.0.2.101) and the request and resulting media session would likely have worked. However, there are difficulties with ALGs including:

1. All the headers and message bodies with private IP addresses must be in the clear to the ALG, or the ALG needs to know the encryption key.
2. The ALG rewriting of some header and message bodies may be interpreted as a man-in-the-middle attack by some security mechanisms.
3. If the ALG does not Record-Route and be a visible SIP intermediary (i.e. acts as a transparent proxy), troubleshooting problems can be extremely difficult since the presence of these devices can only be inferred.
4. ALGs can introduce additional security attack vectors if an internal host is compromised and manipulates the ALG to assist in outside attacks on the network.

STUN —Simple Traversal of UDP through NATs

The STUN (Simple Traversal of UDP through NATs) defined by RFC 3489[17] is a protocol that allows an endpoint to discover and classify any NATs in the path between the endpoint and the STUN server. In addition, the private/public address binding can be determined, and the discovered public IP addresses used in SIP and SDP messages. As a result, STUN easily allows communication between an endpoint behind a NAT and one in the public Internet. In some cases, such as both endpoints behind NATs, a media relay is required, as is discussed in the next section.

The first part of the call flow shown in Figure 13.2 is the interaction between the UA and the STUN server. In this case, the STUN server is located on the public Internet. The address of the STUN server can be provisioned in the UA,

---

[17] RFC 3489: "STUN—Simple Traversal of User Datagram Protocol (UDP) Through Network Address Translators (NATs)," by J.Rosenberg, J. Weinberger, C. Huitema, R. Mahy, IETF, March 2003.

or it can be discovered using a DNS SRV lookup (_stun._udp.example.com would return the STUN servers for the example.com domain).

The first exchange between the UA and the STUN server is a shared secret exchange. The UA opens a TLS connection to the STUN server and validates the server's certificate. This shared secret is provided by the STUN server and is used in future UDP messaging between the UA and the server. Having discovered the STUN server and obtained a shared secret, the UA can now send STUN Binding Request messages to the STUN server to discover the presence and type of NATs.

The BindingRequest messages are sent from the IP address that the UA needs to know the NAT address bindings. The STUN server replies with a BindingResponse message in which the STUN server indicates the IP address and port that the it received the BindingRequest from. By sending BindingRequests to more than one STUN IP address, the UA can determine if it is behind a symmetric NAT or not. By setting a flag to request that the Binding Response be sent from a different IP address, the UA can tell if the NAT is a full cone or restricted cone. Finally, by sending periodic STUN requests, a UA can keep a NAT binding refreshed.

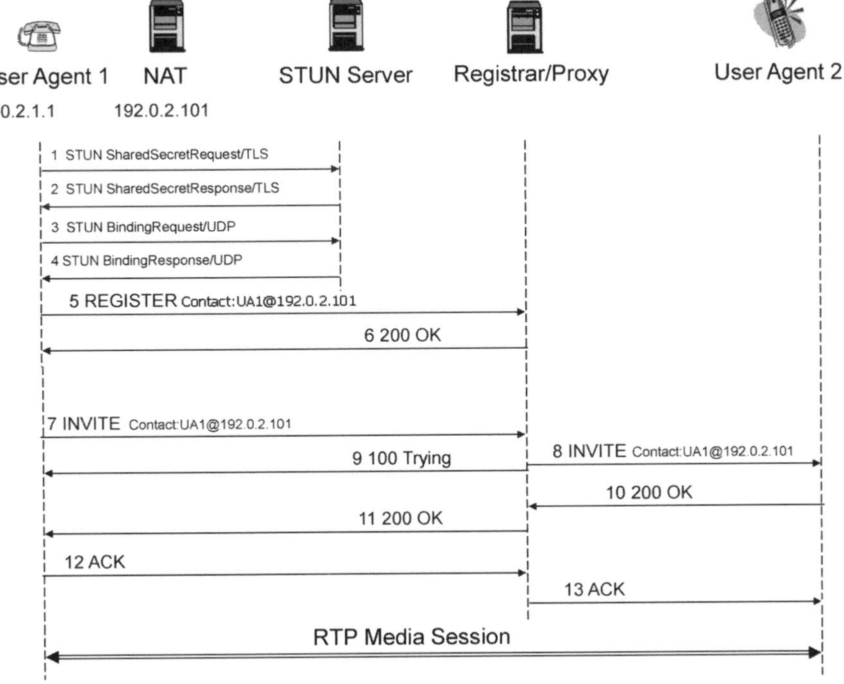

Figure 13.2 – STUN call flow with SIP

The SIP call flow in Figure 13.2 shows how the bindings obtained using STUN can be used in SIP REGISTER and INVITE request to set the Via, Contact, and SDP IP addresses correctly.

The default STUN port is 3478.

Media relays and TURN —Traversal Using Relay NATs

For some topologies of NAT traversal and for some firewall traversal cases, a media relay must be used. The media relay may be introduced by SIP intermediary acting as a Back-to-Back User Agent (B2BUA) such as the call flow described in Section 3.5 of the SIP Call Flows Document.[18] The intermediary changes the IP addresses and port numbers in the SDP to point to the media relay, which forwards the RTP packets from one interface to another to complete the media session.

Alternatively, the TURN (Traversal Using Relay NAT)[19] approach can be used by a UA to obtain transport addresses routable on the public Internet. These addresses would then be inserted into the SIP messages in a similar way to STUN information. In fact, the TURN protocol is designed to be built on top of STUN and reuse the same syntax and structure.

A TURN Allocate Request is sent by a UA to the TURN Server to request the allocation of a transport address, which is returned in the Allocate Response.

Note that the TURN server emulates a port restricted NAT. That is, incoming traffic will only be relayed from an IP address that has received an outgoing packet. As a result, in addition to requesting the allocation, the UA must also send a few packets through the TURN server to the host that will be sending traffic to the TURN server to "open" the port.

ICE—Interactive Connectivity Establishment

By using STUN and TURN, it is possible to traverse all types of NATs for SIP and RTP traffic. However, in some cases, a media relay will be used in topologies in which it could have been avoided. An algorithm for the use of STUN and TURN that guarantees that a media relay will be used only

---

[18] RFC 3665: "Session Initiation Protocol (SIP) Basic Call Flow Examples," by A. Johnston, S. Donovan, R. Sparks, C. Cunningham, and K. Summers, IETF, December 2003.

[19] "Traversal Using Relay NAT," by J. Rosenberg, R. Mahy, and C. Huitema, IETF Internet-Draft, October 2004.

when there is no alternative. This algorithm is known as Interactive Connectivity Establishment or ICE.[20]

ICE uses a modified version of STUN which is run between peers trying to establish communication, not with a STUN server. The basic algorithm has the following steps:

1. Each UA uses STUN and any configuration information to compile a set of possible transport addresses. This set explicitly includes private addresses, since these may be routable if the two UAs are within the same private network. TURN addresses may also be included for last resort use. The addresses are listed in a priority order.
2. During the session establishment, the UAs exchange these two lists of transport addresses. In SIP, these addresses are included in the SDP in the offer/answer exchange.
3. Each UA then sends STUN requests to each of the transport addresses received in turn. Any new transport addresses derived from STUN responses or received STUN requests are then added to the list and STUN requests sent to them.
4. Based on the results of the STUN probing, the highest priority transport address that "works" is selected and the media session begins.

One drawback of ICE is that it requires that STUN be sent and received on the same IP address and ports as used for the media. This introduces a requirement for the UA to demultiplex STUN packets from RTP packets received on the same port.

ICE provides optimal connectivity in a number of important cases without a media relay, such as:

- Both UAs are behind different symmetric NATs.
- Both UAs are behind the same NAT, or are one level of NAT different in a hierarchy of NAT.

The other major drawback of ICE is that it requires that both UAs support it. By themselves, STUN and TURN do not require both UAs to support them.

---

[20] "Interactive Connectivity Establishment (ICE): A Methodology for Network Address Translator (NAT) Traversal for Multimedia Session Establishment Protocols," by J. Rosenberg, IETF Internet Draft, October 2004.

The principles behind ICE have been proven in operation over the Internet in various peer-to-peer applications for file sharing and even VoIP.

The authors expect ICE support to be common in nomadic endpoints which will connect to the Internet in many different ways.

A call flow showing ICE with SIP is shown in Figure 13.3. Note that the peer-to-peer STUN probes can be done as soon as both endpoints exchange SDP offers and answers, so they can begin after the 180 Ringing as shown in the figure, or after the 200 OK or the ACK in other scenarios.

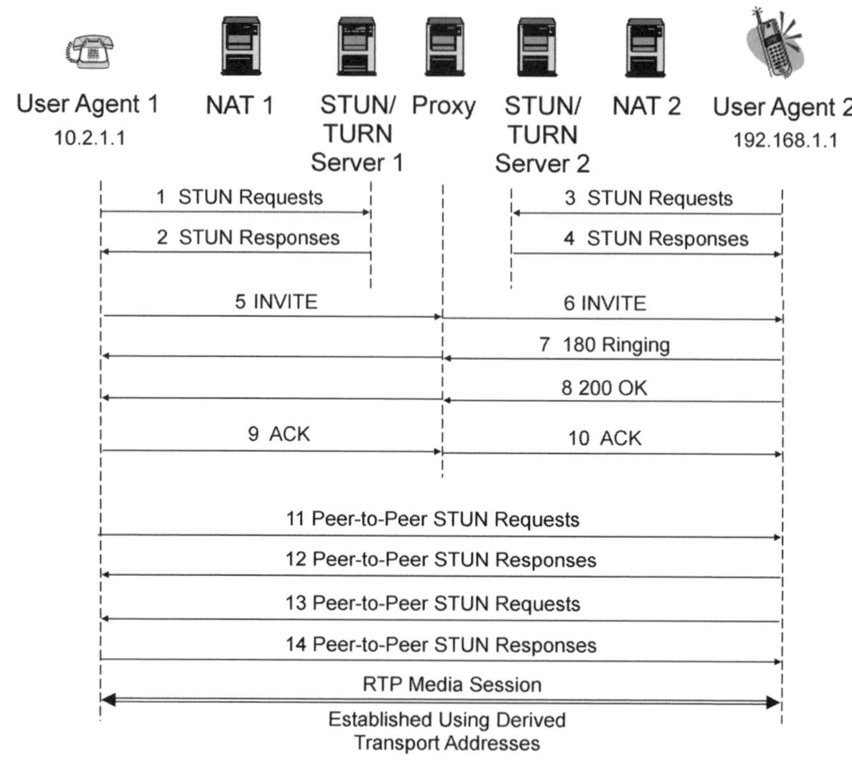

Figure 13.3 – ICE call flow

For a large set of ICE call flows through NAT, see the SIP NAT Scenarios document.[21]

[21] "Best Current Practices for NAT Traversal for SIP," by C. Boulton and J. Rosenberg, IETF Internet Draft, April 2005.

Symmetric SIP is Helpful

An extension to SIP has been developed to simplify SIP traversal through NATs. The received Via parameter might seem to be all that is necessary, but a NAPT will break this by changing the port number that the request must be sent in order to be received inside the NAT at the desired port. In addition, since incoming connections from outside the NAT can not be opened in general, another mechanism is needed to tell a server to keep open and reuse an existing connection opened by a client from behind the NAT.

The SIP extension to do this is the rport Via parameter.[22] A SIP UA which supports this specification includes the rport parameter in its Via header. A SIP server which receives the request writes the IP address it received the request from in the received parameter, and the port it received the request from in the rport parameter. When a response to the request is sent, it is sent to the IP address and port in the received and rport parameters, from the IP address and port number it received the request from. In this way, SIP behaves in a completely symmetric manner. Combining this extension with the connection reuse SIP extension,[23] which uses an alias Via parameter provides complete symmetric SIP operation which is extremely helpful in enabling NAT traversal.

Symmetric RTP is Helpful

One underlying implication in many NAT firewall traversal techniques is that of Symmetric RTP. However, only recently has this property been documented in a standards document.[24]

Symmetric RTP is a property of a UA that says that if it receives RTP on a give UDP port, it will send RTP using that same UDP port. Since the "sent from" port in UDP is often not used, some UAs do not use this symmetric property and use a fixed port number. The use of symmetric RTP is extremely helpful for NAT/Firewall traversal. In many cases, if the media from behind the NAT manages to reach the other side, it is likely that media

[22] RFC 3581: "An Extension to the Session Initiation Protocol (SIP) for Symmetric Response Routing," by J. Rosenberg and H. Schulzrinne. IETF, August 2003.

[23] "Connection Reuse in the Session Initiation Protocol (SIP)," by R. Mahy. IETF Internet Draft, October 2004.

[24] "Symmetric RTP and RTCP Considered Helpful," by D. Wing. IETF Internet Draft, October 2004.

sent back to that same IP address and port number will also work. As a result, symmetric RTP (and RTCP) enable many NAT traversal scenarios.

The authors feel that symmetric RTP should be supported by all SIP UAs in the future, wherever possible. (Note: Some UAs can not support symmetric RTP if the signaling host is different from the media host, as in a fully decomposed PSTN gateway composed of a Media Gateway Controller and a Media Gateway).

Behaved NAT

Even the use of STUN, TURN, and ICE does not guarantee reliable communication through NATs if they do not "behave" in a deterministic way. For example, it has been observed that some currently deployed NATs use different address binding allocation methods depending on how many bindings are established. Others have widely differing values for timeouts and binding intervals.

As a result the IETF has formed the Behavior Engineering for Hindrance Avoidance working group,[25] known as "behave" to develop standards for NATs and how they interact with applications. Behavior covered will include IP fragmentation, UDP, TCP, ICMP, IGMP, etc.

As this working group produces RFCs which are adhered to by NAT builders, the ability to successfully and securely establish communication through NATs will be greatly enhanced.

Firewall Traversal

There are two types of firewall traversal possible, depending on whether the firewall is cooperating or non-cooperating. In the cooperating mode, a firewall may become SIP aware, parse the SIP messages and SDP, opening and closing pin holes to allow media to flow through. The support of symmetric RTP is critical in this case as a firewall tries to "lock down" the pinhole by going from a 3-tuple (destination IP address, destination port, and protocol) to a full 5-tuple (source and destination IP address, source and destination port, and protocol).

A more secure approach is to have a SIP proxy server which authorizes and authenticates SIP and resulting media traffic through the firewall. SIP traffic on ports 5060 and 5061 can be forwarded by the firewall to the proxy, and only proxied traffic passed. This requires a control protocol

[25] http://www.ietf.org/html.charters/behave-charter.html

between the SIP proxy server and the firewall to open and close the pinholes. Currently, there are no such standard protocols, although the IETF MIDCOM (Middlebox Communications) Working Group[26] was originally chartered to produce such a protocol.

The approach with the highest certainty is to implement both a signaling and media relay function, and enforce rules in the firewall that all Internet Communications traffic must go through the relays. This approach is sometimes referred to as "media anchoring" in that all the media appears to terminate and originate from a small set of IP addresses. The downside to this approach is that the signaling and media relay must act as a B2BUA and terminate the signaling and media sessions. Any features and services not understood by the relay will be unavailable to endpoints establishing sessions through the firewall.

In terms of non-cooperating modes, a UA inside the firewall can establish a session through the firewall terminating on a host in the public Internet. Incoming and outgoing traffic is then funneled through this other host. Any open ports in the firewall could be used, even port 80 normally used for HTTP. While this approach works today, the use of deep packet filtering in firewalls will close this hole in the future, as non-web port 80 traffic will be blocked.

The authors believe that cooperative firewall traversal techniques are preferred, as this gives security managers control over their network.

Conclusions

The traversal for SIP messages and the associated media streams of NAT and firewalls is arguably the most complex design problem for Internet communication systems.

The use of recent Internet technologies can, however, solve this problem in a standards compliant way that doe not interfere with other requirements, such as security and end-to-end control:

- STUN servers to inform a UA inside a private IP network about its external transport address on the Internet.
- TURN media relays to anchor the media to/from UA behind symmetric NAT.
- ICE in both UAs behind a NAT, to determine their connectivity and optimum use of STUN and TURN, as required.

---

[26] http://www.ietf.org/html.charters/midcom-charter.html

- Symmetric SIP is helpful.
- Symmetric RTP is helpful.
- Use only "behaved" NAT.
- Do correct firewall traversal using the above and avoid masquerading SIP and RTP flows as HTTP through port 80.

Chapter 14

Peer-to-Peer SIP

Introduction

Peer-to-peer (or P2P as it is commonly known) networks[1] have become a hot topic in the Internet today. P2P gained popularity (and notoriety) in file sharing applications such as Napster, Kazaa, and others. Its use in Internet communications such as VoIP and IM has been shown by Skype[2] and others.[3] While SIP already has many P2P properties, it is possible to replace many client-server (CS) functions with a P2P network. The Chord distributed hash table lookup algorithm is introduced as an example and its usage with SIP is explained. Finally, we will give an example of a popular PBX function, call transfer, using the SIP peer-to-peer call control model.

A Short History of Peer-to-Peer Computing

P2P computing is a natural phenomenon on the Internet where peer computing between endpoints is an architectural principle. Successful P2P Internet applications are USENET and FidoNet that were invented in 1979 and 1984 respectively and are still in use today.[4] Even plain file transfer with FTP, the venerable CS file transfer protocol is mostly used in a P2P mode.

Modern P2P file sharing systems became popular, starting in 1999 when Napster was introduced. Napster was used at its peak by 60 million people. Other systems, such as Gnutella and Kazaa followed, with significant technical improvements and also with various ways to elude the ensuing legal problems that beset P2P applications. BitTorrent[5] is as of this writing probably the most successful and refined P2P content sharing protocol.

Of most interest to Internet communications is however the Skype P2P service that provides presence, IM and VoIP. As of this writing, Skype is reported have 24 million users and is predicted to have 245 million users

---

[1] Dejan Milojicic, Vana Kalogeraki, Rajan M Lukose, Kiran Nagaraja, Jim Pruyne, Bruno Richard, Sami Rollins, and Zhichen Xu, "Peer-to-peer computing," technical report HPL-2002-57 20020315, Technical Publications Department, HP Labs Research Library, March 2002, http://www.hpl.hp.com/techreports/2002/HPL-2002-57.html.

[2] http://www.skype.com

[3] Frank Strauss and S. Schmidt, "P2P CHAT—a peer-to-peer chat protocol." Internet draft, Internet Engineering Task Force, July 2004, Work in progress.

[4] "The Practice of peer-to-peer computing: Introduction and history," by T. Sundsted. IBM developerWorks, March 2001. http://www-106.ibm.com/developerworks/java/library/j-p2p/

[5] "Incentives Build Robustness in BitTorrent," by B. Cohen. May 22, 2003. http://bittorrent.com/bittorrentecon.pdf

by 2008.[6] By these numbers, Skype is by far the biggest VoIP service provider in the world.

Most P2P applications have been invented by solitary innovators, by researchers in academia or small programming teams in startup companies. No telecom company has ever made any contribution to our knowledge to P2P communications. This is one more proof that on the Internet, innovation occurs mostly at the edge, as long as the Internet preserves its transparency to any kind of applications.

Since consumer and business Internet communications have to interoperate seamlessly, the use of standards compliant SIP for both P2P and CS Internet communications is required.

Defining Peer-to-Peer

The peer-to-peer computing (P2P) model is based on peers sharing resources such as computing power, memory and data such as presence information about other peers. This is distinct from the more familiar Client-Server (CS) model used in many protocols, including in SIP that distinguishes the roles of clients and servers. Peers can assume both roles of client and server the same time. In the CS model, the same application can act either as a client or as a server depending on the request and the state of the application.

There is no clear distinction between P2P and CS. In hybrid P2P networks, some peers are 'more equal than others' such as is the case for super nodes for Skype.[7] The definition of P2P is actually quite complicated, depending on the criteria used to define P2P, such as hierarchy *versus* mesh, look-up *versus* discovery, protocols and other. Perspectives on P2P include the historical evolution of computing, services such as content sharing, communications and collaboration, architecture, algorithms and programming models.

P2P is also used in context with other definitions, such as distributed computing, grid computing and *ad hoc* communications. A quite detailed

---

[6] "Skype Lands its First Telecom Partner," in TelecomWeb, February 7, 2005. http://www.telecomweb.com/news/1107801962.htm

[7] "An Analysis of the Skype Peer-to-Peer Internet Telephony Protocol," by S. Baset and H. Schulzrinne. Columbia University Technical Report, September 15, 2004. http://www1.cs.columbia.edu/~library/TR-repository/reports/reports-2004/cucs-039-04.pdf

terminology for P2P computing has been developed[8] and we will use in the following mostly this terminology and also many of the concepts from that paper.

Characteristics of P2P Computing

P2P computing has some specific characteristics that we review here, since they show the value of P2P computing when applied to Internet communications. These characteristics are also of interest when comparing P2P with CS systems. Last but not least, the P2P characteristics are of interest from the point of view of system requirements for SIP-based communications.

Decentralization Traditional computing is based on powerful central servers that are easier to manage and to secure. This comes however at the cost of human resources to maintain them. Decentralized computing is based on user ownership and control of their data, with no cost incurred for central servers. Decentralization is more complex, since there is no global view and no central manageability of the data. Hybrid P2P systems with supernodes are a compromise between the two approaches.

Self organization Self organization is required in P2P systems, to support:

- Scalability,
- Fault resilience,
- Intermittent connection of peers (this includes *ad hoc* additions of peers and mobility),
- Low cost of ownership.

Many successful implementations and publications prove these interesting properties.

Scalability Decentralization brings along the benefit of better scaling, since all new peers contribute with their resources to the system. In new P2P systems, each node maintains information for about a limited number of peers and this improves scalability in a significant way. Such P2P systems are claimed to scale to billions of users.

[8] "Peer-to-Peer Computing," by D. Milojicic, et al. HP Laboratories Report, March 8, 2002. http://www.hpl.hp.com/techreports/2002/HPL-2002-57.pdf

Privacy The legal need of anonymity for P2P content distribution systems has led to the development of powerful techniques to ensure the privacy of data and anonymity of the ownership of the data.

Cost of ownership Sharing of costly resources in large P2P systems makes the cost for each owner very small. P2P computing systems for example can provide supercomputer power to its peers.

Ad hoc connectivity While the disappearance of a resource is an exception in traditional CS systems, leaving and joining of peers to the network is the rather normal behavior in P2P systems. The large number of peers or some adjunct servers in hybrid P2P has to make up for acceptable service levels.

Performance Performance is mostly measured by the delay in satisfying requests to the system, such as call setup delay in P2P VoIP. Performance is influenced by the computing power, storage and network bandwidth available to the peers. Bandwidth is the most critical parameter, when large numbers of messages have to propagate in the P2P system. Performance can be optimized by key approaches, such as:

- Replication,
- Caching,
- Intelligent routing.

Caching and intelligent routing are used in the Chord protocol, also under consideration for P2P SIP.

Security Conventional security requirements for P2P systems include:

- Cryptographic key exchange,
- Digital digests (hashing),
- Encryption,
- Signatures.

Tools developed specifically to P2P computing include:

- Multi-key encryption,
- Sandboxing to protect from malicious code,
- Reputation and accountability,
- Digital rights management for content distribution.

A distinct but critical part of security is NAT and firewall traversal. The introduction of NAT and firewalls has broken the transparency of the Internet and applications could no longer rely on DNS to associate names with IP addresses. P2P systems came up with different naming and discovery schemes. The P2P community was first in inventing NAT and firewall traversal techniques that were later formalized in the SIP community, such as relays and client connectivity discovery: STUN, TURN and ICE.

Usability P2P software should require no understanding or maintenance by its users, although the maintenance responsibility is distributed among all peers. Configuration of peers should be automatic and software updates should also require no skills by the user.

Fault Resilience Fault resilience is a key requirements and strength of P2P systems. Network failures or the loss of certain resources, such as peers or servers with key information must not disable the service.

Interoperability At present no standards for P2P computing exist in any meaningful way, though efforts are ongoing in several industry forums. For example Skype P2P VoIP is not interoperable with SIP systems and this constitutes one of its main weaknesses.

P2P communications systems must be SIP standards compliant, so as to interoperate with CS SIP systems without gateways (in native mode).

The Disruption of the Telephony Business by P2P Internet Communications

Though Skype is not at present based on SIP, its tremendous success is a solid proof of concept for the reasons why P2P Internet communications represent an unprecedented disruption of the telephony business, both for telephony service providers and their vendors: Note, however, that Skype does have a centralized authorization service and as such is not a pure P2P service.

Minimal or no infrastructure cost

Though the overlay network of peers is technically the infrastructure, from a capital cost perspective, Internet P2P communications do not require any new infrastructure and use the Internet 'as is' at present.

All existing VoIP network infrastructure elements, such as the softswitch, the session border controller (SBC), the integrated access device (IAD), various SIP server types for component services, media servers, QoS enabled network elements, QoS monitoring for VoIP, etc. are not required any more. In P2P systems with supernodes, the servers acting as supernodes can be considered infrastructure, though a minimal one.

The software package of the peer node is actually the infrastructure for the overlay network. Software development cost for the peer nodes replaces the infrastructure capital expenses.

Minimal or no operations cost

Since there is a minimal or no infrastructure to operate, there are also no associated operations costs. The self organizing property discussed later makes all the difference for operations cost. Given the high cost of operations personal, the main cost for the service communications provider has disappeared. A very small number of residual servers, such as for user registration and payments can be maintained with minimal cost.

Peers software updates cost may be considered the equivalent of operations cost.

Minimal customer support costs

Customer support, such as in traditional call centers is being replaced by one single piece of high quality software (the peer node) that users can download and operate without any technical support.

It is though feasible for more complex P2P features to provide online resources, such as a knowledge database for customer support.

Minimal IT systems.

Registration and payments are similar to standard e-commerce web sites and therefore of very low cost. This is in stark contrast to the extremely complex and expensive operational support systems (OSS) and the billing system in use by the telephone industry.

No service level agreements

Service level agreements (SLA) are the bread and butter of the telecom industry and are used as a justification for all services that go beyond providing basic best effort Internet service. The good voice quality of Skype, as well as its good availability, is however a proof that Internet best effort service and P2P technology are competing well with costly SLA-based telecom services.

Reminder: QoS services do not create bandwidth, but only re-allocate scarce bandwidth, mainly on the access link.

The service level agreement is therefore not provided by the P2P service, but by the Internet access service provider. One could imagine a possible SLS for the overlay network, but we have not seen this yet in practice.

Minimal customer acquisition cost

All P2P services have not used any significant marketing, or no marketing at all. Incidentally, Skype has not used any expensive marketing campaigns to grow to its astonishing size. This may however change if and when competitors for P2P Internet communications will multiply in the marketplace. Customer acquisition cost will probably always remain lower, since no user devices such as for example IADs, cell phones or PDAs have to be subsidized by the service provider.

The only cost items are gateways to legacy non-Internet networks

Internet P2P communication services require gateways to wired and wireless network to make them attractive as a complete service. This need will go down over time as Internet communications will gradually replaced wired and 2G/3G wireless telephony services.

Note: Standards compliant SIP P2P will probably not require any gateways to standards compliant client-server (CS) SIP systems.

P2P in Consumer and in Business Communications

P2P Internet communications such as Skype may well out-compete all existing infrastructure-based communication services for the reasons shown above.

In the business market however P2P may not be acceptable to any significant degree, at least near term, since CS are a more accountable way of providing critical services that cost more money in exchange for a service level agreement and security that can make IT managers comfortable.

Chord—An Advanced Peer-to-Peer Algorithm

Chord[9] is an example of a structured P2P algorithm. It is of interest because its Distributed Hash Table (DHT) searching has important scalability advantages over unstructured searching P2P algorithms. A number of other structured search algorithms such as CAN,[10] Pastry,[11] could all be used with SIP, although Chord is explained as a representative example.

For more detailed information about Chord, there are a number of excellent tutorials available.[12]

Overlay Networks

All P2P networks use an overlay network, a network structure built dynamically between peers on top of the lower layer connectivity provided by a network such as the Internet. A peer discovers one or more peers in the network then inserts itself into the network. Two extremes over overlay networks are full mesh and ring structures.

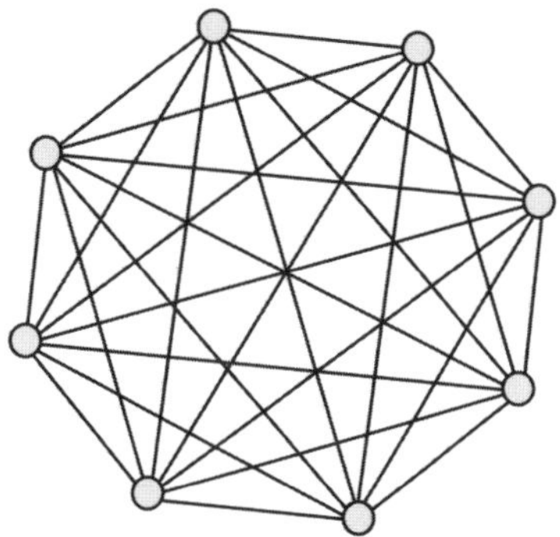

Figure 14.1 – P2P full mesh overlay network

[9] Ion Stoica, Robert Morris, David Karger, M. Frans Kaashoek, Hari Balakrishnan, "Chord: A Scalable Peer-to-Peer Lookup Service for Internet Applications." *Proceedings of ACM SIGCOMM'01*, San Diego, CA, August 2001.

[10] Sylvia Ratnasamy, Paul Francis, Mark Handley, Richard Karp, and Scott Shenker, "A scalable content addressable network," in *SIGCOMM Symposium on Communications Architectures and Protocols*, San Diego, CA, USA, Aug. 2001, ACM.

[11] Antony Rowstron and Peter Druschel, "Pastry: Scalable, distributed object location and routing for large-scale peer-to-peer systems," in *IFIP/ACM International Conference on Distributed Systems Platforms (Middleware)*, Heidelberg, Germany, Nov. 2001, pp. 329–350.

[12] "P2P Systems," by Keith W. Ross and Dan Rubenstein. http://cis.poly.edu/~ross/papers/P2PtutorialInfocom.pdf

In the full mesh shown in Figure 14.1, each node tracks all the other nodes in the network. Searches take only one hop, but the information stored by each node grows linearly with the number of nodes. This network clearly is not scalable.

A more typical P2P structure used by Chord is a ring, in which nodes keep track of at least two neighbor nodes, although additional nodes are also tracked so that if a neighbor node goes away, the ring can be reconstructed.

In its simplest form, a node searches for content or information using a key, and sends the search request to neighbor nodes. In an unstructured search, the request is "flooded" in an analogous way to broadcasting, with a maximum hop count used to limit the search. While responses to the search may be sent back through the ring, the actual content would be sent directly to the peer. This ring structure is shown in Figure 14.2.

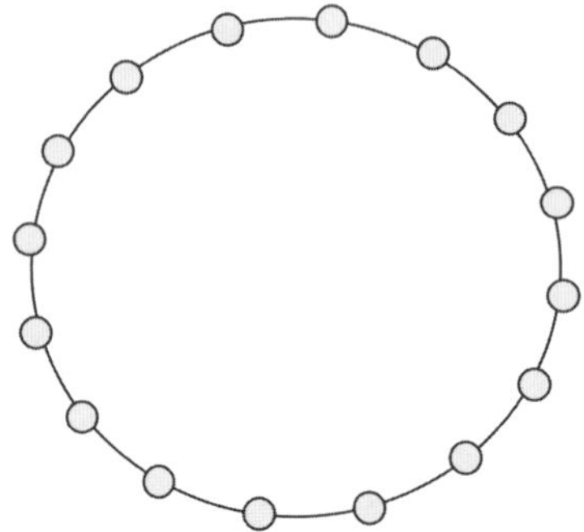

Figure 14.2 – P2P ring overlay network

Each node interacts with only two other nodes. However, searches may take up to N hops where N is the number of nodes in the overlay network. This results in a search time that grows linearly with the number of nodes in the network. While this is scalable, the performance falls off as the network grows large.

Many P2P networks implement smart caching algorithms in order to minimize search delays. In a file sharing network in which there are clearly popular files, this can result in a significant decrease in search time. However, if the content is roughly equally popular, such as location information in a P2P communication or presence network, caching optimizations will not yield such improvements.

An alternative approach is to use a structured search in which a key value is used to compute a hash function which points to a particular node in the ring. The Chord algorithm is a distributed lookup protocol that maps a key onto a node in a network.

Distributed Hash Table Algorithm

The Chord algorithm uses an m-bit SHA-1 (Secure Hash Standard) function.[13]

Each node in the ring has an integer node identifier from 0 to 2^m - 1, where *m* bits are used for the hashing function. The maximum number of nodes in this overlay network N is then 2^m.

Search keys are mapped to a key identifier which has the same range as the node identifier. For example, the search key "Alice" might map using the SHA-1 algorithm to the value 31 in a 5 bit hash. As a result, information or a pointer to Alice would be stored at Node 31 in the overlay network. Since not every node will be present in the ring, nodes also store or point to information about nodes that are not present in the overlay. For example, in the overlay network shown in Figure 14.3, Node 11 stores information whose key identifiers are 12 to 17 in addition to key identifier 11. On the other hand, Node 10 stores information only about key identifier 10 since Node 11 is present in the network.

Each node keeps track of its predecessor and successor in the ring. For example, Node 10 has Node 3 as its predecessor and Node 11 as its successor.

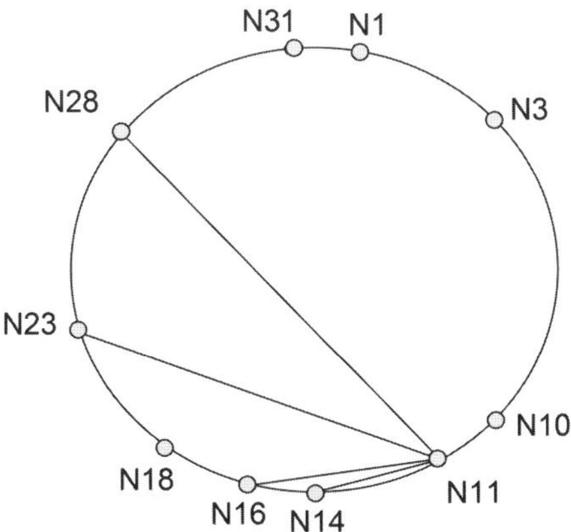

Figure 14.3 – Simple chord ring example with 32 nodes

[13] NIST, FIPS PUB 180-1: Secure Hash Standard, April 1995.

Finger Table

To speed up searching time, the Chord algorithm has each node construct a finger table. The finger table has m entries which jump ahead on the ring in powers of two. The finger table for Node 11 is shown in Table 14.1. For this 5 bit function, the finger table has entries for 2^0 through 2^5.

Table 14.1 – Finger Table for N11

Finger	Reference	Value
1	N11+1	N14
2	N11+2	N14
3	N11+4	N16
4	N11+8	N23
5	N11+16	N28

Thus Node 11 stores information about seven different nodes - the predecessor and successor nodes and the five nodes in the finger table. If Node 11 is searching for information about Node 31, a linear search would have gone through nodes 15, 16, 18, 23, and 28 before reaching 31. However, using the finger table, the search jumps to node 28 then 31.

An important property of the chord algorithm is that the amount of node information a node must store about neighbors grows logarithmically with the maximum number of nodes in a network, i.e. grows with LOG(N) where N is the maximum number of nodes in the P2P overlay network. In addition, the number of search hops needed to locate the search information also scales logarithmically instead of linearly as it does in unstructured searches. Another property is that most of the information in the finger table is about nearby nodes, with a smaller set of information about further away nodes.

In geometry, a chord is a line between two points on the circumference of a circle. It is these "jump ahead" lines that nodes use to track neighbor nodes that give the Chord algorithm its name.

Joining and Leaving the Ring

Nodes joining the ring insert themselves between two nodes. This insertion changes the successor and predecessor tables in two nodes, and the finger tables in a number of other nodes.

As users dynamically join and leave the ring, there may be times when the finger tables are inaccurate. This will result in some extra search hops. However, even in a network in which large numbers of nodes are joining and leaving, searches will still converge and complete.

The stabilization protocol for Chord is run periodically in the background and updates the entries in the finger tables and the pointers to the successor nodes. Should there be a failed lookup before the new entries for nodes that have joined or left the ring have stabilized, the next retry will provide the correct response.[14]

Peer-to-Peer SIP Architecture

Although SIP was designed based on HTTP and uses clients and servers, right from the start SIP had some peer-to-peer capabilities designed in. For example, all SIP servers (proxies, registrars, redirect servers) are purely optional elements. Two UAs can communicate directly in a peer-to-peer manner without having to go through a server. However, this requires a UA know the IP address of the UAs it wishes to communicate with. Using static IP addresses or dynamic DNS clients, the authors have run and used peer-to-peer SIP networks for years for their personal SIP communications as have many others.

To provide for mobile and nomadic UAs, SIP registration and proxy servers were introduced to enable dynamic discovery and mapping of a long lived Address of Record URI for a user to a short lived Contact URI of a particular device as it currently connects to the Internet. However, even when a proxy server is used, the basic design of SIP is for the proxy server or servers to drop out of the exchange starting with the ACK, allowing the endpoints to communicate directly in a peer-to-peer manner. However, many SIP proxy servers have been deployed utilizing Record-Routing in which a proxy server stays in the SIP dialog beyond the initial exchange. While sometimes justified, this is often done just to mimic the control structures and architectures of other networks, and adds little value to the SIP communications. In addition, the proliferation of B2BUA intermediaries can completely obscure the P2P advantages and capabilities inherent in SIP.

---

[14] "Chord: A scalable peer-to-peer look-up protocol for internet applications," by C. Kiefer. MPI Informatik lecure, 2004. http://www.mpi-sb.mpg.de/units/ag5/teaching/ws03_04/p2p-data/11-18-paper1.ppt

SIP has also developed both centralized and peer-to-peer call control. In the centralized model, a third party controller[15] uses a technique of re-INVITEs and SDP mapping to cause two UAs to establish a connection with each other. In peer-to-peer mode call control,[16] SIP call control primitives such as REFER, Replaces, and Join are used by one peer to request an action from another peer without being directly involved.

NAT traversal techniques as discussed in Chapter 13 with SIP can use either a server-based approach (ALG, media proxy, etc.) or a peer-to-peer approach (ICE[17] using STUN and TURN). The addition of unnecessary media relay points can be extremely detrimental to media session quality. As a result, the peer-to-peer approach of ICE is clearly superior, as demonstrated by Skype.

The latest peer-to-peer approaches being applied to SIP relate to the discovery mechanism. That is, replacing the registrar server with a peer-to-peer network for discovering other UAs in a network.

In one approach developed by one of the inventors of SIP,[18] the SIP registrar and proxy server becomes the distributed peer-to-peer network. A P2P SIP UA joins the P2P network and discovers possible registrar servers (possibly chosen at random). These registrar servers are the supernodes of the P2P network. The UA then sends a SIP REGISTER to this supernode which then shares the registration information with other supernodes in the network. When a P2P UA has a SIP URI for resolution, the UA looks it up in the P2P network to discover a supernode which has registration information about the UA identified by the URI. The INVITE is then sent to that supernode. The supernode then redirects (302 Moved) the UA to the current Contact SIP URI for the user, allowing the UA to contact the other UA directly, establishing a P2P SIP and media session.

---

[15] RFC 3725: "Best Current Practices for Third Party Call Control (3pcc) in the Session Initiation Protocol (SIP)," by J. Rosenberg, J. Peterson, H. Schulzrinne, G. Camarillo.

[16] R. Mahy, B. Campbell,R. Sparks, J. Rosenberg, D. Petrie, A. Johnston, "A Call Control and Multi-party usage framework for the Session Initiation Protocol (SIP)." IETF Internet Draft, October 2003, Work in progress.

[17] Jonathan Rosenberg, "Interactive connectivity establishment (ICE): a methodology for network address translator (NAT) traversal for the session initiation protocol (SIP)." Internet draft, Internet Engineering Task Force, July 2003, Work in progress.

[18] Kundan Singh and Henning Schulzrinne, "Peer-to-Peer Internet Telephony using SIP." http://www1.cs.columbia.edu/~library/TR-repository/reports/reports-2004/cucs-044-04.pdf

Another possible approach is to use the P2P network for the UA to directly query for the Contact SIP URI for the user. This would only require supernodes to act as registrars and not as redirect servers.

And yet another approach is to completely separate the SIP signaling and the P2P discovery and lookup function. This approach would require almost no extensions to the SIP protocol itself and could reuse an existing general P2P overlay network

Another outstanding issue of P2P SIP is the question of namespaces and the relation to DNS. Using P2P, it could be possible to create and use a namespace completely outside of DNS and not accessible to non-members of the network. Another approach is to use both DNS and P2P searches.

Role of Supernodes

Supernodes are nodes in a P2P network that have special functions. Instead of the flat peer-to-peer structures discussed in the previous sections, peers are either nodes or supernodes. This structure is shown in Figure 14.4. For example, in a P2P communication network, a supernode could provide proxy and NAT traversal services to other peers. In other networks, a supernode can store pointers to content available at the peers that connect to it. A peer search would first check this local information, then query other supernodes in the network.

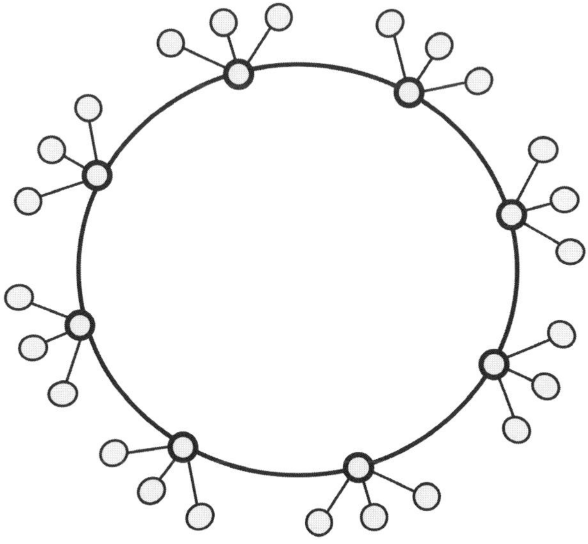

Figure 14.4 – P2P supernode ring

Implementing Advanced VoIP Functions with P2P SIP

The SIP call control and multiparty usage framework explains in detail both the CS central control using 3rd part call control, as well as the P2P call control.[19] It turns out most PBX-like functions can be implemented using P2P call control. One of the key PBX functions is call transfer using the Refer method.[20] We will show here in Fig. 14.5 an example of P2P call transfer using Refer.[21]

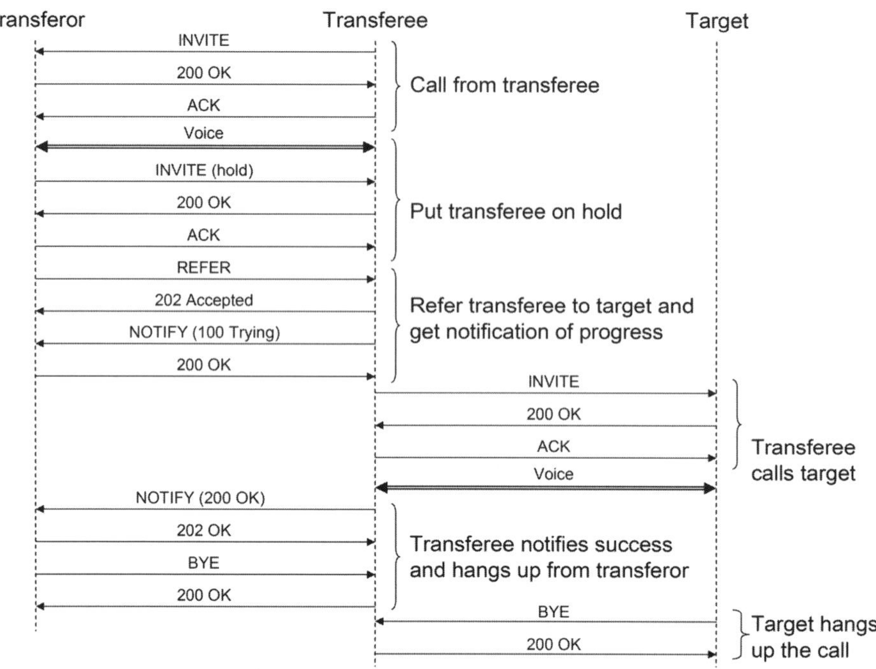

Figure 14.5 – P2P SIP call transfer using the Refer method

The detailed messages for the call transfer example have been described elsewhere.[18]

---

[19] "A Call Control and Multi-party usage framework for the Session Initiation Protocol (SIP)," by R. Mahy. [draft-ietf-sipping-cc-framework-03] (work in progress), October 2003.

[20] RFC 3892: "The Session Initiation Protocol (SIP) Referred-By Mechanism," by R. Sparks. IETF, September 2004. Work in progress.

[21] "Session Initiation Protocol Call Control—Transfer," by R. Sparks, et al. Internet Draft, [draft-ietf-sipping-cc-transfer-03], IETF, October 2004. Work in progress.

The readers may look at the call SIP call flow examples[22] for detailed guidance for a complete set of PBX-like telephony functions and also for conferencing functions as described by Johnston and Levin.[23]

In conclusion, most PBX/Centrex-like functions can be implemented in pure P2P systems.

Future of Peer-to-Peer

P2P networks are likely to continue their disruptive ways for Internet applications. It is very likely that a SIP P2P network or networks will be deployed in the near future.

[22] "Session Initiation Protocol Call Flow examples," by A. Johnston, et al. Internet Draft. IETF, 2004.

[23] Johnston, A. and O. Levin, "Session Initiation Protocol Call Control—Conferencing for User Agents," [draft-ietf-sipping-cc-conferencing-04]. Work in progress, July 2004.

Chapter 15

The Work Ahead and Conclusions

Introduction

The SIP standards are probably 80%-90% developed and some parts are *too* developed in our opinion. For this reason, most work ahead mentioned here is related to the implementation in products of already well-defined SIP features.

The broad acceptance of SIP by practically all vendors and its planned or existing deployment by most service providers is testimony to the success of the technology.

Today, there are hundreds of SIP endpoint, server, test-equipment, and software component providers successfully competing for business. A major component of this success has been an unusual attitude shared by these companies: they all believe it is of the utmost importance to interoperate with each other. And this is really what standards are all about.

Still, the SIP community faces some challenges and some more work ahead. This book would not be adequate without considering the work ahead and the challenges to face.

Short Term Challenges

We will focus here on what we believe to be short term challenges, since all the issues here need to be quickly addressed in today's fast changing communications and Internet industries. We have no complementary section on long term challenges as a result.

The Fixation on Telephony

Even a summary survey of most vendor and service provider web sites will reveal what we believe is the fixation on telephony, expressed in the more marketable term of VoIP. This fixation is understandable given that voice is the biggest part of the over one trillion Dollar global telecommunications industry in 2004. The focus on voice does not take into account however changing user habits and the changing of business models caused by the Internet.

The focus on telephony is also reflected in the IETF related working groups, such as IPTEL, SIP and SIPPING.

We believe that while work on telephony has contributed to the success of SIP, too much time has been spent into making SIP emulate and out-do legacy telephony features, such as found in the ITU-T Intelligent Network standards and in PBXs and Centrex for the enterprise. As a result, these telephony-centric efforts have detracted many from exploring the innovative services enabled by SIP.

The fixation on SIP for telephony, has determined the authors to write this book so as to contribute to some balance when exploring SIP.

Implementing Events and Presence

As described in Chapter 5 on context aware communications, events and presence enable completely new communication models and the integration of communication with applications. Unfortunately, most current VoIP systems are not enabled with events, presence or IM. Furthermore, users are faced with the fact that most public IM systems are still proprietary. Even in the IETF community we are faced with the regrettable fact of having two standards for IM: SIMPLE and XMPP; definitely nothing to write home about from the IETF.

Interconnecting the SIP Islands versus the Walled Gardens

Most public SIP VoIP systems are today walled gardens. Since users don't get URLs, they may not communicate off-net except using the PSTN. Most enterprise VoIP systems are also designed as isolated systems that connect only to the PSTN for off-net communications. 3G mobile networks and cable VoIP systems have gone to great lengths not to provide open communications off-net using the Internet. Much work has been spent in the IETF on developing features of SIP to accommodate the business models of cable and wireless operators. The authors take a dim view of these features.

The obvious technology for connecting all SIP islands is ENUM as discussed in Chapter 7 instead of using designs that are targeted only to meet someone's near term business plan. Such 'special' SIP features, often marked by SIP "P-" headers, for "preliminary," "private," or "proprietary."[1] We recommend avoiding all P- headers where global communications are pursued.

Emergency Services

Though the advantages of migrating the emergency services from the PSTN to the Internet are compelling, this is still in a very early stage, not because of any complex technology issues, but because of the installed base of PSTN base emergency services.

[1] RFC 3427: "Change Process for the Session Initiation Protocol (SIP)," by A. Mankin, et al. IETF, December 2002.

Identity and Security

Interconnecting the SIP islands over the Internet is not practical without solid identity management and encryption of the media streams using Secure RTP (SRTP). Identity management using the SIP certificate service is described in Chapter 12, though we believe the application development for such services has to catch up with the proposed standard.

Migrating to Internet Codecs

Most VoIP codecs deployed today are a legacy from the installed based of early voice over ATM and voice over frame relay gateways to the PSTN. The ITU-T G.7xx family of codecs and are however not optimally designed for the Internet. They also require significant licensing payments to the benefit of legacy telecom vendors that have to be absorbed in the cost of the VoIP service. A summary count of codec types in various VoIP equipments goes up to 25 and more, without even counting all the mobile phone codecs. This chaotic situation has actually opened a whole new industry niche for voice transcoding gateways. The authors believe VoIP should have one single default codec, the Internet Low Bit Rate (iLBC) as specified in RFC 3951 and RFC 3952. A very small number of voice codecs may be acceptable, but of optional nature, depending of the application. An open source wideband codec, such as Speex[2] may for example improve the user experience in IP-IP conference calls.

Similar considerations apply to video codecs. There are many optional annexes to H.263. The SDP markup indicating their support is intricate, and not always explicit, leading to interoperability issues when negotiating a video stream. H.264 moves some of this negotiation into codec parameters, but it adds even more complex and computationally intensive features. The community would benefit greatly from a common, open, simple and efficient video codec.

Configuration Management

Configuring SIP phones and multimedia UAs for the PC is mostly a very complex operation. As a result, service providers or the IT organization in the enterprise are usually performing the complex configuration work for the users, with the undesirable consequence that a SIP phone configured for one VoIP service may not work with another service without the help

[2] See the home page for Speex at http://www.speex.org/

of an expert. The Configuration Framework under development in the IETF SIPPING Working Group[3] is meant to address this problem.

P2P SIP

Though SIP is essentially a protocol that can support the peer-to-peer as well as client-server model, practically all current SIP products support only the client-server model. The rapid growth of Skype as a P2P implementation has posed in our opinion a most welcome challenge to the SIP community, and work on P2P SIP has been recently reported as mentioned in Chapter 14. P2P SIP is however at a very incipient stage as of this writing.

Monitoring the Quality of Service

Changes in network (or even physical environment) characteristics can cause the perception of media quality to degrade. Automated, real-time measurements that estimate human perception of the media quality can be used by the endpoint to adjust its codec parameters or even change to a different kind of codec. Service providers could monitor these measurements, allowing them to quickly discover problem regions and better respond to support calls. The AVT working group has defined the RTP Control Protocol Extended Reports (RTCP XR) in RFC 3611.[4]

The RTCP XR can be used for monitoring the quality of service as experienced by the user by implementing a suitable application that resides in the SIP phone or UA in the PC.[5] Such an application, co-resident with the SIP UA can issue QoS reports to the service provider on a call by call basis and provide mid-call alerts if a quality threshold is passed.

Any quality metric can be conveyed. Work needs to be done to standardize a minimal set of metrics that all endpoints will support. The SIPPING working group is developing a SIP Events package that allows elements not on the media path to monitor summaries of these quality scores, receiving notification when scores become exceptional. Work remains too on the filters that define these exceptional conditions.

---

[3] "A Framework for Session Initiation Protocol User Agent Profile Delivery," by D. Petrie. Internet Draft, IETF, October 2004. Work in progress.

[4] RFC 3611: "RTP Control Protocol Extended Reports (RTCP XR)," by T. Friedman, et al. IETF, November 2003.

[5] "SIP Service Quality Reporting Event," by A. Johnston, et al. Internet Darft, January 2005. Work in progress.

Refining SIP Interoperability

Twice a year, the implementation community gets together for a week at the SIP Forum's SIPit[6] interoperability test event and also for the SIMPLEt test events. There have been over a hundred distinct implementations and around two hundred participants at the recent events. Engineers from each company bring their current products and their cutting edge research code and test with as many other implementations as they can. The SIP Forum designs special test scenarios to simulate real world deployments and push each implementation to the edge. The participants help each other get the protocol fundamentals right–without interoperability there is no market. In the process, they discover and fix flaws in their products. They also uncover places in the standards where the language is vague or even incorrect. The feedback from these events has drastically improved the quality of work coming from the SIP related working groups.

The test events have been and will continue to be one of the major drivers for the success of SIP, but they are not enough. By their nature, the events are a closed, technical event. What two companies learn about each other's implementation stays between those companies. The event reports on the overall state of implementation, and any specification bugs that are discovered, but not information about individual products.

Consumers and service providers need a companion tool that gives them visibility into the quality of the products they might buy. Pulver.com has held SIPOp events in tradeshow environments, publicly simulating deployments and allowing vendors to show off their goods playing various roles in those deployments. These events have not been sufficient either.

Potential customers need a standard suite of tests to independently apply to a product. This set of tests should focus primarily on interoperability issues that could affect deployment. The SIP Forum has started work on such a test suite, initially defining a set of tests for a basic SIP user agent. The SIP Forum also seeded development of the SIP Forum Test Framework (SFTF), software to execute these tests. The SFTF is currently an open source project hosted at the SIPfoundry.[7] These tests report potential problems and allow implantations to be compared by category, but they do not result in a "score."

---

[6] See the notices from the SiPit and SIMPLEt interoperability test events at http://www.sipforum.org/

[7] See http://www.sipfoundry.org/

Future work may involve defining a score-based test system, but such work must be done with extreme care. It is very easy to accidentally define the tests based on current services rather than core protocol interoperability. Such mistakes could ossify the implementation base where it is now, instead of continuing to promote the evolution of communications that is underway.

In the long run, such a score-based test system could be used as the basis for a certification program. Industry forums like the SIP Forum will continue to debate when and whether a certification program is appropriate. At this time, the consensus is that a certification program would do more harm than good.

Core Protocol Work

Specifying Presence Composition

The SIMPLE working group has completed definition of a system that allows the basic behavior of the currently deployed proprietary presence systems to be realized in a standard way. Presence in these systems is very simple, often consisting only of online or offline and a status string. These systems base usually base presence on exactly one input. Those that allow multiple inputs take a "last input to speak wins" approach to resolving conflicts.

SIMPLE may bring a much richer type of presence to users. Inputs from multiple sources, including home and work computers, calendars, mobile handsets and GPS units can be sewn together, or composed, into one statement of and individual's availability for communication.

However, there is not yet agreement on exactly how such composition should take place. There are ongoing fundamental discussions about the role of the user and the service provider in establishing and enforcing policy around composition. There are arguments in progress over how much information composition can hide or even throw away. The outcome of these arguments will refine the Presence Data Model being forged in SIMPLE. Once these questions are addressed, mechanisms to express and convey composition policy will need to be developed.

Improvements to the Core Protocol and its Applications

As we gain knowledge from deployment and focused testing such as the SIPits, we will identify areas where the protocol needs maintenance. Two significant adjustment efforts are currently underway. The first focuses on improving the overall behavior of non-INVITE transactions in SIP networks.

The second addresses some subtle and surprising complexity stemming from using the same dialog for INVITE usages and subscriptions.

The SIP non-INVITE transaction has a fixed maximum duration. If a final response hasn't arrived to finish the transaction within 32 seconds of a request being sent, the transaction is considered a failure. Because networks hops and transiting intermediaries introduce delay, these transactions have a race condition allowing a responder to believe it has responded in time, but the requestor sees a timeout. This race condition triggers a potentially huge and totally unnecessary 408 Request Timeout response storm when multiple proxies were in the path. Furthermore, a single lost race can cause service providers to temporarily black-list each other's proxies, stopping interdomain communication unnecessary. The SIP working group is recommending changes that address several of these issues[8, 9] but some work, particularly around solving the blacklisting issue, remains.

At one point very early in the design of SIP, the Call-ID uniquely identified each association (call) between any two endpoints. Forking quickly broke that concept, leading to the introduction of the From and To tags. Each branch of a fork that led to such an association became known as a dialog. Each dialog maintains its own state, including such things as the current CSeq value for that branch. Transfer came along with two problems. First, how can you get a REFER request to the same endpoint that accepted an earlier INVITE? Second, how do you recognize this REFER has something to do with one of the sessions currently in progress? The answer was to send the REFER in the same dialog as the original accepted INVITE. This causes the subscription created by the REFER to share the same dialog state as the session (or dialog-usage) created with the INVITE. Deployment experience showed that this sharing leads to confusion. It is unclear for several failure codes if the failure applies only to the subscription, the Invite usage, or both. The working group is refining mechanisms like GRUU and header fields similar to Replaces and Join to allow a REFER for transfer to be sent in its own dialog. SIPPING is also working to clarify the meaning of various response codes when a dialog is shared by more than one usage.[10]

---

[8] "Future work addressing issues with the Session Initiation Protocol's non-INVITE Transaction," by R. Sparks. Internet Draft, IETF, February 2005. Work in progress.

[9] "Actions addressing identified issues with the Session Initiation Protocol's non-INVITE Transaction," by R. Sparks. Internet Draft, IETF, January. Work in progress.

[10] "Multiple Dialog Usages in the Session Initiation Protocol," by R. Sparks. Internet Draft, IETF, February 2005. Work in progress.

Conclusions

SIP is a very general protocol for establishing sessions between any type of application, in a standard way across the Internet and in private IP networks. SIP events and presence enable new communication services and the integration of communications and applications.

Most of the SIP protocol work is now done and SIP is quite mature. Naturally, it will take some time to get this powerful technology from the standards stage to market and to leverage the whole potential of SIP in commercial products.

Index

Numbers

A

Index

Index

D

Q

R

T